Brief Menu

W9-CET-996

How can I write a stronger thesis? See 1c or 6c.

What's the difference between affect *and* effect? *See 19.*

How do periods and commas work with quotation marks? See 34d.

How should I format my essay? See 51 (MLA) or 53 (APA).

Where can I see model citations? See 50 (MLA) or 52 (APA).

THE
BEDFORD
Handbook
Twelfth Edition

Diana Hacker

Nancy Sommers
Harvard University

bedford/st.martin's
Macmillan Learning

Boston | New York

Vice President: Leasa Burton
Senior Program Manager: Laura Arcari
Director of Content Development: Jane Knetzger
Development Editor: Melissa Rostek
Associate Editor: Aislyn Fredsall
Director of Media Editorial: Adam Whitehurst
Media Editor: Julia Domenicucci
Marketing Manager: Vivian Garcia
Senior Director, Content Management Enhancement: Tracey Kuehn
Senior Managing Editor: Michael Granger
Executive Content Project Manager: Gregory Erb
Lead Digital Asset Archivist and Senior Workflow Project Manager: Jennifer
    L. Wetzel
Production Supervisor: Brianna Lester
Director of Design, Content Management: Diana Blume
Interior Design: Claire Seng-Niemoeller
Cover Design: William Boardman
Text Permissions Editor: Allison Ziebka-Viering
Photo Permissions Associate: Maisie Howell
Photo Researcher: Krystyna Borgen, Lumina Datamatics, Inc.
Director of Digital Production: Keri deManigold
Senior Media Project Manager Training Specialist: Allison Hart
Copyeditor: Arthur Johnson
Indexer: Ellen Kuhl Repetto
Composition: Lumina Datamatics, Inc.
Printing and Binding: LSC Communications

Library of Congress Control Number: 2022932924
ISBN 978-1-319-33202-0

Printed in the United States of America.

1   2   3   4   5   6   27   26   25   24   23   22

Acknowledgments

Jonathan H. Adler, excerpt from "Little Green Lies: The Environmental Miseducation of America's Children," *Policy Review*, Summer 1992. Copyright © 1992 by the Heritage Foundation. Used with permission. All rights reserved.

Michele Berger, "Volunteer Army," *Audubon*, November–December 2010. Copyright © 2010 by Michele Berger. Used with permission. All rights reserved.

Betsy Taylor, "Big Box Stores Are Bad for Main Street," *CQ Researcher*, November 1999. Copyright © 1999 by CQ Press, a division of Sage Publications. Republished with permission of CQ Press, a division of Sage Publications. Permission conveyed through Copyright Clearance Center, Inc.

Art acknowledgments and copyrights appear on the same page as the art selections they cover; these acknowledgments and copyrights constitute an extension of the copyright page.

For information, write: Bedford/St. Martin's, 75 Arlington Street, Boston, MA 02116

Preface for instructors

Dear Colleagues:

Welcome to the twelfth edition of *The Bedford Handbook*. Over twelve editions, this trusted writing guide has transformed into a complete teaching package. The book has taken on a more concise, "less is more" identity, giving students exactly the instruction they need. You have the handbook you love available as both an interactive e-book and a print handbook. And you have **Achieve**, Macmillan's digital course experience, easy and intuitive to use, to help you design assignments, comment on students' drafts, and measure students' writing progress.

What hasn't changed is the book's dedication to answering students' essential question: *How do I write a good college paper?* As students learn the expectations for college writing, they need support for researching, documenting sources, creating arguments, and building paragraphs and punctuating sentences. With its practical, straightforward instruction, *The Bedford Handbook* provides this support, guiding students in writing with purpose and clarity. Achieve supports these goals with a suite of tools—including adaptive quizzing, diagnostics, customizable assignments, and revision tools—that drive students' learning. Everything you need to make college success achievable for all students is yours with the twelfth edition of *The Bedford Handbook*.

This beloved handbook has been shaped by the students and instructors who use it. As we craft a new edition, my Macmillan editors and I listen and learn; we reimagine and revise—just like our students. For this edition, our Diversity, Equity, and Inclusion (DEI) Board, a talented team of writing faculty, advised us on how to widen our language and usage instruction to stress the importance of equity and respect in writing. We made it our mission to ensure that students can see themselves in the handbook. We took a close look at how we phrased our grammar instruction and at the examples presented. And we expanded our research instruction on entering research conversations to guide students in seeking out and incorporating diverse perspectives and underrepresented voices.

In the twelfth edition of *The Bedford Handbook*, you'll find other new features, including more how-to instruction on annotating, analyzing, and summarizing sources, particularly for online sources. Achieve includes new auto-graded activities that bring our how-to boxes to life for students, illustrating important skills such as evaluating online sources and revising a thesis statement. Chapter 6 features a new researched argument essay about the relationship between zoos and endangered animals. In Achieve, students can follow the student writer's process, see drafts and important documents from her research, and hear her talk about how she found, across drafts, a position to argue. Students have an opportunity to learn alongside the writer with scorable activities on establishing common ground, balancing rhetorical appeals, contributing to research conversations, and more.

The Hacker tradition is one of innovation, and the twelfth edition of *The Bedford Handbook*, combined with Achieve's digital tools, will transform the way we teach and the way students learn. I am eager to share this new edition with you, confident that you will find everything here that you and your students value in *The Bedford Handbook*. Our handbook supports students' progress as college writers, providing structure and building confidence. I can't imagine teaching without it.

With every good wish,

Nancy Sommers

Nancy Sommers

Welcome to the Twelfth Edition

Achieve with The Bedford Handbook

Achieve is a dedicated composition space for writing instructors and students of all comfort levels with course technology. It provides trusted content with a robust e-book, as well as diagnostics with personalized study plans. Achieve's writing tools break down the writing process for students, make revision choices more visible to instructors, and guide students through drafting, peer review, plagiarism avoidance, reflection, and revision. Achieve supports instructors with prebuilt writing assignments and rubrics, engages students in and outside of class, and helps to promote equity in the classroom.

- *Reflection*: Allows students to articulate the choices they're making as writers and promotes the transfer of skills to writing in other courses and beyond the classroom environment.

- *Feedback and Commenting Tools*: Allow instructors to provide feedback that's efficient and effective; ties to draft goals for greater focus; links to e-book content for reference within the platform.

- *Revision Plan*: Helps students engage meaningfully in the revision process by translating instructor and peer feedback into actionable revision strategies.

- *Peer Review*: Gives students a scaffolded framework for providing feedback to their peers using the same tools their instructor has already modeled; allows instructors to monitor student progress and to comment on feedback students give to their peers.

- *Seamless and Connected Drafting Experience*: With Achieve, everything is in one place and the writing process is made transparent, with next steps for action clear.

What's new in the book?

- *A new argument essay and a look into the writing process.* Section 6, Writing Arguments, features a new student essay. The chapter is built around examples from the writer's essay and process. A companion case study in Achieve brings the writer's process to life for students, from developing a working thesis and organizing an argument to selecting and integrating evidence. Videos, notes, and drafts from the writer illustrate concepts, and the corresponding exercises have students apply what they've learned and test their understanding.

- *More help finding and working with sources.* Instruction on widening the research conversation helps students conduct research and seek out sources from diverse viewpoints (see pp. 268–269). A new feature highlights how to use quotation marks with other punctuation while quoting sources (see p. 302). Two new "How to" boxes in Academic Reading and Writing take students through the steps needed to effectively annotate (p. 43) and summarize (p. 45) texts.

- *"How-to" help brought to life in Achieve.* Built around the book's how-to boxes, a new set of activities illustrates the steps needed to build effective writing skills. Covering topics from revising a thesis statement to evaluating a source for false information, these digital tutorials give students the opportunity to practice the skills laid out in one of the book's most helpful features.

- *Up-to-date MLA and APA formatting and documentation guidelines.* The advice, models, and student essays in the twelfth edition of *The Bedford Handbook* align with MLA's 2021 update and APA's 2020 guidelines.

A new resource for corequisite composition

Writers develop over time — and some writers need more time and more practice to develop the skills and habits that help them meet the challenges of the first-year writing course. For those students enrolled in paired, corequisite, or ALP sections of composition, *A Student's Companion to Hacker Handbooks* offers practical support that will help them get up to speed and perform on-level. The workbook offers college success and reading strategies; graphic organizers for many kinds of writing; opportunities for reflection; and more than sixty exercises covering everything from thesis statements and plagiarism to fragments, run-ons, commas, and verb tenses.

A Student's Companion to Hacker Handbooks is available as a print workbook, as a convenient e-book, or as a module through Achieve. Even better, the print companion is available packaged with the handbook at no additional cost to students.

What hasn't changed?

Neither Google nor an OWL can give students the confidence that comes with a coherent reference that covers all the topics they need in a writing course. *The Bedford Handbook* supports students as they compose for different purposes and audiences and in a variety of genres, and as they collaborate, revise deeply, conduct research, document sources, format their writing, and edit for clarity. The eleventh edition's authoritative and trustworthy instruction, brief and accessible explanations, and step-by-step help in writing guides and how-to boxes are still here in the twelfth. With examples that teach and plenty of boxes, checklists, and navigation tools, the book is easy to use and understand. It also comes with the service and support you have come to expect from Bedford/St. Martin's — including professional resources, training for digital tools, and quick, personal service when you need it.

Bedford/St. Martin's puts you first

From day one, our goal has been simple: to provide inspiring resources that are grounded in best practices for teaching reading and writing. For more than 40 years, Bedford/St. Martin's has partnered with the field, listening to teachers, scholars, and students about the support writers need. No matter the moment or teaching context, we are committed to helping every writing instructor make the most of our resources — resources designed to engage every student.

How can we help you?

- Our editors can align our resources to your outcomes through correlation and transition guides for your syllabus. Just ask us.

- Our sales representatives specialize in helping you find the right materials to support your course goals.

- Our learning solutions and product specialists help you make the most of the digital resources you choose for your course.

- Our *Bits* blog on the Bedford/St. Martin's English Community (community.macmillan.com) publishes fresh teaching ideas regularly. You'll also find easily downloadable professional resources and links to author webinars on our community site.

Contact your Bedford/St. Martin's sales representative or visit macmillanlearning.com to learn more.

Digital and print options for The Bedford Handbook

Digital

- **Achieve with The Bedford Handbook.** Achieve offers a dedicated composition space for writing instructors and students of all comfort levels with course technology. It provides trusted content with a robust e-book, as well as diagnostics with personalized study plans. Achieve's writing tools break down the writing process for students, make revision choices more visible to instructors, and guide students through drafting, peer review, plagiarism avoidance, reflection, and revision. Fully editable pre-built assignments support the book's approach. To order Achieve with *The Bedford Handbook*, use **ISBN 978-1-319-41297-5.** For details, visit macmillanlearning.com/college/us/achieve/english.

- **Popular e-book formats.** For details about our e-book partners, visit macmillanlearning.com/ebooks.

- **Inclusive Access.** Enable every student to receive their course materials through your LMS on the first day of class. Macmillan Learning's Inclusive Access program is the easiest, most affordable way to ensure all students have access to quality educational resources. Find out more at macmillanlearning.com/inclusiveaccess.

Print

- *The Bedford Handbook.* To order the paperback text, use **ISBN 978-1-319-33202-0.** To order the paperback text packaged with Achieve, use **ISBN 978-1-319-51319-1.**
- *A Student's Companion to Hacker Handbooks,* **Second Edition.** To order the paperback workbook, use **ISBN 978-1-319-24421-7.** To package the workbook with the print handbook at no additional cost, contact your sales representative.

Your Course, Your Way

No two writing programs or classrooms are exactly alike. Our Curriculum Solutions team works with you to design custom digital (e-book and Achieve) and print options that provide the resources your students need. (Options below require enrollment minimums.)

- *ForeWords for English.* Customize any print resource to fit the focus of your course or program by choosing from a range of prepared topics, such as Sentence Guides for Academic Writers.
- *Macmillan Author Program (MAP).* Add excerpts or package acclaimed works from Macmillan's trade imprints to connect students with prominent authors and public conversations. A list of popular examples or academic themes is available upon request.
- *Mix and Match.* With our simplest solution, you can add up to 50 pages of curated content to your Bedford/St. Martin's text. Contact your sales representative for additional details.

Instructor Resources

You have a lot to do in your course. We want to make it easy for you to find the support you need—and to get it quickly.

Teaching with Hacker Handbooks is available as a PDF that can be downloaded from macmillanlearning.com and is also available in Achieve.

In addition to chapter overviews and teaching tips, this instructor's manual includes sample syllabi, correlations to the Council of Writing Program Administrators' Outcomes Statement, and classroom activities.

Acknowledgments

I am grateful for the expertise, enthusiasm, and classroom experience that so many individuals brought to the tenth edition.

Meet our Advisory Board for Diversity, Equity, and Inclusion

The following fellow teachers of writing worked with us to make sure students can see themselves and their experiences represented in the handbook, to review terminology and instruction, and to promote inclusion and openness. We are grateful for their important contributions.

Kendra N. Bryant, North Carolina Agricultural and Technical State University

Javier Dueñas, Miami Dade College, North

Symmetris Jefferson Gohanna, Calhoun Community College

David F. Green, Howard University

Jamila Kareem, University of Central Florida

Esther Milu, University of Central Florida

Kristin vanEyk, University of Michigan

Reviewers

Preston L. Allen, Miami Dade College; Chuck Baker, Greenville Technical College; Lori Bongiorno, Greenville Technical College; Jim Burns, University of Delaware; Cornelius Collins, Fordham University; Natalie Dorfeld, Florida Institute of Technology; Javier Dueñas, Miami Dade College; Edward Glenn, Miami Dade College; Kimberley M. Holloway, King College; John F. Jebb, University of Delaware; Peter Krause,

Fordham University; Debbie Lelekis, Florida Institute of Technology; Yousi Mazpule, Miami Dade College; Jason Newport, Meredith College; Maria Orban, Fayetteville State University; Kalen R. Oswald, Albion College; Faye Pelosi, Palm Beach State College–Lake Worth; Tiffany E. Probasco, University of Delaware; R. Joseph Rodriguez, Saint Edward's University; Kevin M. Rulo, Catholic University of America; George Shamshayooadeh, Evergreen Valley College; David A. Stivers, Savannah College of Art And Design; Kyle D. Torke, Eastern New Mexico University–Roswell; David C. Wright, Monmouth College.

Contributors

I thank the following fellow writing teachers for important content and smart revisions. Our exciting new resource for corequisite composition, *A Student's Companion to Hacker Handbooks*, was made possible with the help of Sylvia Basile (Midlands Technical College), who wrote material on integrating sources; Sandra Chumchal (Blinn College), who wrote advice and activities for two chapters on active reading; Sarah Gottschall (Prince George's Community College), who contributed content to help students avoid plagiarism and write stronger thesis statements; and Paul Madachy (Prince George's Community College), who wrote an important chapter on audience awareness. I am also grateful to colleagues who have contributed to the previous editions, as their important work informs the tenth edition: Margaret Price (The Ohio State University) helped us to think about gender and pronouns and inclusivity; Kimberli Huster (Robert Morris University and Duquesne University) updated advice for multilingual writers; and Sara McCurry laid the groundwork for the current version of *Teaching with Hacker Handbooks*.

Student Contributors

Including sample student writing in each edition of the handbook and its media makes these resources more useful for you and your students. I would like to thank these students for letting us adapt their work as models: Sophie Harba, Dan Larson, Michelle Nguyen, Margaret Peel, Julia Riew, Emilia Sanchez, April Bo Wang, and Ren Yoshida.

Bedford/St. Martin's

Developing handbooks, e-books, and digital writing tools is a highly collaborative business, and it is my pleasure to acknowledge and thank the enormously talented Bedford/St. Martin's media and editorial teams, whose commitment to student success informs each new feature of *The Bedford Handbook* and Achieve for *The Bedford Handbook*. Leasa Burton, vice president for Humanities, generously offers her deep knowledge of composition to help us understand how the field continues to transform. Leasa's leadership is a source of inspiration and instruction for those who work with her. Adam Whitehurst, director of media editorial for Humanities, is a constant source of practical answers to our media questions. I thank him for his creative energy and his dedication to engaging instructors and students in the process of building Achieve. Laura Arcari, program manager for English, offers her superb judgment and big-picture thinking to make sure that *The Bedford Handbook* remains the handbook instructors trust and love. I am grateful for Laura's commitment to our handbooks, especially her deep understanding of our digital writing tools to build students' success and confidence. Many thanks to Bedford marketing colleagues Joy Fisher Williams and Vivian Garcia for their treasured advice and feedback. Doug Silver, product manager, helps us to reimagine writers' and teachers' opportunities with digital tools.

Michelle Clark, senior executive editor, is the editor every author dreams of having. She manages to be exacting and endearing all at once—a treasured friend and colleague and an endless source of creativity. Melissa Rostek, development editor and lead editor of the twelfth edition, brings her excellent editorial instincts and bold questions to our collaboration. Always an advocate for students, she is a close reader extraordinaire who knows how to make every idea more interesting and every sentence more precise. Thank you, Melissa, for your unshakable optimism and steadiness, for being such an awesome editor, and for our friendship. Julia Domenicucci, media editor, managed content development for Achieve and all things digital. I thank her for her positivity and guidance throughout the process. Thanks also to Aislyn Fredsall, associate editor, for developing the new researched argument paper, overseeing the review and permissions processes, and developing ancillary materials. Aislyn jumps in to assist on any project with her "can do" spirit, always showing us how to accomplish a task better than we imagined. She suggests innovative ways to make our handbook smarter.

Many thanks to the media production team, especially Allison Hart, senior media project manager, for delivering engaging and accessible handbook tools for students composing in the digital age. Thanks also to Gregory Erb, executive content project manager, for his experience with our handbooks and for his careful eye and smart management of the content production process; to Arthur Johnson, copy editor, for his thoroughness and attention to detail; to Claire Seng-Niemoeller, who kept our design clean, simple, and elegant—as always; and to Billy Boardman, senior design manager, who has created a striking new cover for the twelfth edition.

Last, but never least, I offer thanks to my own students who, over many years, have shaped my teaching and helped me understand their challenges. Thanks to my friends and colleagues Jenny Doggett, Sarah Garfinkel, Joan Feinberg, Elisabeth McKetta, Maxine Rodburg, Laura Saltz, Dawn Skorczewski, and Kerry Walk for sustaining conversations about the teaching of writing. And thanks to my family: to Joshua Alper, an attentive reader of life and literature, for his steadfastness across the drafts, and for his grace and good humor; to my parents, Walter and Louise Sommers, who encouraged me to write and set me forth on a career of writing and teaching; to my extended family, Ron, Charles Mary, Demian, Liz, Devin, Yuval, Kate, Nik, Sam, Steve, and Alexander, for their encouragement and affection; and to Rachel, Alexandra, and Brian, world-class listeners, witty and wise beyond measure, always generous with their instruction and inspiration in all things that matter. They give point and purpose to writing and share my thrill when they hold this handbook in their hands. And to my grandchildren, Lailah and Oren, thanks for the joy and sweetness you bring to life.

Nancy Sommers

Contents

PART 6   ## Punctuation   185

PART 1

A Process for Writing

> # 1 Exploring, planning, and drafting

Welcome to *The Bedford Handbook*—your college writing guide. One of the pleasures of college writing is exploring ideas and discovering what you think about a subject.

You may find that the writing process leads you in unexpected directions. The more you learn, the more questions you form. It's in the process of writing and thinking about ideas that you discover what's interesting in a subject and why you care about it.

Since it's not possible to think about everything all at once, start by assessing your writing situation and composing a piece of writing in stages—planning, drafting, revising, and editing.

1a Assess your writing situation.

Before composing a first draft, spend time asking questions about your writing situation. The key elements include your subject, purpose, audience, and genre.

Subject

Often your subject will be assigned to you. When you are free to choose what to write about, select subjects that interest or puzzle you. Writing is much more interesting when you explore questions you don't have answers to.

Purpose

All writing has a purpose or reason—to inform, to analyze, to persuade, to propose, to call readers to action, and so on. The wording of an assignment may suggest its purpose. You may need to ask yourself, "What do I want to accomplish?" and "What do I want to communicate to my audience?"

Audience

You are always writing to readers, so take time to consider their interests and expectations. What do they know or believe about your subject? What kind of information will they need to understand your ideas? What kind of response do you want from your readers? Make choices that show respect for your readers' values and perspectives.

Genre

Pay attention to the genre, or type of writing, assigned. Each genre is a category of writing meant for a specific purpose and audience, with its own set of agreed-upon expectations for style, structure, and format. Genres include essays, lab reports, business memos, research proposals, and position papers.

Writing for an audience: Emails and other messages

When you write a message to an instructor, a classmate, or a potential employer, respect your audience by using a concise subject line, stating your main point at the beginning of the message, keeping paragraphs brief, proofreading for errors, and paying attention to your tone. If you include someone else's words, let your reader know the source.

EXERCISE 1–1   Narrow the following subjects into topics that would be manageable for an essay of two to five pages. For each of the five narrowed topics, suggest a purpose and an audience.

1. The minimum wage
2. Immigration
3. Mandated vaccinations
4. Racial profiling
5. Internet privacy

Checklist for assessing your writing situation

Subject

- Has the subject been assigned, or are you free to choose your own?
- Why is your subject worth writing about?
- What questions would you like to explore?
- Do you need to narrow your subject to a more specific topic?

Purpose

- Why are you writing? To inform? To analyze? To argue? To call readers to action? For some combination of purposes?
- What message do you want to communicate?

Audience

- Who are your readers? How well informed are they about your subject?
- What information do readers need to understand your ideas?
- Will your readers resist your ideas? What objections might you need to anticipate and counter?

Genre

- What genre or type of writing is required? Essay? Report? Speech or presentation? Something else?
- What are the expectations for the genre? For example, what type of evidence is typically used? What style and organization are used?

Length and format

- Are there length requirements? Format requirements?
- What documentation style is required: MLA, APA, or another style?
- Do you have guidelines or examples to consult?

Deadlines

- Do you know the rough draft due date? The final due date?
- How should you submit your writing—by printing, posting, emailing, or sharing?

1b Explore your subject.

Experiment with strategies for exploring your subject and discovering your purpose. You might find it useful to explore your subject with sentence starters. In the examples below, "X" is the subject you're interested in:

> Here's something I would like to understand about X: _____.
>
> What doesn't make sense about X is _____.
>
> Why hasn't anyone asked this question about X: _____?

The following strategies will help you generate ideas for your writing.

Asking questions

Questions are the engines of writing. Try asking *why* and *how* questions that cannot be answered with a simple yes or no. Ask questions that allow you to enter debates and deepen your understanding of what's at stake in the topic.

Talking and listening

Talking about your ideas can help you develop your thoughts and discover what your listeners find interesting, what they are curious about, and where they disagree with you. If you are writing an argument, try describing it to listeners who have other points of view to hear their ideas.

Reading and annotating texts

Reading is an important way to deepen your understanding of a topic, learn from the insights and research of others, and expand your perspective. Annotating (making notes on) a text encourages you to read actively—to highlight key concepts, to note possible contradictions in an argument, or to raise questions for further research and investigation.

Brainstorming and freewriting

Brainstorming and freewriting are good ways to figure out what you know and what questions you have. Write quickly and freely, without pausing to think about word choice, to discover what questions are on your mind and what directions you might pursue.

Keeping a journal or a blog

A journal is a collection of informal or exploratory writing. You might pose questions, comment on an interesting idea from one of your classes, or keep a list of observations that occur to you while reading. You might imagine a conversation between yourself and your readers or stage a debate to understand opposing positions.

Although a blog is a type of journal, it is a public rather than a private writing space. In a blog, you can explore an idea for a paper by writing posts from different angles. Since most blogs allow commenting, you can start a conversation by inviting readers to give you feedback in the form of questions, counterarguments, or links to other sources on a topic.

1c Draft and revise a working thesis statement.

For many types of writing, you will be able to state your central idea in a sentence or two. Such a statement, which ordinarily appears at the end of your introduction, is called a *thesis statement* or simply a *thesis*.

Understanding what makes an effective thesis statement

An effective thesis statement is a central idea that conveys your purpose, or reason for writing, and that requires support. An effective thesis should

- state a position that needs to be supported.
- use concrete language and be sharply focused.
- let your readers know what to expect.
- be appropriate for the assignment's length requirements, and not too broad or too narrow.
- pass the "So what?" test (see p. 10).

Drafting a working thesis statement

As you explore your topic, you will begin to see ways to focus your material.

You'll find that the process of answering a question or taking a position on a debatable topic will focus your thinking and lead you to develop a working thesis. For example, here are the efforts of a student, Jared, to pose a question and draft a working thesis for an essay in his composition course.

QUESTION
Should the federal government enact legislation to prevent social media companies from selling users' personal data?

WORKING THESIS
The federal government should enact legislation to prevent social media companies from selling users' personal data.

The working thesis offers a useful place to start writing, a way to narrow the topic and focus a first draft. However, it doesn't respond to readers who will ask why this topic matters or why these laws should be created. To fully answer his own question, Jared pushed his thinking with the word *because*.

STRONGER WORKING THESIS
The federal government should enact legislation to prevent social media companies from selling users' personal data because such selling practices harm the privacy of citizens who may not know their personal information is being spread.

Revising a working thesis statement

As you move toward a clearer and more specific position you want to take, you'll start to see ways to revise your working thesis. As your ideas develop, your working thesis will change, too. You may find that the evidence you have collected supports a different thesis, or that your position has changed as you have learned more about your topic. Or you might find instead that your position isn't clear and needs to become more specific.

Solve five common problems with thesis statements

Revising a working thesis is easier if you have a method or an approach. The following problem/solution approach can help you recognize and solve common thesis problems.

1 Common problem: **The thesis is a statement of fact.**

Solution: Enter a debate by posing a question about your topic that has more than one possible answer. For example: Should the polygraph be used by private employers? Your thesis should be your answer to the question.

Working thesis: *The first polygraph was developed by Dr. John Larson in 1921.*

Revised: *Private employers should be banned from using the polygraph because it has not been proved reliable, even under controlled conditions.*

2 Common problem: **The thesis is a question.**

Solution: Take a position on your topic by answering the question you have posed. Your thesis should be your answer to the question.

Working thesis: *Why did so many companies release ads about racism in 2020 and 2021?*

Revised: *Because corporate social responsibility matters to both customers and employees, companies in the United States advertised their values more than their products in 2020 and 2021, using their platforms to speak out against racism.*

→

❸ **Common problem: The thesis is too broad.**

Solution: Focus on a subtopic of your original topic. Once you have chosen a subtopic, take a position in an ongoing debate and pose a question that has more than one answer. For example: Should people be tested for genetic diseases? Your thesis should be your answer to the question.

Working thesis: *Mapping the human genome has many implications for health and science.*

Revised: *Now that scientists can detect genetic predisposition for specific diseases, policymakers should establish clear guidelines about whom to test and under what circumstances.*

❹ **Common problem: The thesis is too narrow.**

Solution: Identify challenging questions that readers might ask about your topic. Then pose a question that has more than one answer. For example: Do the risks of genetic testing outweigh its usefulness? Your thesis should be your answer to the question.

Working thesis: *A person who carries a genetic mutation linked to a particular disease might or might not develop that disease.*

Revised: *Avoiding genetic testing is a smart course of action because of both its emotional risks and its medical limitations.*

❺ **Common problem: The thesis is vague.**

Solution: Focus your thesis with concrete language and clues about where the essay is headed. Pose a question about the topic that has more than one answer. For example: How does the physical structure of the Vietnam Veterans Memorial shape the experience of visitors? Your thesis — your answer to the question — should use specific language.

Working thesis: *The Vietnam Veterans Memorial is an interesting structure.*

Revised: *By inviting visitors to see their own reflections in the wall, the Vietnam Veterans Memorial creates a link between the present and the past.*

One effective way to revise a working thesis is to put it to the "So what?" test below.

Putting your working thesis to the "So what?" test

Use the following questions to help you revise your working thesis.

- Why would readers want to read an essay with this thesis?
- How would you respond to a reader who hears your thesis and asks "So what?" or "Why does it matter?"
- Is your thesis debatable? Can you anticipate counterarguments (objections) to your thesis?
- How will you establish common ground with readers who may not agree with your argument?

1d Draft a plan.

To develop your thesis, try listing and organizing ideas. An informal outline can be drafted and revised quickly to help you identify how the different ideas fit together to support your thesis.

Here is one student's informal outline.

Working thesis: Animal testing should be banned because it is bad science and doesn't contribute to biomedical advances.

- Most animals don't serve as good models for the human body.
- Drug therapies can have vastly different effects on different species—92 percent of all drugs shown to be effective in animal tests fail in human trials.
- Some of the largest biomedical discoveries were made without the use of animal testing.
- The most effective biomedical research methods—issue engineering and computer modeling—don't use animals.
- Animal studies are not scientifically necessary.

A formal outline may be useful later in the writing process, after you have written a rough draft, to help you see the logic and organization of your draft and to help you identify any gaps.

EXERCISE 1-2 In each of the following pairs, which sentence would be an effective working thesis for a short paper? Why would the other sentence be ineffective? Is it too factual? Too broad? Too vague? Use the problem/solution approach from pages 8–9 to evaluate each thesis.

1. a. Many drivers use their cell phones irresponsibly while driving.

   b. Current state laws are inadequate to punish drivers who use their cell phones irresponsibly to text, read email, or perform other distracting activities.

2. a. The electoral college creates imbalanced elections because it gives disproportionate decision-making power to states with fewer people.

   b. The electoral college was created to make presidential elections more balanced.

3. a. As we search to define the intelligence of animals, we run the risk of imposing our own understanding of intelligence on animals.

   b. How does the field of animal psychology help humans define intelligence?

4. a. The high cost of college needs to be reduced because it affects students and their families.

   b. To reduce the high cost of college, more students should be offered opportunities for dual-enrollment courses and a three-year college degree.

5. a. Opioid addiction affects people of all ages and from every socio-economic group.

   b. The most effective way of treating opioid addiction is with combination therapies; often a single therapy is not enough.

1e Draft an introduction.

Introductions are often called *hooks* because their purpose is to capture the attention of readers and give them a reason to say "I want to read this essay." Your introduction will usually be a paragraph of 50 to 150 words (in a longer paper, it may be more than one paragraph) and will include your thesis statement. The most common strategy is to open with a few sentences that engage readers, establish your purpose for writing, and lead readers to your thesis.

Strategies for drafting an introduction

- Offer a surprising statistic or an unusual fact
- Ask a question
- Introduce a quotation
- Establish common ground with readers
- Provide historical background
- Define a key term or concept
- Point out a problem or contradiction
- Use a vivid example or image

In the following introduction, which opens with an engaging question, the thesis is highlighted.

Opening question engages readers.

Should the government enact laws to regulate healthy eating choices? Many Americans would answer an emphatic "No," arguing that what and how much we eat should be left to individual choice rather than unreasonable laws. Others might argue that it would be unreasonable for the government not to enact legislation, given the rise of chronic diseases that result from harmful diets. In this debate, both the definition of reasonable regulations and the role of government to legislate food choices are at stake. In the name of public health and safety, state governments have the responsibility to shape health policies and to regulate healthy eating choices, especially since doing so offers a potentially large social benefit for a relatively small cost.

Shows two sides of the debate to establish common ground.

All the sentences lead readers to the thesis.

Thesis answers the question and offers the writer's position.

—Sophie Harba, student

TIP: For more examples of effective introductions, see pages 48, 55, and 72.

> **Academic Writing**
>
> Depending on your past experiences with writing, you may feel that asserting a thesis in your introduction sounds impolite or even rude. Don't be afraid to use a direct approach. Make your position clear with a strong thesis in your introduction.

1f Draft the body.

As you draft the body of your essay, you might naturally ask: What should I say? How will I write an entire essay on my topic? You will find the process easier if you have a working thesis to guide the drafting process. If your thesis suggests a plan (see 1d), or if you have sketched a preliminary outline, try to organize your paragraphs accordingly. Draft the body of your essay by writing at least one paragraph about each supporting point you listed in the planning stage.

As you draft, keep asking questions: What is my purpose? What does my thesis promise readers? How will I support my position? Keep anticipating what information your readers will need to understand your ideas. Remember that first drafts aren't finished drafts; they're just *first,* a place to begin. Find your momentum and keep writing.

If you decide that support for your thesis could come from one or more visuals, such as a table or an infographic, keep in mind that a visual should support your writing, not substitute for it. See the student paper in 51b; the writer uses a graph to help develop her point.

For more detailed help with drafting and developing paragraphs, see section 2.

USING SOURCES RESPONSIBLY: As you draft, keep notes about sources you read and consult. If you quote, paraphrase, or summarize a source, include a citation, even in your draft (see sections 45 and 48). You will save time and avoid plagiarism if you do so.

1g Draft a conclusion.

A conclusion reminds readers of the essay's main idea without repeating it. By the end of the essay, readers should already understand your position, so the concluding paragraph is often relatively short. An effective conclusion rounds out an essay by giving readers a sense of completion or by issuing a call to action.

Always end your essay on a strong, positive note. You don't need to use phrases such as *In conclusion* or *In summary* because your readers will understand that your essay is concluding. The conclusion is your chance to have the last word on the subject and remind readers why your essay was worth reading.

Strategies for drafting a conclusion

In addition to echoing your main idea, a conclusion might do any of the following:

- Briefly summarize your essay's key points
- Return to the hook used in the introduction
- Propose a course of action
- Offer a recommendation
- Suggest the topic's wider significance or implications

For examples of effective conclusions, see pages 49–50, 57, and 77.

---

2 Writing effective paragraphs

▸ Writing focused and unified paragraphs, 16
▸ Common transitions, 20

A paragraph is a group of sentences that focuses on one main point or example. Except for special-purpose paragraphs, such as introductions and conclusions (see 1e and 1g), paragraphs are units of organization that develop and support an essay's main point, or thesis. Aim for paragraphs that are well developed, organized, coherent, and neither too long nor too short for easy reading.

2a Focus on a main point.

An effective paragraph is unified around a main point. The point should be clear to readers, and all sentences in the paragraph should relate to it.

Stating the main point in a topic sentence

A clear topic sentence, a one-sentence summary of the paragraph's main point, tells readers what to expect. It acts as a signpost pointing in two directions: backward toward the thesis of the essay and forward toward the body of the paragraph.

Usually the topic sentence comes first in the paragraph.

> All living creatures manage some form of communication. The dance patterns of bees in their hive help to point the way to distant flower fields or announce successful foraging. Male stickleback fish regularly swim upside-down to indicate outrage in a courtship contest. Male deer and lemurs mark territorial ownership by rubbing their own body secretions on boundary stones or trees. Everyone has seen a frightened dog put his tail between his legs and run in panic. We, too, use gestures, expressions, postures, and movement to give our words point.
>
> —Olivia Vlahos, *Human Beginnings*

In college writing, topic sentences are often necessary for advancing or clarifying lines of an argument and introducing evidence from a source. In the following paragraph on the effects of the 2010 oil spill in the Gulf of Mexico, the writer uses a topic sentence to state that the extent of the threat is unknown, before quoting three sources that illustrate her point.

> To date, the full ramifications [of the oil spill] remain a question mark. An August report from the National Oceanic and Atmospheric Administration estimated that 75 percent of the oil had "either

evaporated or been burned, skimmed, recovered from the wellhead, or dispersed." However, Woods Hole Oceanographic Institution researchers reported that a 1.2-mile-wide, 650-foot-high plume caused by the spill "had and will persist for some time." And University of Georgia scientists concluded that almost 80 percent of the released oil hadn't been recovered and "remains a threat to the ecosystem."

—Michele Berger, "Volunteer Army"

Sticking to the point

Sentences that do not support the topic sentence destroy the unity of a paragraph. In the following paragraph describing the switch to online learning at a high school, the information about the chemistry instructor is clearly off the point.

As the result of the emergency move to online learning in 2020, students enrolled at Lincoln High School had to make important adjustments. Students suddenly were put in charge of their own learning and working space, sometimes having to compete with siblings for a suitable place to do schoolwork, for example. Also, students in classes with hands-on labs, such as biology and chemistry, had to adjust to learning by simulation. The chemistry instructor left to have a baby at the beginning of the semester, and most of the students don't like the substitute. For students who learn better in groups, the move to online learning left them feeling disconnected and uncertain.

Writing focused and unified paragraphs

A strong paragraph supports a thesis, opens with a topic sentence, focuses on and develops a main point, and holds together as a unit. As you build and revise your paragraphs, ask these questions:

- Does each paragraph support the thesis?
- Does each paragraph open with a clear topic sentence?
- Does each paragraph focus on a main point and develop the point?
- Is each paragraph organized and coherent?
- Is each paragraph the right length for its topic?
- Does each paragraph contain transitions to help readers move from sentence to sentence and between paragraphs?

EXERCISE 2–1   Underline the topic sentence in the following paragraph, and cross out any sentences that do not support the main idea.

Quilt making has served as an important means of social, political, and artistic expression for women. In the nineteenth century, quilting circles provided one of the few opportunities for women to forge social bonds outside of their families. Once a week or more, they came together to sew as well as trade small talk, advice, and news. They used dyed cotton fabrics much like the fabrics quilters use today; surprisingly, quilters' basic materials haven't changed that much over the years. Sometimes the women joined their efforts in support of a political cause, making quilts that would be raffled to raise money for temperance societies, hospitals for sick and wounded soldiers, and the fight against slavery. Quilt making also afforded women a means of artistic expression at a time when they had few other creative outlets. Within their socially acceptable roles as homemakers, many quilters subtly pushed back at the restrictions placed on them by experimenting with color, design, and technique.

2b Make paragraphs coherent.

When sentences and paragraphs flow from one to another logically and clearly, without discernible bumps, gaps, or shifts, they are said to be coherent. Coherence can be improved by strengthening the ties between old information and new. A number of techniques for strengthening those ties are detailed in this section.

Linking ideas clearly

Readers expect to learn a paragraph's main point in a topic sentence early in the paragraph. Then, as they move into the body of the paragraph, they expect to encounter specific details, facts, or examples that support the topic sentence — either directly or indirectly. If a sentence does not support the topic sentence directly, readers expect it to support another sentence in the paragraph and therefore to support the topic sentence indirectly.

The following paragraph begins with a topic sentence. The highlighted sentences are direct supports, and the rest of the sentences are indirect supports.

> There are several things that college students taking online classes can do to stay involved socially. First, they can use technology to support their studies outside of the classroom. Instead of meeting in the library for a study session, students can meet over video. Class members can use chat software or social media groups to discuss the week's lecture, ask questions, or organize group work. Second, students can move their extracurriculars online alongside their classes. Clubs can meet virtually and complete club activities over video, or students can simply stay in touch with friends and classmates they have not met in person. Finally, students can stay informed on what is happening at their schools. Many schools and colleges have blogs, social media pages, or online newsletters. Such platforms deliver school updates, inform students of both in-person and virtual events that they can attend, and—through pictures, videos, and more—provide a piece of campus life, however small.
>
> —Margaret Smith, student

Repeating key words

Repetition of key words is an important technique for gaining coherence. To prevent repetitions from becoming dull, you can use variations of a key word (*hike, hiker, hiking*), pronouns referring to the word (*gamblers . . . they*), and synonyms (*run, spring, race, dash*). In the following paragraph describing plots among indentured servants in the seventeenth century, historian Richard Hofstadter binds sentences together by repeating the key word *plots* and echoing it with a variety of synonyms.

> Plots hatched by several servants to run away together occurred mostly in the plantation colonies, and the few recorded servant uprisings were entirely limited to those colonies. Virginia had been forced from its very earliest years to take stringent steps against mutinous plots, and severe punishments for such behavior were recorded. Most servant plots occurred in the seventeenth century: a contemplated uprising

was nipped in the bud in York County in 1661; apparently led by some left-wing offshoots of the Great Rebellion, servants plotted an insurrection in Gloucester County in 1663, and four leaders were condemned and executed; some discontented servants apparently joined Bacon's Rebellion in the 1670s.

—Richard Hofstadter, *America at 1750*

Providing transitions

Transitions are bridges between what has been read and what is about to be read. They help readers move from sentence to sentence and from paragraph to paragraph.

Sentence-level transitions   Certain words and phrases signal connections between (or within) sentences. Frequently used transitions are included in the chart on page 20.

In the following paragraph about social psychology research, the authors use transitions to guide readers from one idea to the next.

> Social psychologists conduct research because many of the things we think we know to be true turn out to be false, or more nuanced than we originally thought, when subjected to investigation. For example, it seems reasonable that people who are threatened with punishment for doing something forbidden, illegal, self-defeating, or fattening might eventually stop, and the more severe the punishment, the more likely they will be to comply. After all, they would now associate the activity with fear or pain. But when tested empirically, this assumption turns out to be dead wrong.
>
> —Elliot and Joshua Aronson, *The Social Animal*

Paragraph-level transitions   Paragraph-level transitions usually link the *first* sentence of a new paragraph with the *first* sentence of the previous paragraph. In other words, the topic sentences signal global connections.

Look for opportunities to echo the subject of a previous paragraph (as summed up in its topic sentence) in the topic sentence of the next one.

In the excerpt below, the author uses this paragraph-level transition strategy to link topic sentences.

> Consider aseptic packaging, the synthetic packaging for the "juice boxes" so many children bring to school with their lunch. One criticism of aseptic packaging is that it is nearly impossible to recycle, yet on almost every other count, aseptic packaging is environmentally preferable to the packaging alternatives. Not only do aseptic containers not require refrigeration to keep their contents from spoiling, but their manufacture requires less than one-tenth the energy of making glass bottles.
>
> What is true for juice boxes is also true for other forms of synthetic packaging. The use of polystyrene, which is commonly (and mistakenly) referred to as "Styrofoam," can reduce food waste dramatically due to its insulating properties. (Thanks to these properties, polystyrene cups are much preferred over paper for that morning cup of coffee.) Polystyrene also requires significantly fewer resources to produce than its paper counterpart.
>
> —Jonathan H. Adler, "Little Green Lies"

Common transitions	
TO SHOW ADDITION	and, also, besides, further, furthermore, in addition, moreover, next, too, first, second
TO GIVE EXAMPLES	for example, for instance, in fact, specifically, to illustrate
TO COMPARE	also, in the same manner, likewise, similarly
TO CONTRAST	although, but, even though, however, in contrast, nevertheless, on the other hand, still, though, yet
TO SUMMARIZE OR CONCLUDE	in conclusion, in short, in summary, therefore, to sum up
TO SHOW TIME	after, as, before, during, finally, immediately, later, meanwhile, next, then, when, while
TO SHOW PLACE OR DIRECTION	above, below, beyond, close, nearby, opposite, to the left
TO INDICATE LOGICAL RELATIONSHIP	as a result, because, consequently, for this reason, if, since, so, therefore, thus

2c Choose a suitable strategy for developing paragraphs.

Although paragraphs and essays may be developed in any number of ways, certain methods of organization occur frequently, either alone or in combination: illustrations, narration, description, process, comparison and contrast, analogy, cause and effect, classification, and definition. These strategies for developing paragraphs have different uses, depending on the writer's subject and purpose.

Illustrations

Illustrations are extended examples and can be a vivid and effective means of developing a point. The writer of the following paragraph uses illustrations to support his point that Harriet Tubman was a genius at eluding her pursuers.

> Part of [Harriet Tubman's] strategy of conducting was, as in all battle-field operations, the knowledge of how and when to retreat. Numerous allusions have been made to her moves when she suspected that she was in danger. When she feared the party was closely pursued, she would take it for a time on a train southward bound. No one seeing Negroes going in this direction would for an instant suppose them to be fugitives. Once on her return she was at a railroad station. She saw some men reading a poster and she heard one of them reading it aloud. It was a description of her, offering a reward for her capture. She took a southbound train to avert suspicion. At another time when Harriet heard men talking about her, she pretended to read a book which she carried. One man remarked, "This can't be the woman. The one we want can't read or write." Harriet devoutly hoped the book was right side up.
>
> —Earl Conrad, *Harriet Tubman*

Narration

A paragraph of narration tells a story or part of a story. Narrative paragraphs are usually arranged in chronological order, but they may also contain flashbacks, interruptions that take the story back to an earlier time. The following paragraph recounts the author's experiences in the wilderness of Tanzania.

> One evening when I was wading in the shallows of the lake to pass a rocky outcrop, I suddenly stopped dead as I saw the sinuous black body of a snake in the water. It was all of six feet long, and from the slight hood and the dark stripes at the back of the neck I knew it to be a Storm's water cobra—a deadly reptile for the bite of which there was, at that time, no serum. As I stared at it an incoming wave gently deposited part of its body on one of my feet. I remained motionless, not even breathing, until the wave rolled back into the lake, drawing the snake with it. Then I leaped out of the water as fast as I could, my heart hammering.
>
> —Jane Goodall, *In the Shadow of Man*

Description

A descriptive paragraph sketches a portrait of a person, place, or thing by using concrete and specific details that appeal to one or more of our senses—sight, sound, smell, taste, and touch. Consider, for example, the following description of the grasshopper invasions that devastated the Midwestern landscape in the United States in the late 1860s.

> They came like dive bombers out of the west. They came by the millions with the rustle of their wings roaring overhead. They came in waves, like the rolls of the sea, descending with a terrifying speed, breaking now and again like a mighty surf. They came with the force of a williwaw and they formed a huge, ominous, dark brown cloud that eclipsed the sun. They dipped and touched earth, hitting objects and people like hailstones. But they were not hail. These were *live* demons. They popped, snapped, crackled, and roared. They were dark brown, an inch or longer in length, plump in the middle and tapered at the ends. They had

transparent wings, slender legs, and two black eyes that flashed with a
fierce intelligence.

—Eugene Boe, "Pioneers to Eternity"

Process

A process paragraph is structured in chronological order. A writer may
choose this pattern either to describe how something is made or done or
to explain to readers, step by step, how to do something. Here is a paragraph explaining how to perform a "roll cast," a fly-fishing technique.

> Begin by taking up a suitable stance, with one foot slightly in front
> of the other and the rod pointing down the line. Then begin a smooth,
> steady draw, raising your rod hand to just above shoulder height and
> lifting the rod to the 10:30 or 11:00 position. This steady draw allows a
> loop of line to form between the rod top and the water. While the line
> is still moving, raise the rod slightly, then punch it rapidly forward and
> down. The rod is now flexed and under maximum compression, and
> the line follows its path, bellying out slightly behind you and coming
> off the water close to your feet. As you power the rod down through
> the 3:00 position, the belly of line will roll forward. Follow through
> smoothly so that the line unfolds and straightens above the water.
>
> — *The Dorling Kindersley Encyclopedia of Fishing*

Comparison and contrast

To compare two subjects is to draw attention to their similarities, although
the word *compare* also has a broader meaning that includes a consideration of differences. To contrast is to focus only on differences.

Whether a paragraph stresses similarities or differences, it may be
patterned in one of two ways. The two subjects may be presented one at a
time, as in the following paragraph of contrast.

> So Grant and Lee were in complete contrast, representing two dia-
> metrically opposed elements in American life. Grant was the modern
> man emerging; beyond him, ready to come on the stage, was the great
> age of steel and machinery, of crowded cities and a restless, burgeoning

vitality. Lee might have ridden down from the old age of chivalry, lance in hand, silken banner fluttering over his head. Each man was the perfect champion of his cause, drawing both his strengths and his weaknesses from the people he led.

—Bruce Catton, "Grant and Lee: A Study in Contrasts"

Alternatively, a paragraph may proceed point by point, treating the two subjects together, one aspect at a time. The following paragraph uses the point-by-point method to compare speeches given by Abraham Lincoln in 1860 and Barack Obama in 2008.

Two men, two speeches. The men, both lawyers, both from Illinois, were seeking the presidency, despite what seemed their crippling connection with extremists. Each was young by modern standards for a president. Abraham Lincoln had turned fifty-one just five days before delivering his speech. Barack Obama was forty-six when he gave his. Their political experience was mainly provincial, in the Illinois legislature for both of them, and they had received little exposure at the national level—two years in the House of Representatives for Lincoln, four years in the Senate for Obama. Yet each was seeking his party's nomination against a New York senator of longer standing and greater prior reputation—Lincoln against Senator William Seward, Obama against Senator Hillary Clinton.

—Garry Wills, "Two Speeches on Race"

Analogy

Analogies draw comparisons between items that appear to have little in common. Writers use analogies to make something abstract or unfamiliar easier to grasp or to provoke fresh thoughts about a common subject. In the following paragraph, physician Lewis Thomas draws an analogy between the behavior of ants and that of humans.

Ants are so much like human beings as to be an embarrassment. They farm fungi, raise aphids as livestock, launch armies into wars, use chemical sprays to alarm and confuse enemies, capture slaves. The families of weaver ants engage in child labor, holding their larvae like shuttles to spin out the thread that sews the leaves together for their fungus gardens. They exchange information ceaselessly. They do everything but watch television.

—Lewis Thomas, "On Societies as Organisms"

Cause and effect

A paragraph may move from cause to effects or from an effect to its causes. The topic sentence in the following paragraph mentions an effect; the rest of the paragraph lists several causes.

The fantastic water clarity of the Mount Gambier sinkholes results from several factors. The holes are fed from aquifers holding rainwater that fell decades—even centuries—ago, and that has been filtered through miles of limestone. The high level of calcium that limestone adds causes the silty detritus from dead plants and animals to cling together and settle quickly to the bottom. Abundant bottom vegetation in the shallow sinkholes also helps bind the silt. And the rapid turnover of water prohibits stagnation.

—Hillary Hauser, "Exploring a Sunken Realm in Australia"

In the following paragraph, the topic sentence identifies a cause; the rest of the paragraph lists the effects.

The rise of rail transport in the nineteenth century forever changed American farming—for better and for worse. Farmers who once raised crops and livestock to sustain just their own families could now make a profit by selling their goods in towns and cities miles away. These new markets improved the living standard of struggling farm families and encouraged them to seek out innovations that would increase their profits. On the downside, the competition fostered by the new markets sometimes created hostility among neighboring farm families where there had once been a spirit of cooperation. Those farmers who couldn't compete with their neighbors left farming forever, facing poverty worse than they had ever known.

—Chris Mileski, student

Classification

Classification is the grouping of items into categories according to some consistent principle. The principle of classification that a writer chooses ultimately depends on the writer's purpose. The following paragraph classifies types of intelligence.

> Robert Sternberg has introduced his three-part theory of successful intelligence. *Analytical* intelligence is our ability to complete problem-solving tasks such as those typically contained in tests; *creative* intelligence is our ability to synthesize and apply existing knowledge and skills to deal with new and unusual situations; *practical* intelligence is our ability to adapt to everyday life — to understand what needs to be done in a specific setting and then to do it; what we call street smarts. Different cultures and learning situations draw on these intelligences differently, and much of what's required to succeed in a particular situation is not measured by standard IQ or aptitude tests, which can miss critical competencies.
>
> —Peter C. Brown, Henry L. Roediger III, and Mark A. McDaniel,
> *Make It Stick: The Science of Successful Learning*

Definition

A definition puts a word or concept into a general class and then provides enough details to distinguish it from others in the same class. In the following paragraph, the writer defines *Punk* as a subculture.

> Quickly expanding beyond its garage rock origins, Punk was an attitude, subculture and übercult — an anti-authoritarian backlash of nihilist aggression. It began to take hold in New York around 1973 and by the end of the decade had cultivated not only its own abrasive sound, but also its own in-your-face visual aesthetics. Like the Hippies that came before them, the Punks, and their New Wave sidekicks, were ready to change the world, though less with peace and love than with a slap up the side of the head.
>
> —Ann Fensterstock, *Art on the Block*

3   Revising, editing, and proofreading

To revise is to *re-see*, and the comments you receive from reviewers — instructors, peers, and writing center tutors — will help you re-see your draft through readers' eyes. Asking your readers simple questions such as "Do you understand my main idea?" and "Is my draft organized?" will help you revise your draft to clarify and organize your ideas. Writing multiple drafts allows you to write in stages, seek feedback, and strengthen your work through revising and editing.

3a   Use peer review: Give constructive comments.

Peer review offers you an opportunity to read the work of your classmates. When you review a peer's work, you not only help your classmate but also benefit from the process of thinking strategically about revision. As you offer advice about how to strengthen a thesis, for example, or how to use a visual to convey information, you are learning, too, about the purpose of a thesis or about the role of visuals. The box on the next page will guide you in providing helpful peer review comments.

3b   Learn from peer review: Revise with comments.

Peer review gives you an opportunity to learn what's working and not working in your draft. Your peers will offer their suggestions, answer your questions, and help you strengthen your essay.

The guidelines beginning on page 29 will help you learn from your reviewers' comments and revise successfully.

Write helpful peer review comments

1 **View yourself as a coach, not a judge.** Think of yourself as asking questions and proposing possibilities, not dictating solutions. Help your peer identify the strengths of a draft and build on those strengths. Try phrasing comments this way: "Have you thought about . . . ?" or "How can you help a reader understand this point?"

2 **Pay attention to global issues first.** Focus on the big picture—purpose, thesis, organization, and evidence—before sentence structure, word choice, and grammar. You might, for instance, offer counterarguments to a peer's thesis, or you might suggest places where additional evidence would make an argument more persuasive. Use the checklist for global revision on page 31 to help you focus comments on global issues.

3 **Restate the writer's main idea.** As a reader, you can help the writer see whether points are expressed clearly. Can you follow the writer's train of thought? Restate the writer's thesis to check your understanding.

4 **Be specific.** Point to specific places in a draft to show your peer how, why, and where a draft is effective or confusing. Instead of saying "I like your introduction," say exactly what you like: "You use a surprising statistic in your introduction, and it really hooks me as a reader." Always end your comments with specific recommendations for revising.

Be active.   Help reviewers understand your purpose for writing, including why you chose your topic and what you hope to accomplish in your draft. Tell reviewers your specific questions and concerns so they can focus their feedback, and ask questions to make sure you understand your reviewers' comments.

Have an open mind.   After you've worked hard on a draft, you might be surprised to hear reviewers tell you it still needs more development. Don't take criticism personally. Responding to readers' objections instead of dismissing them will strengthen your ideas and make your essay more persuasive.

Weigh feedback carefully.   Your reviewers will offer more suggestions than you can use, so be strategic. Sort through all the comments you receive with your original goals in mind, and focus on global concerns first.

Keep a revision and editing log.   To help you learn about your strengths and challenges as a writer, make a list of the global and sentence-level concerns that keep coming up in your reviewers' comments. For advice on keeping an editing log, see page 33.

Revise with comments: What does "be specific" mean?

Often the comments you'll receive are written as shorthand commands, such as "Be specific!" Such comments don't show you how to revise, but they do identify where you want to focus your attention. When reviewers say that you need to "be specific," the comment often signals that you could strengthen your writing by including additional evidence or by analyzing the evidence.

Strategies for revising

- Reread your topic sentence to understand the focus of the paragraph. (See 2a.)

- Ask questions. Does the paragraph contain claims that need support? Have you provided evidence—specific examples, vivid details and illustrations, statistics and facts—to help readers understand your ideas and find them persuasive? (See 6e.)

- Analyze your evidence. Remember that details and examples don't speak for themselves. You will need to show readers how evidence supports your claims. (See 4c.)

An excerpt from an online peer review session below shows a peer reviewer offering constructive comments that lead the writer to a stronger idea about how to connect to her audience.

Excerpt from an online peer review session

Juan (peer reviewer): Rachel, your essay makes a great point that credit card companies often hook students on a cycle of spending. But it sounds as if you're blaming students for their spending habits and credit card companies for their deceptive actions. Is this what you want to say?

Rachel (writer): No, I want to keep the focus on the credit card companies. I didn't realize I was blaming students. What could I change?

Juan (reviewer): In paragraphs three and four, you group all students together as if all students have the same bad spending habits. If students are your audience, you'll be insulting them. What reader is motivated to read something that's alienating? What is your purpose for writing this draft?

Rachel (writer): Well . . . It's true that students don't always have good spending habits, but I don't want to blame students. My purpose is to call students to action about the dangers of credit card debt. Any suggestions for narrowing the focus?

Juan (reviewer): Most students know about the dangers of credit card debt, but they might not know about specific deceptive practices companies use to lure them. Maybe ask yourself what would surprise your audience about these practices.

Rachel (writer): Juan, that's a good idea. I'll try it.

|

POST COMMENT

Peer reviewer restates writer's main point and asks a question to help her clarify her ideas.

Writer takes comment seriously and asks reviewer for specific suggestion.

Peer reviewer points to specific places in the draft and asks questions to help writer focus on audience and purpose.

Writer is actively engaged with peer reviewer's comments and doesn't take criticism personally.

Peer reviewer responds as a reader and acts as a coach to suggest possible solutions.

Writer thanks reviewer for his help and leaves session with a specific revision strategy.

3c Approach global revision in cycles.

Revision is more effective when you approach it in cycles, rather than attempting to change everything all at once. You may, for example, take one pass through your draft to make sure you are addressing the expectations of a particular audience, and then a second pass to make sure the draft is focused on one central idea or argument. Yet a third pass or cycle may be dedicated to thinking through the logic or the evidence. As you revise, use the following checklist to help you focus on global issues.

Checklist for global revision

Purpose and audience

- Does the draft address a question, a problem, or an issue that readers care about?
- Is the draft appropriate for its audience? Does it account for the audience's knowledge of and possible attitudes toward the subject?

Focus

- Is the thesis clear? Is it prominently placed?
- Does the thesis answer a reader's "So what?" question? (See 1c.)

Organization and paragraphing

- Is each paragraph unified around a main point?
- Have you stated the main point of each paragraph in a topic sentence?
- Does each paragraph support and develop the thesis with evidence?
- Have you presented ideas in a logical order?
- Does each paragraph flow from one to another without gaps or bumps?

Content

- Is the supporting material relevant and persuasive?
- Which ideas need further development? Have you left readers with any unanswered questions?

CHECKLIST FOR GLOBAL REVISION (*cont.*)

• Do major ideas receive enough attention?

• Where might you delete redundant or irrelevant material?

Point of view

• Is the dominant point of view—first person (*I* or *we*), second person (*you*), or third person (*he, she, it, one,* or *they*)—appropriate for your purpose and audience? (See 13a.)

Academic Writing

When reviewing your draft, carefully consider the language you've used when discussing others. Have you made any assumptions about groups of people that are stereotypical or too general? Have you used any language that might be disrespectful or noninclusive of your readers? See 17e.

3d Revise globally by making a reverse outline.

Outlines are useful before you write a first draft to help you focus and structure your ideas. They are useful, too, *after* you have written a draft to reveal the organization and logic of your essay. A *reverse outline* helps you see how the parts of your essay work together so you can determine where to focus your revision efforts. To make a reverse outline, reread your draft and write your main points in the margin. Evaluate each paragraph and ask yourself questions, such as: What is the topic sentence and main idea of each paragraph? Have you provided sufficient support for your thesis? Did you leave anything out? The answers to these questions will shape your revision.

3e Revise and edit sentences.

When you *revise* sentences, you focus on clarity and effectiveness; when you *edit*, you check for correctness. Read each sentence slowly to determine whether it uses correct grammar and punctuation and whether it communicates your meaning clearly and specifically.

Improve your writing with an editing log

An important aspect of becoming a college writer is learning how to identify the grammar, punctuation, and spelling errors that you make frequently and that may make your writing hard to read. You can use an editing log to keep a list of your common errors and learn the rules needed to make corrections or changes. When you receive a draft with feedback, take the following steps.

1 **Review any errors** that your instructor or tutor has identified.

2 **Note which errors you commonly make.** For example, have you seen "run-on sentence" or "need a transition" marked in other drafts?

3 **Identify the advice in the handbook** that will help you correct the errors.

4 **Make an entry in your editing log** to identify each error. A suggested format appears below.

SAMPLE EDITING LOG PAGE

Original Sentence

Most consumer goods companies have social media accounts many of them do not use social media effectively to build their brand recognition.

Edited Sentence

Most consumer goods companies have social media accounts , **but** *many of them do not use social media effectively to build their brand recognition.*

Rule or Pattern Applied

To edit a run-on sentence, use a comma and a coordinating conjunction (and, but, or).

The Bedford Handbook, section 21a

3f Proofread and format the final version of your essay.

Proofreading is a special kind of reading: a slow and methodical search for misspellings, typos, and omitted words or word endings. Such errors can be difficult to spot in your own work because you may read what you intended to write, not what is actually on the page.

PROOFREADING TIPS

- Remove distractions and allow yourself ten to fifteen minutes of pure concentration—without your cell phone.
- Proofread out loud, articulating each word as it is actually written.
- Proofread your sentences in reverse order.
- Don't rely too heavily on spell checkers and grammar checkers. Before accepting their changes, consider the accuracy and appropriateness of the suggestions.
- Ask a volunteer (a friend, roommate, or co-worker) to proofread after you. A second reader may catch something you didn't.

Before turning in your essay, make sure that it is formatted correctly. Use the format recommended by your instructor or for your academic discipline. For an example of formatting in MLA style, see 51b. For an example that shows APA formatting, see 53b.

3g Reflect on your writing.

Reflection—the process of stepping back to examine your decisions, preferences, strengths, and challenges as a writer—helps you recognize your progress as a writer. Thinking about what you've learned about writing makes it possible for you to transfer your learning from one writing assignment to the next. When you complete a piece of writing, reflect on questions such as the following:

- What have you learned about yourself as a writer?

- What parts of the writing process are easy for you? What parts are challenging?

- What do you want to do differently the next time you write?

- Can you identify two or three decisions you made that were successful?

- Can you identify two or three pieces of feedback that helped you revise? What did the feedback teach you?

PART 2

Academic Reading and Writing

4 Reading critically; writing analytically

One of the best ways to become a successful college writer is to become a critical reader. When you read critically, you read with an open, curious mind, trying to understand not only what is written but also why and how it is written. When you write analytically, you respond to a text and its author with your thoughtful observations and insights. The more you take from your reading, the more you have to give as a writer.

4a Read actively.

Reading, like writing, is an active process that happens in steps. For most texts, such as the ones assigned in college, a single quick reading is often not enough. Many such texts require you to read and reread to comprehend their ideas and the evidence used to support their claims.

The guidelines on the next page will help you read actively—previewing, annotating, and conversing with a text you read, whether it is a traditional text composed solely of words or a multimodal text composed of any combination of words, static images, moving images, and sound.

Guidelines for active reading

Preview the text.

- Who is the author? What are the author's credentials?
- What is the author's purpose: To inform? To persuade? To call to action?
- Who is the expected audience?
- When was the text written or created? Where was it published or posted?
- What kind of text is it: A book? A scholarly article? An ad? A public service video? An online news report?

Annotate the text.

- What surprises, puzzles, or intrigues you about the text?
- What question does the text attempt to answer, or what problem does it attempt to solve?
- What is the author's thesis, or main idea?
- What type of evidence does the author provide to support the thesis? How persuasive is this evidence?
- If the text includes sound or images, what purpose do they serve?
- What do you notice about design details?

Converse with the text.

- What are the strengths and limitations of the text?
- If it is a multimodal text, has the author chosen the best combination of modes for the message?
- Has the author drawn conclusions that you question? Do you have a different interpretation of the evidence?
- Does the text raise questions that it does not answer?
- Does the author consider opposing points of view and treat sources fairly?

Ask "So what?"

- Why does the author's thesis need to be argued, explained, or explored? What's at stake?
- What has the author overlooked in presenting this thesis? What's missing?
- Could a reasonable person draw different conclusions?

Read like a writer

Reading like a writer helps you identify the techniques writers use so that you can use them, too. To read like a writer is to pay attention to *how* a text is written and *how* it creates an effect on you.

1 **Review any notes you've made on a text.** What passages do you find effective? What words or sentences did you underline? If you think the text is powerful or well written, figure out *why* and *how* the text works.

2 **Ask *what*, *why*, and *how* questions about the techniques writers use.** *What* techniques do writers use in their introductions, for instance, to hook readers? How does a writer's use of a surprising statistic capture your attention? Identify the specific techniques you appreciate as a reader—and name them—so that they become part of your repertoire as a writer.

3 **Observe how writers use specific academic writing techniques you want to learn.** For instance, if you're interested in learning how writers introduce and respond to counterarguments or how they quote and para-phrase sources, pay attention to these academic writing techniques when you read.

4 **Use your own experiences as a reader to plan the effect you want to create for *your* readers.** As you draft and revise your writing, make deliberate choices to create this effect.

The following example shows how one student, Emilia Sanchez, practiced active reading by annotating an article from *CQ Researcher*, a newsletter about social and political issues.

ANNOTATED ARTICLE

Big Box Stores Are Bad *for Main Street*

BETSY TAYLOR

Title gives away Taylor's position.

There is <u>plenty of reason to be concerned</u> about the proliferation of Wal-Marts and other so-called "big box" stores. The question, however, is not whether or not these types of stores create jobs (although several studies claim they produce a net job loss in local communities) or whether they ultimately save consumers money. The real **concern about having a 25-acre slab of concrete with a 100,000 square foot box of stuff land on a town is whether it's good for a community's soul.

*Main point of article. But what does she mean by "community's soul"?

Assumes readers are concerned.

The worst thing about "big boxes" is that they have a tendency to produce Ross Perot's famous "big sucking sound"—sucking the life out of cities and small towns across the country. On the other hand, small businesses are great for a community. They offer more personal service; they won't threaten to pack up and leave town if they don't get tax breaks, free roads and other blandishments; and small-business owners are much more responsive to a customer's needs. (Ever try to complain about bad service or poor quality products to the president of Home Depot?)

Lumps all big boxes together.

Assumes all small businesses are attentive.

"Either/or" argument— Main Street is good, big boxes are bad.

Yet, if big boxes are so bad, why are they so successful? One glaring reason is that we've become a nation of hyper-consumers, and the big-box boys know this. Downtown shopping

True?

districts comprised of small businesses take some of the efficiency out of overconsumption. There's all that hassle of having to travel from store to store, and having to pull out your credit card so many times. Occasionally, we even find ourselves chatting with the shopkeeper, wandering into a coffee shop to visit with a friend or otherwise wasting precious time that could be spent on acquiring more stuff.!

Word choice makes author seem sentimental.

Author's argument seems one-sided and makes assumptions about consumers.

But let's face it—bustling, thriving city centers are fun. They breathe life into a community. They allow cities and towns to stand out from each other. They provide an atmosphere for people to interact with each other that *just cannot be found at Target, or Wal-Mart or Home Depot.

*Shopping at Target to save money—is that bad?

Is it anti-American to be against having a retail giant set up shop in one's community? Some people would say so. On the other hand, if you board up Main Street, what's left of America?

Ends with emotional appeal. Seems too simplistic!

4b Summarize to deepen your understanding.

Reading critically leads you to understand a text's key points. When you summarize, you test your understanding of the text by putting the main ideas in your own words—concisely, objectively, and accurately—and distinguishing between the text's major and minor points. You'll find advice for summarizing effectively in the box on page 45.

Annotate a text effectively

When you annotate a text with your words, symbols, and responses, you slow down your reading and think critically about the source. You understand the text's meaning better—and you are better prepared to write about it. The following strategies will help you annotate a text.

1 **Circle, underline, or bracket the text's thesis, key words, and major pieces of evidence** to help you distinguish the main idea from the supporting ideas.

2 **Use the text's margins to ask questions** about the author's purpose and argument.

3 **Note what surprises or puzzles you** about the text, or where you agree or disagree with the author's points.

4 **Use symbols to visualize your responses,** such as asterisks (*) for important ideas, exclamation points (!) for information that surprises you, and question marks (?) for points that confuse you.

5 **Experiment with annotation tools.** Sometimes a pen on a printed article is all you'll need. But when you read an online source, annotating digitally can be just as effective. Adobe Reader, for example, is a free program that offers annotation tools for PDFs. Smartphones have built-in annotation tools for text and images. Remember to save your annotated files.

6 **Avoid multitasking.** Focus your full attention on the source and your annotations. Close messaging and social media apps to avoid any distractions.

4c Analyze to demonstrate your critical reading.

Whereas a summary most often answers the question of *what* a text says, an analysis looks closely at the parts of a text to examine *how* the text conveys its main idea. Start with questions and observations you have about the text. What puzzles you or doesn't make sense about the text? What are the strengths of the text? What parts of the text stand out and need close examination? Do you have questions about the author's thesis or use of evidence?

Balancing summary with analysis

Summary and analysis need each other in an analytical essay; you can't have one without the other. Your readers may not be familiar with the text you are analyzing, so you should briefly summarize the text to orient readers and help them understand the basis of your analysis. To balance summary with analysis, try the following strategies:

- Pose *why* and *how* questions that lead to an interpretation of the text rather than to a summary.
- Formulate a strong position (thesis) to answer your questions about the text.
- Make sure your summary sentences serve a purpose and provide a context for analysis.
- Focus your analysis on the text's main ideas or some prominent feature.
- Pay attention to your topic sentences to make sure they signal analysis.

Drafting an analytical thesis statement

An effective thesis statement for analytical writing responds to a question about a text or tries to resolve a problem in the text. Remember that your thesis isn't the same as the text's thesis or main idea. Your thesis presents your judgment of the text's argument.

Summarize effectively

1 **Mention the title of the text, the name of the author, and the author's thesis** in the first sentence.

2 **Maintain a neutral tone;** be objective, and avoid adding your own views to the summary.

3 **Keep your focus on the text.** Don't state the author's ideas as if they were your own.

4 **Use the third-person point of view and the present tense** to present the author's ideas: *Taylor argues . . . , Taylor explains . . .* (If you are writing in APA style, see 49c.) Because the ideas are the author's, avoid writing sentences that begin with *The article says . . .*

5 **Put all or most of your summary in your own words.** If you borrow a phrase or a sentence from the text, put it in quotation marks and give the page number in parentheses. Use a signal phrase to introduce any borrowed language: *According to Singh, immigration data "reflect a slow move away from . . ."*

6 **Limit yourself to presenting the text's key points,** not every detail.

Draft an analytical thesis statement

Analysis begins with asking questions about a text. Answering these questions will help you form a judgment about the text. Let these steps guide you as you develop an analytical thesis statement.

1 **Review your notes to remind yourself of the author's main idea,** supporting evidence, purpose (reason for writing), and audience (intended reader).

2 **Ask *what, why,* or *how* questions to show readers what in the text needs to be questioned and is open to debate.** How do the author's perspective and thesis clarify or complicate your understanding of the subject? Why might a reasonable person agree or disagree with the author? Look for patterns among your questions and annotations to help you discover what interests you about the text.

3 **Write your thesis as an answer to the questions** you have posed or as the resolution of a problem you have identified in the text. Remember that your thesis isn't the same as the author's thesis. Your thesis is your position and presents your judgment of the text.

4 **Test your thesis.** An analytical thesis is arguable, one with which readers might disagree, and not a summary of the text. Is your position clear? Is your position debatable? The answer to both questions should be yes.

5 **Revise your thesis.** Examine your thesis to make sure you state your position clearly. Why does your position matter? Put your working thesis to the "So what?" test (see 1c). Consider adding a *because* clause to your thesis to answer a reader's "So what?" question.

If student writer Emilia Sanchez had started her analysis of "Big Box Stores Are Bad for Main Street" (pp. 41–42) with the following draft thesis statement, she merely would have repeated the main idea of the article.

INEFFECTIVE THESIS STATEMENT (REPEATS AUTHOR'S ARGUMENT)

Big-box stores such as Wal-Mart and Home Depot promote consumerism by offering endless goods at low prices, but they do nothing to promote community.

Instead, Sanchez wrote this analytical thesis statement, which offers *her judgment* of Taylor's argument.

REVISED THESIS STATEMENT (WRITER'S JUDGMENT OF AUTHOR'S ARGUMENT)

By ignoring the complex economic relationship between large chain stores and their communities, Taylor incorrectly assumes that simply getting rid of big-box stores would have a positive effect on America's communities.

4d Sample student writing: Analysis of an article

Following is Emilia Sanchez's analysis of the article by Betsy Taylor (see pp. 41–42). Sanchez used MLA (Modern Language Association) style to format her paper and cite the source.

Emilia Sanchez

Professor Goodwin

English 10

22 October 2015

Rethinking Big-Box Stores

In her essay "Big Box Stores Are Bad for Main Street," Betsy Taylor focuses not on the economic effects of large chain stores but on the effects these stores have on the "soul" of America. She argues that stores like Home Depot, Target, and Wal-Mart are bad for America because they draw people out of downtown shopping districts and cause them to focus on consumption. In contrast, she believes that small businesses are good for America because they provide personal attention, encourage community interaction, and make each city and town unique. But Taylor's argument is unconvincing because it is based on sentimentality—on idealized images of a quaint Main Street— rather than on the roles that businesses play in consumers' lives and communities. By ignoring the complex economic relationship between large chain stores and their communities, Taylor incorrectly assumes that simply getting rid of big-box stores would have a positive effect on America's communities.

Taylor's use of colorful language reveals that she has a sentimental view of American society and does not understand economic realities. In her first paragraph, Taylor refers to a big-box store as a "25-acre slab of concrete with a 100,000 square foot box of stuff" that "land[s] on a town," evoking images of a powerful monster crushing the American way of life. But she oversimplifies a complex issue. Taylor does not consider that many downtown business districts failed long before chain

Summary of the article's thesis orients readers and prepares them for analysis.

Sanchez begins to analyze Taylor's argument.

Thesis expresses Sanchez's judgment of Taylor's article.

Signal phrase introduces quotations from the source.

In MLA style, no page number is needed in an in-text citation for a one-page source.

Marginal annotations indicate MLA-style formatting and effective writing.

Sanchez 2

stores moved in, when factories and mills closed and workers lost their
jobs. In cities with struggling economies, big-box stores can actually
provide much-needed jobs. Similarly, while Taylor blames big-box stores
for harming local economies by asking for tax breaks, free roads, and
other perks, she doesn't acknowledge that these stores also enter into
economic partnerships with the surrounding communities by offering
financial benefits to schools and hospitals.

> Sanchez
> identifies and
> challenges
> Taylor's
> assumptions.

Taylor's assumption that shopping in small businesses is always
better for the customer also seems driven by nostalgia for an old-
fashioned Main Street rather than by the facts. While she may be right
that many small businesses offer personal service and are responsive
to customer complaints, she does not consider that many customers
appreciate the service at big-box stores. Just as customer service is
better at some small businesses than at others, it is impossible to
generalize about service at all big-box stores. For example, customers
depend on the lenient return policies and the wide variety of products at
stores like Target and Home Depot.

> Clear topic
> sentence
> announces a
> shift to a new
> point.

> Sanchez refutes
> Taylor's claim.

Taylor blames big-box stores for encouraging American "hyper-
consumerism," but she oversimplifies by equating big-box stores with
bad values and small businesses with good values. Like her other points,
this claim ignores the economic and social realities of American society
today. Big-box stores do not force Americans to buy more. By offering
lower prices in a convenient setting, however, they allow consumers to
save time and purchase goods they might not be able to afford from
small businesses. The existence of more small businesses would not
change what most Americans can afford, nor would it reduce their desire
to buy affordable merchandise.

Taylor may be right that some big-box stores have a negative
impact on communities and that small businesses offer certain

> Sanchez treats
> the author fairly.

Sanchez 3

Conclusion returns to the thesis and shows the wider significance of Sanchez's analysis.

advantages. But she ignores the economic conditions that support big-box stores as well as the fact that Main Street was in decline before the big-box store arrived. Getting rid of big-box stores will not bring back a simpler America populated by thriving, unique Main Streets; in reality, Main Street will not survive if consumers cannot afford to shop there.

Sanchez 4

Work Cited

Work cited page is in MLA style.

Taylor, Betsy. "Big Box Stores Are Bad for Main Street." *CQ Researcher,* vol. 9, no. 44, 1999, p. 1011.

How to write an analytical essay

An **analysis** of a text allows you to examine the parts of a text to understand *what* it means and *how* it makes its meaning. Your goal is to offer your judgment of the text and to persuade readers to see it through your analytical perspective. Sample analytical essays begin on pages 48 and 55.

Key features

- **A careful and critical reading** of a text reveals what the text says, how it works, and what it means. In an analytical essay, you pay attention to the details of the text, especially its thesis, evidence, and—in the case of a multimodal text—its visual or audio presentation.

- **A thesis that offers a clear judgment** of the text anchors your analysis. Your thesis might be the answer to a question you have posed about the text or the resolution of a problem you have identified in the text.

- **Support for the thesis** comes from evidence in the text. You summarize, paraphrase, and quote passages that support the claims you make about the text.

- **A balance of summary and analysis** helps readers who are not familiar with the text you are analyzing. Summary answers the question of *what* a text says; analysis looks at *how* a text makes its point.

Thinking ahead: Presenting and publishing

You may have the opportunity to present or publish your analysis in the form of a multimodal text such as a video or a slide show. Consider how adding images or sound might strengthen your analysis or help you to better reach your audience.

→

Writing your analytical essay

Explore

Generate ideas for your analysis by responding to questions such as the following:

- What is the text about?
- What do you see as the strengths of the text?
- What do you find most interesting, surprising, or puzzling about this text?
- What is the author's thesis, purpose, or central idea? Put the author's thesis to the "So what?" test.
- What do your annotations of the text reveal about your response to it?

Draft

- Draft a working thesis to focus your analysis. Remember that your thesis is not the same as the author's thesis or message. Your thesis presents *your* judgment of the text.
- Draft a plan to organize your paragraphs. Your introductory paragraph will briefly summarize the text and offer your thesis. Your body paragraphs will support your thesis with evidence from the text. Your conclusion will pull together the major points and show the significance of your analysis.
- Identify specific words, phrases, sentences, or design features as evidence to support your thesis.

Revise

Ask your reviewers to give you specific comments. You can use the following questions both to guide their feedback and to guide your own revision plan.

- Is the introduction effective and engaging?
- Is summary balanced with analysis?
- Does the thesis offer a clear judgment of the text?
- What objections might your readers have to your analysis?
- Is the analysis well organized? Are there clear topic sentences and transitions?
- Have you provided sufficient evidence? Have you analyzed the evidence?
- Have you cited words, phrases, or sentences that are summarized or quoted?

4e Read and write about multimodal texts.

In many of your college classes, you'll have the opportunity to read and write about multimodal texts, such as advertisements, podcasts, videos, or websites. Multimodal texts combine two or more of the following modes: words, static images, moving images, and sound. Like a print text, a multimodal text can be read carefully to understand *what* it says and *how* it communicates its purpose and reaches its audience.

Use the guidelines for active reading on page 39 to help you preview, annotate, and converse with a multimodal text.

Annotate a multimodal text to understand the message and ask questions

The first step is to become familiar enough with the text that you can state its central idea and key points simply and objectively. Taking notes on the text will help you do that. One student, Ren Yoshida, annotated an advertisement for fairly traded coffee. In his annotations, which appear alongside the ad on the next page, you'll see how Yoshida jotted down his observations of the ad's design features and questioned some of the ad's language.

Analyze a multimodal text to demonstrate your critical reading

When you analyze a multimodal text, you say to readers: "Here's my reading of this text. This is what the text means and why it matters." Analysis begins with asking *why* and *how* questions about the text to help you form a judgment about it. When Ren Yoshida analyzed the Equal Exchange advertisement, he asked questions about the ad's design details and its emotional and logical appeals, and he focused his thesis by questioning a single detail in the ad. On the following pages is the Equal Exchange advertisement with Yoshida's notes, followed by his analysis of the ad.

ANNOTATED ADVERTISEMENT

When you choose Equal Exchange
fairly traded coffee, tea or
chocolate, you join a network that
empowers farmers in Latin America,
Africa, and Asia to:
- **Stay on their land**
- **Care for the environment**
- **Farm organically**
- **Support their family**
- **Plan for the future**

www.equalexchange.coop

Photo: Jesus Choqueheranca de Quevera,
Coffee farmer & CEPICAFE Cooperative member, Peru

What is being exchanged?

Why is "fairly traded" so hard to read?

"Empowering"—why in an elegant font? Who
is empowering farmers?

"Farmers" in all capital letters—shows
strength?

Straightforward design and not much text.

Outstretched hands. Is she giving a gift?
Inviting partnership?

Hands: heart-shaped, foregrounded.

Raw coffee beans are red: earthy,
natural, warm.

Positive verbs: consumers choose, join,
empower; farmers stay, care, farm, support,
plan.

How do consumers know their money helps
farmers stay on their land?

Yoshida 1

Ren Yoshida

Professor Marcotte

English 101

4 November 2021

Sometimes a Cup of Coffee Is Just a Cup of Coffee

A farmer, her hardworking hands full of coffee beans, reaches out from an Equal Exchange advertisement (Advertisement). The hands, in the shape of a heart, offer to consumers the fruit of the farmer's labor. The ad's message is straightforward: in choosing Equal Exchange, consumers become global citizens, partnering with farmers to help save the planet. Suddenly, a cup of coffee is more than just a morning ritual; a cup of coffee is a moral choice that empowers both consumers and farmers. This simple exchange appeals to a consumer's desire to be a good person—to protect the environment and do the right thing. Yet the ad is more complicated than it first seems, and its design raises some logical questions about such an exchange. Although the ad works on an emotional level, it is less successful on a logical level because of its promise for an equal exchange between consumers and farmers.

The focus of the ad is a farmer, Jesus Choqueheranca de Quevero, and, more specifically, her outstretched, cupped hands. Her hands are full of red, raw coffee, her life's work. The ad successfully appeals to consumers' emotions, assuming they will find the farmer's welcoming face and hands, caked with dirt, more appealing than startling statistics about the state of the environment or the number of farmers who lose their land each year. It seems almost rude not to accept the farmer's generous offering since we know her name and, as the ad implies, have the choice to "empower" her. In fact, how can a consumer resist helping the farmer "[c]are for the environment" and "[p]lan for the future," when it is a simple matter of choosing the right coffee? The ad sends

Source is cited in the text. No page number is available for the online source.

Yoshida summarizes the content of the ad.

Thesis expresses Yoshida's analysis of the ad.

Details show how the ad appeals to consumers' emotions.

Yoshida interprets details such as the farmer's hands.

Marginal annotations indicate MLA-style formatting and effective writing.

Yoshida 2

the message that our future is a global future in which producers and consumers are bound together.

First impressions play a major role in the success of an advertisement. Consumers are pulled toward a product, or pushed away, by an ad's initial visual and emotional appeal. Here, the intended audience is busy people, so the ad tries to catch viewers' attention and make a strong impression immediately. Yet with a second or third viewing, consumers might start to ask some logical questions about Equal Exchange before buying their morning coffee. Although the farmer extends her heart-shaped hands to consumers, they are not actually buying a cup of coffee or the raw coffee directly from her. In reality, consumers are buying from Equal Exchange, even if the ad substitutes the more positive word *choose* for *buy*. Furthermore, consumers aren't actually empowering the farmer; they are joining "a network that empowers farmers." The idea of a network makes a simple transaction more complicated. How do consumers know their money helps farmers "[s]tay on their land" and "[p]lan for the future" as the ad promises? They don't.

The ad's design elements raise questions about the use of the key terms *equal exchange* and *empowering farmers*. The Equal Exchange logo suggests symmetry and equality, with two red arrows facing each other, but the words of the logo appear almost like an eye exam poster, with each line decreasing in font size and clarity. The words *fairly traded* are tiny. Below the logo, the words *empowering farmers* are presented in contradictory fonts. *Empowering* is written in a flowing, cursive font, almost the opposite of what might be considered empowering, whereas *farmers* is written in a plain, sturdy font. The ad's varying fonts communicate differently and make it hard to know exactly what is being exchanged and who is becoming empowered.

Marginal annotations:

Yoshida begins to challenge the logic of the ad.

Words from the ad serve as evidence.

Clear topic sentence announces a shift to a new point.

Summary of the ad's key features serves Yoshida's analysis.

Yoshida 3

What is being exchanged? The logic of the ad suggests that consumers will improve the future by choosing Equal Exchange. The first exchange is economic: consumers give one thing—dollars—and receive something in return—a cup of coffee—and the farmer stays on her land. The second exchange is more complicated because it involves a moral exchange. The ad suggests that if consumers don't choose "fairly traded" products, farmers will be forced off their land and the environment destroyed. This exchange, when put into motion by consumers choosing to purchase products not "fairly traded," has negative consequences for both consumers and farmers. The message of the ad is that the actual exchange taking place is not economic but moral; after all, nothing is being bought, only chosen. Yet the logic of this exchange quickly falls apart. Consumers aren't empowered to become global citizens simply by choosing Equal Exchange, and farmers aren't empowered to plan for the future by consumers' choices. And even if all this empowerment magically happened, there is nothing equal about such an exchange.

> Yoshida shows why his thesis matters.

Advertisements are themselves about empowerment—encouraging viewers to believe they can become someone or do something by identifying, emotionally or logically, with a product. In the Equal Exchange ad, consumers are emotionally persuaded to identify with a farmer whose face is not easily forgotten and whose heart-shaped hands hold a collective future. On a logical level, though, the ad raises questions because empowerment, although a good concept to choose, is not easily or equally exchanged. Sometimes a cup of coffee is just a cup of coffee.

> Conclusion includes a detail from the introduction.
>
> Conclusion returns to Yoshida's thesis.

Yoshida 4

Work Cited

Advertisement for Equal Exchange. *Equal Exchange*, equalexchange.coop. Accessed 14 Oct. 2021.

5 Reading arguments

Many of your college assignments will ask you to read and write arguments about debatable issues. The questions being debated might be matters of public policy (*Should law enforcement officers be allowed to seek no-knock warrants?*), or they might be scholarly issues (*What role does social responsibility play in determining behavior in a pandemic?*). On such questions, reasonable people may disagree. You'll find the critical reading strategies introduced in section 4 to be useful as you enter debates and ask questions about an argument's logic, evidence, and use of appeals.

5a Read with an open mind and a critical eye.

As you read arguments and enter into academic or public policy debates, keep an open mind about opposing viewpoints. Be curious about and open to the wide range of positions in the arguments you are reading. Examine an author's assumptions (ideas the author accepts as true), assess the evidence, and weigh conclusions. Reading with an open mind means doing the following:

- **Read carefully.** Read to understand an author's argument and point of view. Ask questions: What is the author's thesis? What evidence does the author use to support the thesis?

- **Read skeptically.** Read to test the strengths and weaknesses of an author's argument. Ask questions: Are any of the author's assumptions or conclusions problematic? Is the author's evidence persuasive and sufficient? How does the author handle opposing views?

- **Read evaluatively.** Read to evaluate the usefulness and significance of an author's argument. Put the argument to the "So what?" test: Why does the thesis matter? Why does it need to be argued?

> ## Recognizing logical fallacies
>
> When you evaluate an argument, look closely at the reasoning behind it. Some arguments use unreasonable argumentative tactics known as *logical fallacies*.
>
> A **hasty generalization** is a conclusion based on insufficient or unrepresentative evidence.
>
> *In a single year, scores on standardized tests in California's public schools rose by ten points. Therefore, more children than ever are succeeding in America's public school systems.*
>
> A **stereotype** is a hasty generalization about a group.
>
> *All politicians are corrupt.*
>
> A **false analogy** is a comparison that points out a similarity between two things that are unrelated.
>
> *If we can send a spacecraft to Mars, we should be able to find a cure for the common cold.*
>
> A *post hoc* **fallacy** assumes that because one event follows another, the first is the cause of the second.
>
> *Since Governor Cho took office, unemployment within communities of color has decreased by seven percent. Governor Cho should be applauded for reducing unemployment.*
>
> An **either/or fallacy** oversimplifies an argument by suggesting that there are only two alternatives, when in fact there are more.
>
> *Many attempted solutions to opioid addiction have not worked. We should either stop manufacturing opioid drugs or give everyone access to naloxone, the overdose-preventing drug.*
>
> ***Non sequitur*** is Latin for "It does not follow." When a statement or conclusion is an assertion that does not logically follow what came before it, we call it a non sequitur.
>
> *State governments should not require vaccines in schools because the flu is not usually fatal.*

5b Evaluate ethical, logical, and emotional appeals.

Ancient Greek rhetoricians distinguished among three kinds of appeals used to influence readers: ethical, logical, and emotional. As you evaluate arguments, identify these appeals and question their effectiveness. Are they appropriate for the audience and the argument? Are they balanced and legitimate or lopsided and misleading?

Evaluating ethical, logical, and emotional appeals as a reader

Ethical appeals (*ethos*)

Ethical arguments call upon a writer's character, knowledge, and authority. Ask questions such as the following when you evaluate the ethical appeal of an argument.

- Is the writer informed and trustworthy? How does the writer establish authority and credibility?
- Does the writer use sources knowledgeably and responsibly?
- How does the writer describe the views of others and deal with opposing views?

Logical appeals (*logos*)

Reasonable arguments appeal to readers' sense of logic, rely on evidence, and use inductive and deductive reasoning. Ask questions such as the following to evaluate the logical appeal of an argument.

- Is the evidence sufficient, representative, and relevant?
- Is the reasoning sound?
- Does the argument contain any logical fallacies or unwarranted assumptions?
- Are there any missing or mistaken premises?

Emotional appeals (*pathos*)

Emotional arguments appeal to readers' beliefs and values. Ask questions such as the following to evaluate the emotional appeal of an argument.

- What values or beliefs does the writer address, either directly or indirectly?
- Is the emotional appeal legitimate and fair?
- Does the writer oversimplify or dramatize an issue?
- Does the emotional argument highlight or shift attention away from the evidence?

THIS SEASON, SHARE SOME VALUES
Learn more about our Common Threads Initiative,
and take the pledge to reduce consumption

TAKE THE PLEDGE

Advertising makes use of ethical, logical, and emotional appeals to persuade consumers to buy a product or embrace a brand. This Patagonia ad makes an ethical appeal with its copy that invites customers to rethink their purchasing practices.

EXERCISE 5–1 In the following paragraph, identify the type of appeal used in each sentence that ends with three choices: *ethos* (ethical appeal), *logos* (logical appeal), or *pathos* (emotional appeal).

Elderspeak, the use of pet names such as "dear" and "sweetie" directed toward older adults, is generally intended as an endearment. However, the use of such language suggests a view of seniors as childlike or cognitively impaired. It should be no surprise, then, that older adults find these pet names condescending and demeaning (*ethos / logos / pathos*). Unfortunately, the effects of elderspeak go far beyond insulting older adults. Health care professionals have found that residents in nursing facilities, even those with dementia, respond to patronizing language by becoming uncooperative, aggressive, or depressed. In a 2009 study published in the *American Journal of Alzheimer's Disease and Other Dementias*, Ruth Herman and Kristine N. Williams reported that older adults responded to elderspeak by resisting care, yelling, or crying ("Elderspeak's Influence") (*ethos / logos / pathos*). Surprisingly, despite widely published research on the negative effects of elderspeak, the worst offenders are health care workers, the very people we trust to treat our elderly family members with respect and dignity—and the very people who are old enough to know better (*ethos / logos / pathos*).

5c Evaluate the evidence behind an argument.

Writers draw on facts, statistics, examples, expert opinion, and appeals to support their arguments. As you read an argument, look closely at the evidence behind the argument. Ask questions:

- Is the evidence **accurate** and **fair**?
- Is the evidence **sufficient**?
- Is the evidence **representative**?
- Is the evidence **relevant**?

The chart on the next page offers an example of how to evaluate evidence in the arguments you read. See also section 46 for more on identifying false and misleading sources.

5d Evaluate how fairly a writer handles opposing views.

The way in which a writer deals with opposing views is telling. Some writers address the arguments of the opposition fairly, conceding points when necessary and countering others, all in a civil spirit. Other writers will do almost anything to win an argument: either ignoring opposing views altogether or misrepresenting such views and attacking their proponents.

Writers build credibility — *ethos* — by addressing opposing arguments fairly. As you read arguments, evaluate how writers deal with views that don't line up with their own. Credible writers deal with opposing arguments by

- respectfully acknowledging alternative positions
- incorporating elements of the opposition into their own arguments
- using precise language to describe opposing views
- quoting opposing views accurately and fairly
- not misrepresenting a source by taking it out of context
- finding common ground among differing positions

Questioning the evidence behind a conclusion

When authors construct an argument, they often use *inductive reasoning*—
drawing a conclusion based on a piece of evidence. You can test the evidence
and the conclusion an author has made with the questions that follow.

Conclusion

*The majority of students on our campus would volunteer at least five hours a
week in a community organization if the school provided a placement service for
volunteers.*

Evidence

*In a recent survey of students on our campus, 723 of 1,215 participants said they
would volunteer at least five hours a week in a community organization if the school
provided a placement service for volunteers.*

1. **Is the evidence accurate and unbiased?** The evidence is trustworthy if the author has conducted the survey fairly and objectively,
without bias. In weighing the accuracy of survey evidence, ask questions
about the author's purpose for conducting the survey and the methods
used to collect data.

2. **Is the evidence sufficient?** That depends. On a small campus (say,
3,000 students), the pool of students surveyed would be sufficient for
research, but on a large campus (say, 30,000 students), 1,215 students
would be only 4 percent of the population. If those 4 percent were known
to be truly representative of the other 96 percent, however, even such
a small sample would be sufficient.

3. **Is the evidence representative?** The evidence is representative if
those responding to the survey reflect the entire student population with
respect to the characteristics of age, gender, race, field of study, number
of extracurricular commitments, and so on. If most of those surveyed
major in a field such as social work, you should question the survey's
conclusion.

4. **Is the evidence relevant?** Yes. The survey results are directly linked
to the conclusion. A survey about the number of hours students work for pay,
by contrast, would not be relevant because it would not be about *choosing to
volunteer.*

> Checklist for reading and evaluating arguments

- What is the writer's purpose and thesis?
- Are there any gaps in reasoning? Does the argument contain any logical fallacies?
- On what assumptions does the argument rest? Are any of the assumptions unstated?
- What appeals—ethical, logical, or emotional—does the writer make? Are these appeals effective?
- What evidence does the writer use? Could there be alternative interpretations of the evidence?
- How does the writer handle opposing views?
- If you are not persuaded by the writer's argument, what counterarguments would you make to the writer?

6 Writing arguments

- ▶ Using ethical, logical, and emotional appeals as a writer, 66
- ▶ How to draft a thesis statement for an argument, 68
- ▶ Anticipating and countering opposing arguments, 71
- ▶ Writing guide: How to write an argument essay, 79

Writing an argument gives you the opportunity to contribute to the ongoing conversation around a debatable issue. You take a position in a debate, provide evidence that supports your position, and respond to other positions on the issue.

Just as you evaluate arguments with an open mind, construct your own arguments with the same openness. Throughout this chapter, you will see the work of a student writer, Julia Riew, who chose to write a researched argument essay about zoos. Her original position treated the issue as either right or wrong. However, her argument became more complex and her writing became more open minded as she developed her essay. You'll find Julia Riew's argument essay in 6h.

6a Identify your purpose and context.

Your purpose in constructing an argument is to support your position and persuade your readers. As you consider possible topics, start by informing yourself about the debate or conversation around a subject, sometimes called its *context*. Read sources that will help you understand the issues and approaches—the ongoing conversation—surrounding a topic. For example, student writer Julia Riew started with the position that zoos are always unethical. However, as she researched the fierce debates around zoos, she learned from experts with differing points of view. She read about the extinction rates of many species and the conservation efforts of some zoos. With the context of the debate more clear, she revised her original position—zoos are unethical—to a new one: It would be unethical for zoos not to save endangered animals.

6b View your audience as a panel of jurors.

As you build your argument, think about how you will appeal to your audience. It is useful to envision your audience as skeptical readers who, like a panel of jurors, will make up their minds after listening to all sides of the argument. To construct a convincing argument, you need to establish your credibility (*ethos*) and appeal to your readers' sense of logic and reason (*logos*) as well as to their values and beliefs (*pathos*). The box below will help you do so.

6c In your introduction, establish credibility and state your position.

When you construct an argument, make sure your introduction includes a thesis statement, a signpost that lets readers know your position. In the sentences leading up to the thesis, establish your credibility (*ethos*) with readers by showing that you are fair-minded and knowledgeable about

Using ethical, logical, and emotional appeals as a writer

Ethical appeals (*ethos*)

To accept your argument, a reader must see you as trustworthy, fair, and reasonable. When you acknowledge alternative positions, you build common ground with readers and gain their trust by showing that you are knowledgeable. And when you use sources responsibly and respectfully, you inspire readers' confidence in your judgment.

> However, not everyone agrees. Critics point out, rightly so, that eliminating grades in academic environments would require massive system-wide rethinking.

Logical appeals (*logos*)

To persuade readers, you need to appeal to their sense of logic and reason. When you provide evidence, you offer readers logical support for your argument. And when you clarify the assumptions (ideas that you accept as true or certain) that underlie your arguments, you appeal to readers' desire for reason.

> A recent study showed that an overemphasis on grades — and not learning — has led 87 percent of the study participants to cheat on or consider cheating on an exam.

Emotional appeals (*pathos*)

To establish common ground with readers, you need to appeal to their beliefs and values as well as to their minds. When you offer vivid examples and illustrations, surprising statistics, or compelling visuals, you engage readers in your argument. And when you balance emotional appeals with logical appeals, you highlight the human dimension of an issue to show readers why they should care about your argument.

> Why continue to promote a culture of fear and intimidation with *report-card Fridays*, days when American students are concerned less with what they've learned than with how they've scored?

the various positions in a debate. By building common ground (*pathos*) with readers who at first may not agree with your views, you show them why they should consider your thesis.

Student writer Julia Riew built credibility in her argument essay by using her introduction to introduce both sides of the debate around zoos and endangered animals. She defined important terms and presented herself as a fair-minded writer. She connected with readers by emphasizing the severity of the extinction rate and establishing the common ground she discovered—that humans are also harmed by animal extinctions. To read Julia's introduction, see 6h.

6d Back up your thesis with persuasive lines of argument.

An argument of any complexity contains lines of argument that, when taken together, might reasonably persuade readers that the thesis has merit. You can think of lines of argument as your *reasons*. The following, for example, are the main lines of argument that student writer Julia Riew uses in her paper about the role of zoos in saving endangered species.

THESIS: CENTRAL CLAIM

When zoos protect animals with compassion and consideration for their needs, they encourage concern for the environment and increase financial support for conservation projects—saving not only endangered species but also the planet and humankind in turn.

SUPPORTING CLAIMS

- While some critics believe all zoos are inhumane, zoos can treat animals humanely—keeping animals in *custody* rather than in *captivity*—with oversight and regulations.
- Zoos protect endangered species by providing safe alternatives to their natural habitats, which may no longer exist.
- Although these animals may no longer be able to survive in the wild, zoos help the conservation effort by educating society about the dangers of extinction and humanity's own hand in causing it.
- Zoos also raise money for conservation efforts through sales and donations.

Draft a thesis statement for an argument

1 **Identify the various positions in the debate you're writing about.** At the heart of a good argument are debate and disagreement. An argumentative thesis takes a clear position on a debatable issue and is supported by evidence. Identify the points in the debate on which there is disagreement. Consider your own questions and thoughts about the topic.

2 **Ask a question that doesn't have an easy yes or no answer.** An open-ended question that doesn't have just one correct answer will lead you to developing a stronger thesis. If your question can be answered with a yes or no response, add *why* or *how* to the question to provide an argumentative edge.

3 **Determine where you stand on the issue.** Consider how the sources you have read provide support for your position. Also consider how the sources make you think further about your position.

4 **Write your thesis as an answer to your question.** Your thesis should be arguable, one with which readers might disagree. Ask questions: Is your position debatable? Does your thesis state your position specifically and clearly? Will readers understand why your thesis matters?

5 **Test your thesis with a counterargument.** View your argument through the eyes of readers who disagree with you. Try to imagine a reader's counterargument to your argument.

6 **Revise your thesis.** Why does your position matter? Put your working thesis to the "So what?" test (1c). Consider adding *because* or *although* to your thesis to show readers the importance of your position or to set it in the context of an opposing view.

6e Support your thesis with specific evidence.

You will support your thesis with evidence: facts and statistics, examples and illustrations, visuals (charts, graphs, photos), expert opinion, and so on.

Using facts and statistics

A fact is something that is known with certainty because it has been objectively verified: carbon has an atomic weight of 12; Georgia congressman John Lewis passed away on July 17, 2020. Statistics are based on data and might or might not be factual, depending on the source of the data. If you choose to use statistics, look closely at the source of the statistics. Ask questions: Where do the statistics come from? Can they be verified? If you suspect that a writer's handling of statistics is not fair, track down the original sources for those statistics or read authors with opposing views, as they may give you a fuller understanding of the numbers.

Using examples

Examples rarely prove a point by themselves, but when used in combination with other forms of evidence, they add detail to an argument and bring it to life. Because examples are often concrete and sometimes vivid, they can reach readers in ways that statistics and abstract ideas cannot.

Using visuals

Visuals can support your argument by providing vivid and detailed evidence and by capturing your readers' attention. Bar or line graphs, for instance, can describe and organize complex statistical data; photographs can convey abstract ideas; maps can illustrate geography. As you consider using visual evidence, ask whether the evidence will appeal to readers logically, ethically, or emotionally.

In her essay, Riew uses a graph to show readers the dramatic increase in extinction rates of vertebrates, supporting her argument that the "current extinction rate is an unprecedented crisis that impacts all creatures." To see the visual in Riew's paper, see page 76.

Citing expert opinion

Although they are no substitute for careful reasoning of your own, the views of an expert can contribute to the force of your argument. To help readers recognize the expert, provide credentials showing why the source is worth listening to—why the expert is, in fact, an expert—perhaps by listing their title or expertise. For example, Riew cites a geological expert who studies ecosystems and provides his credentials.

> Geologist and environmental researcher Paul B. Wignall designates "human activities" such as poaching, climate change, "habitat destruction, the introduction of invasive species . . . , and the general over-exploitation of natural resources" as the primary causes of this increase (17).

6f Anticipate objections; counter opposing arguments.

No argument is complete without anticipating, acknowledging, and countering opposing arguments. It might seem at first that drawing attention to an opposing point of view or contradictory evidence would weaken your argument. But if you don't acknowledge counterarguments, your readers may ask, "Have you thought about this other point of view?" By acknowledging that not everyone draws the same conclusion or holds the same point of view, you show your *ethos* as a reasonable, fair, and well-informed writer who wants to establish common ground with readers.

There is no best place in an essay to deal with opposing views. Often it is useful to summarize the opposing position early in your essay. After stating your thesis but before developing your own arguments, you might include a paragraph that addresses the most important counterargument. Or you can anticipate objections paragraph by paragraph as you build your case. Wherever you decide to address opposing arguments, you will enhance your credibility if you explain the arguments of others accurately and fairly.

> **Anticipating and countering opposing arguments**
>
> To anticipate a possible objection to your argument, consider the following questions.
>
> - Could a reasonable person draw a different conclusion from your facts or examples?
> - Might a reader question any of your assumptions or offer an alternative explanation?
> - Is there any evidence that might weaken your position?
>
> The following questions may help you respond to a potential objection.
>
> - Can you concede the point to the opposition but challenge the point's importance or usefulness?
> - Can you explain why readers should consider a new perspective or question a piece of evidence?
> - Should you explain how your position responds to contradictory evidence?
> - Can you suggest a different interpretation of the evidence?
>
> Use sentence openers to signal to readers that you're about to present an objection.
>
> - Critics of this view argue that _____.
> - Some readers might point out that _____.
> - Researchers challenge these claims by _____.

6g Build common ground with your audience.

As you construct your argument and counter opposing arguments, try to establish common ground with readers. If you can show that you share their concerns, your readers will be more likely to accept your argument. For example, to convince readers of the important role zoos play in protecting and saving endangered species, Riew asked herself, "Why should readers care about the issue of endangered species?" She reasoned that some readers might not care about saving animals, but most readers care about saving themselves from extinction. Through her research, she learned about the connections between the rapid rate of extinctions and the threat to humans' access to food, medicine, and clean water. By asking "Why should readers care?" she found her shared concerns with readers, leading her to argue that, in saving animals from extinction, we are also saving ourselves and our ecosystem.

6h Sample student writing: Argument

In the following paper, student writer Julia Riew argues that zoos have an important mission to offer safe, compassionate custody to shelter and save endangered species and protect our ecosystem. Riew appeals to readers by presenting opposing views fairly before providing her own arguments.

When Riew quotes, summarizes, or paraphrases information from a source, she cites the source with an in-text citation formatted in MLA style. Citations in the paper refer readers to the list of works cited at the end of the paper.

Julia Riew

Professor Pine

Composition I

28 April 2020

From Captors to Custodians: How Zoos Protect Animals,

People, and the Planet

The Tasmanian tiger: extinct. The Japanese sea lion: extinct. The

Pyrenean ibex: extinct. The roster of extinct species goes on: the Saudi

gazelle, the Cape Verde giant skink, the passenger pigeon, and countless

others. The rate of extinction has risen rapidly within the last three

centuries, and it signifies a crisis known as Earth's sixth mass extinction

(Wignall 19–20). This crisis threatens not only animals but also our

ecosystem as a whole, which in turn threatens our access to clean water,

clean air, food, and medicine. In response, many zoos have shifted

their mission from pure entertainment to conservation. Supporters of

the conservation mission claim that zoos possess enormous potential

to save endangered species. Critics claim that zoos should have no role

in conservation, arguing that animals should be free to roam in their

natural habitats, not captive or caged. In this debate, the word *captivity*

often conjures images of fear-stricken animals behind bars, gawked at by

tourists and eager to escape. However, what if we shift our understanding

of *captivity* from imprisonment to compassionate protection, or *custody*?

When zoos protect animals with compassion and consideration for their

needs, they encourage concern for the environment and increase financial

support for conservation projects—saving not only endangered species

but also the planet and humankind in turn.

Despite the intentions of zoo conservation programs to protect

animals, some animal rights advocates object to any form of captivity,

arguing that zoos have a long history of animal abuse and mistreatment.

In 2019, hundreds of zoos affiliated with the World Association of Zoos

Riew introduces a problem and explains why it matters.

Riew summarizes the debate.

Riew defines two key terms, captivity and custody.

Thesis takes a position in the debate.

Riew presents a counterargument fairly.

Marginal annotations indicate MLA-style formatting and effective writing.

and Aquariums (WAZA) faced criticism for mistreating animals, reportedly using training methods such as "premature separation from mothers, physical restraint, and pain- and fear-based conditioning" in order to allow humans to feed, pet, and even ride the animals (Fobar). Such treatment—"inherently stressful," according to one director at the Animal Welfare Institute—harms the animals both physically and psychologically (Fobar). With a legacy of animal rights violations, zoos have earned their poor reputation among many animal rights activists.

> Sources are cited in MLA style.

However, captivity does not have to be—and should not be—inhumane. Rather than thinking of housing endangered species in zoos as harmful *captivity*, we might instead think of zookeeping as *custody*—raising, protecting, and caring for animals with no place to go. A new level of care can be the reality of all zoos with the help of strict regulations provided by animal welfare programs. The American Humane Conservation program, developed by experts in animal welfare and conservation, evaluates and certifies leading zoos all over the world based on several criteria, including "excellent health and housing; positive social interactions . . . ; [and] safe and stimulating environments" (American Humane). Regulations are a step in the right direction.

> Transition moves from introducing the counter-argument to addressing it.

With animal welfare regulations, zoos will protect animals at a higher standard than they have in the past—sometimes at a higher standard than animals can find in the wild if their habitat has been disrupted. Ron Kagan, CEO of the Detroit Zoological Society, points to the success of the Arctic Ring of Life, the largest polar bear facility in the United States. The facility provides chilled seawater and a safe environment for bears whose polar habitats have been destroyed by climate change (00:07:40–08:36). Kagan argues that by putting the needs of the animals first, regulated zoos create living environments that can be both safe and comfortable for animals, giving them access to shelter and space that they may no longer find in the wild.

> Riew backs up her argument with a specific example.

Riew 3

To some critics, capturing and breeding endangered animals in such situations—when the animals may no longer be able to survive in their natural habitats—is pointless. These critics argue that breeding and captive protection can be permissible only if zoos eventually release the animals. However, research indicates that the majority of captive species fail to flourish once reintroduced into their natural habitats: one particularly devastating reintroduction study revealed that "only 16 out of 145 reintroduction projects using captive-born animals were successful" (Keulartz 341). Once in captivity, animals tend to remain in captivity for life.

Why, then, do zoos keep these animals? Despite critics' claims, zoo animals help environmentalists achieve a key goal: to educate the general public about the importance of wildlife and the dangers of extinction. Although some level of extinction is natural, the current extinction rate is an unprecedented crisis that impacts all creatures, including humans—and we are largely to blame. Figure 1 demonstrates the dramatic increase in the extinction rates of vertebrates after the start of the Industrial Revolution. Geologist and environmental researcher Paul B. Wignall designates "human activities" such as poaching, climate change, "habitat destruction, the introduction of invasive species . . . , and the general over-exploitation of natural resources" as the primary causes of this increase (17). Animal extinction disrupts the overall ecosystem and directly impacts us in ways we might not realize. For example, anthropologist Thom Van Dooren notes that predators such as vultures play "an important role in containing disease of various kinds" and their decline "may lead to rises in . . . scavengers and in the incidence of diseases." Furthermore, each time a species goes extinct, the event lowers the overall biodiversity of the region and contributes to "an unraveling of cultural and social relationships that ripples out into the world"—an environmental effect that impacts us all (Van Dooren).

Riew acknowledges a second counter-argument.

Riew refutes the counterargument and develops the thesis.

Riew calls out and describes a figure, located at the top of the next page.

Riew supports her argument's "So what?" factor—why readers should care.

Riew 4

Visual presents specific data that back up Riew's point.

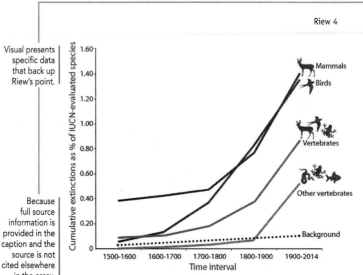

Because full source information is provided in the caption and the source is not cited elsewhere in the essay, no entry for the source is needed in the works cited list.

Fig. 1. Gerardo Ceballos et al. Fig. 1A, "Accelerated Modern Human-Induced Species Losses: Entering the Sixth Mass Extinction." *Science Advances*, vol. 1, no. 5, 19 June 2015, https://doi.org/10.1126/sciadv.1400253.

To reduce future losses of endangered species, people must gain a better understanding of the environment and animals' roles in it, and zoos help with that education. In 2015, a team researching the educational impacts of zoos surveyed more than six thousand visitors to thirty institutions around the globe. Their study found that "biodiversity understanding and knowledge of actions to help protect biodiversity both significantly increased over the course of single zoo and aquarium visits. . . . In other words, zoos and aquariums can and do make a positive contribution" (Moss et al. 243). By exposing people to different animals and educating people about the negative impacts of extinction, zoos can prompt visitors to care more for wildlife.

Riew 5

Zoos can also directly increase financial support for conservation efforts. Not only can their educational efforts lead visitors to donate to conservation organizations, but zoos also can raise funds with ticket, food, and souvenir sales that they then pass on to conservation projects. For example, each year the Oakland Zoo donates a portion of every ticket to conservation organizations through a program called Quarters for Conservation. In 2018, Quarters for Conservation raised $332,000 to help save at-risk species ("Oakland Zoo"). As environmental philosopher Jozef Keulartz points out, "to reach the aim of species conservation, [zoos] need to attract visitors"; thus zoos often house not only animals that need protection but also those that will make people want to buy tickets (347). Traditionally, large "charismatic mammals" can "act as flagship species" to attract visitors, while a variety of species and "imaginative displays" can also increase attendance (Keulartz 347). Higher attendance and ticket sales mean zoos can donate more of their proceeds to a range of conservation initiatives.

> Riew uses specific evidence for support.

By raising animals in regulated and certified habitats, zoos can play a critical role in the conservation cause and can help shift our impressions of zookeepers from captors to custodians. Opponents worry about the necessity of zoos and the health of animals within them. However, with an informed understanding of animal welfare needs, such establishments not only provide animals with humane habitats that no longer exist in the wild but also promote empathy and financial support for conservation. Each day, as the threat of mass extinction continues to sweep the globe and irreversibly damage the worldwide ecosystem, it becomes increasingly urgent for humans to understand the importance of wildlife. With the help of zoos, we can take action to protect animals— and thus ourselves. Perhaps our action today will keep us off the extinction roster tomorrow.

> Conclusion echoes the introduction without repeating it.

> Riew ends by emphasizing why the argument matters.

Riew 6

Works Cited

American Humane. "Twenty-Five Leading Zoological Facilities Receive
        Coveted American Humane Conservation Certification for Humane
        Animal Care in Inaugural Year." *PR Newswire*, Cision, 2 Oct.
        2017, www.prnewswire.com/news-releases/twenty-five-leading
        -zoological-facilities-receive-coveted-american-humane
        -conservation-certification-for-humane-animal-care-in-inaugural
        -year-300529156.html. Press release.

Fobar, Rachel. "Hundreds of Zoos and Aquariums Accused of Mis-
        treating Animals." *National Geographic*, 15 Aug.2019,
        www.nationalgeographic.com/animals/2019/08/
        waza-zoos-accused-of-mistreating-animals-wap-report/.

Kagan, Ron. "Animal Welfare and the Future of Zoos, Ron Kagan,
        TEDxOaklandUniversity." *YouTube*, uploaded by TEDx Talks, 30 Nov.
        2015, www.youtube.com/watch?v=h_FRY4FIkws.

Keulartz, Jozef. "Captivity for Conservation? Zoos at a Crossroads."
        Journal of Agricultural and Environmental Ethics, vol. 28, no. 2,
        Apr. 2015, pp. 335–51. *SpringerLink*, https://doi.org/10.1007/
        s10806-015-9537-z.

Moss, Andrew, et al. "Impact of a Global Biodiversity Education Campaign
        on Zoo and Aquarium Visitors." *Frontiers in Ecology and the Envi-
        ronment*, vol. 15, no. 5, June 2017, pp. 243–47. *Ecological Society
        of America*, https://doi.org/10.1002/fee.1493.

"Oakland Zoo Raises Record-Breaking $332,000 for Wildlife Conserva-
        tion." *Oakland Zoo*, 30 Oct. 2018, www.oaklandzoo.org/news/
        oakland-zoo-raises-record-breaking-332-000-for-wildlife
        -conservation. Press release.

Van Dooren, Thom. "How the Current Mass Extinction of Animals Threat-
        ens Humans." Interview by Simon Worrall. *National Geographic*, 20
        Aug. 2014, www.nationalgeographic.com/news/2014/8/140820-
        extinction-crows-penguins-dinosaurs-asteroid-sydney-booktalk/.

Wignall, Paul B. *Extinction: A Very Short Introduction*. Oxford UP, 2019.
        Very Short Introductions.

Works cited list
is in MLA style.

List is
alphabetized
by authors'
last names (or
by title when
a work has no
author).

How to write an argument essay

When you compose an **argument**, you take a position on a debatable issue. You state your position, provide evidence to support it, and respond to opposing views on the issue. A sample argument essay begins on page 73.

Key features

- **A thesis, stated as a clear position on a debatable issue**, frames an argument essay. The issue is debatable because reasonable people disagree about it.

- **An examination of the issue's context** indicates why the issue is important, why readers should care about it, or how your position fits into the debates surrounding the topic.

- **Sufficient, representative, and relevant evidence** supports the argument's claims. Evidence needs to be specific and persuasive; quoted, summarized, or paraphrased fairly and accurately; and cited correctly.

- **Opposing positions are summarized and countered.** By anticipating and countering objections to your position, you establish common ground with readers and show yourself to be a reasonable and well-informed writer.

Thinking ahead: Presenting or publishing

You may have some flexibility in how you present or publish your argument. If you submit your argument as an audio or video essay, make sure you understand the genre's conventions and think through how your voice or a combination of sounds and images can help you establish your credibility. If you are taking a position on a local issue, consider publishing your argument in the form of a newspaper opinion piece or a public service video to provide a real-world audience.

→

Writing your argument

Explore

Generate ideas by responding to questions such as the following:

- What is the debate around your issue? What sources will help you learn more about your issue?
- What position will you take? Why does your position need to be argued?
- How will you establish common ground with your readers?
- What evidence supports your position? What evidence makes you question your position?
- What types of appeals—*ethos, logos, pathos*—might you use to persuade readers?

Draft

Try to figure out the best way to structure your argument. A typical approach might include the following steps: capture readers' attention; state your thesis; give background information; support your major claims with specific evidence; recognize and respond to opposing points of view; and end by reinforcing your thesis and reminding readers why it matters.

Revise

Ask your reviewers for specific feedback. Here are some questions to guide their comments.

- Is the thesis clear? Is the issue debatable?
- Is the evidence persuasive? Is more needed?
- Is your argument organized logically?
- Are there any flaws in your reasoning or assumptions that weaken the argument?
- Have you presented yourself as a knowledgeable, trustworthy writer?
- Does the conclusion pull together your entire argument? How might the conclusion be made more effective?

7 Writing in the disciplines

College courses introduce you to the thinking of scholars in many disciplines, such as the humanities (literature, music, art), the social sciences (psychology, anthropology, sociology), and the sciences (biology, physics, chemistry). No matter what you study, you will be asked to write for a variety of audiences in a variety of formats and to practice the methods used by the discipline's scholars and practitioners. In a criminal justice course, for example, you may be asked to write a policy memo or a legal brief; in a nursing course, you may be asked to write a treatment plan or a case study. To write in these courses is to think like a criminologist or a nurse and to engage in the debates of the discipline.

7a Recognize the questions that writers in a discipline ask.

Disciplines are characterized by the kinds of questions their scholars and practitioners attempt to answer. For example, social scientists, who analyze human behavior, might ask about the factors that cause people to act in certain ways. Historians, who seek an understanding of the past, often ask about the causes and effects of events and about connections between current and past events.

Whenever you write for a college course, try to determine the kinds of questions scholars in the field might ask about a topic. You can find clues in assigned readings, lecture topics, discussion groups, and the writing assignment itself. If you are writing about literature, the following box will guide you through what questions to ask about literary works.

82   **7a**
wid
Writing in the disciplines

Questions to ask about literature

All good writing about literature attempts to answer a question about the text—for example, how does Black language function in Gwendolyn Brooks's "We Real Cool"? The goal of a literature analysis is to answer such questions with a meaningful and persuasive interpretation. Focus your reading by asking questions about the text. Keep in mind that readers are interested in your ideas about a work; pose questions that lead to your interpretation or a judgment of the work rather than to a summary. The following list can help you get started.

Questions about technique

PLOT What conflicts drive the plot? Are they internal (within a character) or external (between characters or between a character and a force)? How are conflicts resolved? Why do events happen in a particular order?

SETTING Does the setting (time and place) create an atmosphere, give insight into a character, suggest symbolic meaning, or hint at the theme?

CHARACTER What seems to motivate the central characters? Do any characters change significantly? If so, what have they learned from their experiences? Do contrasts between characters highlight important themes?

POINT OF VIEW Does the point of view—the perspective from which the story is narrated or the poem is spoken—influence our understanding of events? Does the narration reveal the character traits of the speaker, or does the speaker merely observe others?

THEME Does the work have an overall theme (a central insight about people or a truth about life, for example)? If so, how do details in the work serve to illuminate this theme?

LANGUAGE Does language—formal or informal, standard or dialect, ordinary or poetic—reveal the character of speakers? How do metaphors, similes, and sensory images contribute to the work? How do recurring images enrich the work and hint at its meaning?

Questions about social context

HISTORICAL CONTEXT What does the work reveal about—or how was it shaped by—the time and place in which it was written? Does the work appear to promote or undermine a philosophy that was popular in its time, such as social Darwinism in the late nineteenth century or feminism in the mid-twentieth century?

QUESTIONS TO ASK ABOUT LITERATURE (*cont.*)

CLASS How does social class shape or influence characters' choices and actions? How does class affect the way characters view—or are viewed by—others?

RACE AND CULTURE Are any characters portrayed as being caught between cultures: between a traditional and an emerging culture, for example? Are any characters engaged in a conflict with society because of their race or ethnic background? Does the work celebrate a specific culture and its traditions?

GENDER Are any characters' choices limited because of gender? What are the power relationships between the sexes, and do these change during the course of the work? Do any characters resist the gender roles assigned to them? Do other characters choose to conform to those roles?

ARCHETYPES (OR UNIVERSAL TYPES) Does a character, an image, or a plot fit a pattern—a type—that has been repeated in stories throughout history and across cultures? (For example, nearly every culture has stories about heroes, quests, redemption, and revenge.) How is an archetypal character, image, or plotline similar to or different from others like it?

7b Understand the kinds of evidence that writers in a discipline use.

Regardless of the discipline in which you are writing, you must support any claims with evidence—facts, data, examples, and expert opinion.

The kinds of evidence used in different disciplines commonly overlap. Students of geography, media studies, and political science, for example, might use census data to explore different topics. The evidence that one discipline values, however, might not be sufficient to support an interpretation or a conclusion in another field. You might use interviews in an anthropology paper, for example, but such evidence would be irrelevant in a biology lab report. The box on the next page lists the kind of evidence used in various disciplines.

What counts as evidence in various disciplines?

Humanities: literature, art, film, music, philosophy

- Passages of text or lines of a poem
- Passages of a musical composition
- Details from an image or a work of art
- Critical essays that analyze original works

Humanities: history

- Primary sources such as photographs, letters, maps, and government documents
- Scholarly books and articles that interpret evidence

Social sciences: psychology, sociology, political science, anthropology

- Data from original experiments
- Results of field research such as interviews or surveys
- Statistics from government agencies
- Scholarly books and articles that interpret findings from other researchers' studies
- Primary sources such as maps, artifacts, or government documents

Sciences and health fields: biology, chemistry, physics, nursing

- Data from original experiments
- Models, diagrams, or animations
- Notes from lab or clinical work
- Scholarly articles that report findings from experiments

7c Become familiar with a discipline's language conventions.

Every discipline has a specialized vocabulary. As you read the articles and books in a field, you'll notice that certain words and phrases come up repeatedly. Sociologists, for example, use terms such as *independent variables* and *dyads* to describe social phenomena; computer scientists might refer to *algorithm design* and *loop invariants* to describe programming methods. Practitioners in health fields such as nursing use terms like *treatment plan* and *systemic assessment* to describe patient care. Use discipline-specific terms only when you are certain that you and your readers fully understand their meaning.

7d Use a discipline's preferred citation style.

In any discipline, you must give credit to those whose ideas or words you have borrowed. It is your responsibility to avoid plagiarism by citing sources honestly and accurately.

While all disciplines emphasize careful documentation, each follows a particular system of citation that its members have agreed on. Writers in the humanities usually use the system established by the Modern Language Association (MLA). Scholars in some social sciences, such as psychology and anthropology, follow the style guidelines of the American Psychological Association (APA). Scholars in history and in some humanities typically follow *The Chicago Manual of Style*.

PART 3

Clear Sentences

8 Prefer active verbs.

Choose an active verb whenever possible. Active verbs express meaning more vigorously than forms of the verb *be* or verbs in the passive voice. Forms of *be* (*be, am, is, are, was, were, being, been*) lack vigor because they convey no action. Passive verbs lack strength because their subjects receive the action instead of doing it.

PASSIVE	The pumps *were destroyed* by a surge of power.
BE VERB	A surge of power *was* responsible for the destruction of the pumps.
ACTIVE	A surge of power *destroyed* the pumps.

8a Choose the active voice or the passive voice, depending on your writing situation.

In the active voice, the subject does the action; in the passive voice, the subject receives the action. Although both voices are grammatically correct, the active voice is usually more effective because it is clearer and more direct.

ACTIVE	Hernando *caught* the fly ball.
PASSIVE	The fly ball *was caught* by Hernando.

In passive sentences, the actor (in this case, *Hernando*) frequently does not appear: *The fly ball was caught.*

Most of the time, you will want to emphasize the actor, so you should use the active voice. To replace a passive verb with an active one, make the actor the subject of the sentence.

> The settlers stripped the land of timber before realizing
> ▶ ~~The land was stripped of timber before the settlers realized~~
> the consequences of their actions.

The revision emphasizes the actors (*settlers*) by naming them in the subject.

The decision to use the active or the passive voice will be influenced not only by your purpose but also by your audience's expectations. In much scientific writing, for example, the passive voice properly emphasizes an experiment or a process, not the researcher: *Just before harvest, the tobacco plants are sprayed with a chemical to prevent the growth of suckers.*

8b Replace *be* verbs that result in dull or wordy sentences.

Not every *be* verb needs replacing. The forms of *be* (*be, am, is, are, was, were, being, been*) work well when you want to link a subject to a noun that clearly renames it or to an adjective that describes it: *Orchard House was the home of Louisa May Alcott. The harvest will be bountiful this year.*

If using a *be* verb makes a sentence needlessly wordy, consider replacing it. Often a phrase following the verb contains a noun or an adjective (such as *violation* or *resistant*) that suggests a more vigorous, active verb (*violate, resist*).

▶ Burying nuclear waste in Antarctica would be in violation of an international treaty. [*violate* written above, replacing *be in violation of*]

▶ When Rosa Parks was resistant to giving up her seat on the bus, she became a civil rights hero. [*resisted* written above, replacing *was resistant to*]

EXERCISE 8–1   Revise any weak, unemphatic sentences by replacing passive verbs or *be* verbs with active alternatives. If a sentence is emphatic, do not change it. Possible revisions appear in the back of the book.

The ranger doused the campfire before giving us
The campfire was doused by the ranger before we were given a ticket for unauthorized use of a campsite.

a. The Saxons were defeated by the Prussians in 1745.
b. The entire operation is managed by Ahmed, the producer.

c. The sea kayaks were expertly paddled by the tour guides.

d. At the crack of rocket and mortar blasts, I jumped from the top bunk and landed on my buddy below, who was crawling on the floor looking for his boots.

e. The protestors' shouts were heard by the congresswoman as she walked up the Capitol steps.

---

9 Balance parallel ideas.

If two or more ideas are parallel, they should be expressed in parallel grammatical form. Single words should be balanced with single words, phrases with phrases, clauses with clauses.

There is more work to be done, more justice to be had, more barriers to break.

—Barack Obama

This novel is not to be tossed lightly aside, but to be hurled with great force.

—Dorothy Parker

9a Balance parallel ideas in a series.

Balance all items in a series by presenting them in parallel grammatical form.

▶   Children who study music also learn confidence,
                                    creativity.
    discipline, and ~~they are creative.~~
                       ^

The revision presents all the items in the series as nouns: *confidence*, *discipline*, and *creativity*.

▶ Racing to get to work on time, Sam drove down the middle of the
                                                        ignored
road, ran a red light, and two stop signs.
                      ^

The revision adds a verb to make the three items parallel: *drove, ran,*
and *ignored.*

9b Balance parallel ideas presented as pairs.

When pairing ideas, underscore their connection by expressing them in
similar grammatical form. Paired ideas are usually connected with coordinating conjunctions, with correlative conjunctions, or with *than* or *as.*

Parallel ideas linked with coordinating conjunctions

Coordinating conjunctions (*and, but, or, nor, for, so,* and *yet*) link ideas of
equal importance. When those ideas are closely parallel in content, they
should be expressed in parallel grammatical form.

                                               encouraging
▶ Many colleges are making SAT scores optional and ~~encourage~~
                                               ^

alternative application materials.

The revision balances the verb *making* with the verb *encouraging.*

Parallel ideas linked with correlative conjunctions

Correlative conjunctions come in pairs: *either . . . or, neither . . . nor, not only
. . . but also, both . . . and, whether . . . or.* Make sure that the grammatical
structure following the second half of the pair is the same as that following the first half.

▶ Thomas Edison was not only a prolific inventor but also ~~was~~ a

successful entrepreneur.

The words *a prolific inventor* follow *not only,* so *a successful entrepreneur*
should follow *but also.*

▶ The counselor reminded me either to submit my class registration
                      to
forms online or drop off the paperwork at her office.
        ^

To submit my class registration forms online, which follows *either*, should be
balanced with *to drop off the paperwork at her office*, which follows *or*.

Comparisons linked with than or as

In comparisons linked with *than* or *as*, the elements being compared
should be expressed in parallel grammatical structure.

▶ For some situations, it is easier to talk on the phone than
to text.
~~texting.~~
^

To talk is balanced with *to text*.

EXERCISE 9–1   Edit the following sentences to correct faulty parallelism.
Possible revisions appear in the back of the book.

Rowena began her workday by refilling the hand sanitizer stations
        setting up
and ~~set up~~ the cash register.
  ^

a. Bluetooth technology is used with personal computers, mobile phones,
   and listening to audio devices.

b. Hannah told her rock-climbing partner that she bought a new harness and
   of her desire to climb Otter Cliffs.

c. It is more difficult to sustain an exercise program than starting one.

d. During basic training, I was not only told what to do but also what to
   think.

e. Jan wanted to drive either to wine country or Sausalito.

10 Add needed words.

Sometimes a writer leaves words out of a sentence without affecting its meaning. But often the result is confusing or ungrammatical. Readers need to see at a glance how the parts of a sentence are connected.

10a Add words needed to complete compound structures.

In compound structures, words are often left out for economy: *Horatio is a man who means what he says and [who] says what he means.* Such omissions are acceptable as long as the omitted words are common to both parts of the compound structure.

If omitting a word from a sentence would make the sentence ungrammatical because the word is not common to both parts of the compound structure, the word must be left in.

> *accepted*
> ▶ Mayor Davis never has and never will accept a bribe.
>   ∧

Has . . . accept is not grammatically correct.

10b Add the word *that* where needed for clarity.

Include the word *that* if there is any danger of misreading without it.

> ▶ In his famous obedience experiments, psychologist Stanley Milgram
>   *that*
> discovered ordinary people were willing to inflict physical pain on
>   ∧
> strangers.

Milgram didn't discover ordinary people; he discovered that ordinary people were willing to inflict pain on strangers.

10c Add words needed to make comparisons logical and complete.

Comparisons should be made between items that are alike. To compare unlike items is illogical and distracting.

▶ The forests of North America are much more extensive
    those of
than Europe.
  ^

Forests must be compared with forests, not with all of Europe.

                                        baker's
▶ My grandfather's pies were better than any other ~~baker~~ in the
                ^
neighborhood.

The grandfather's pies cannot logically be compared with a baker. The revision uses the possessive form *baker's*, with the word *pies* being implied.

            as
▶ The city of Lowell is as old, if not older than, the neighboring city of
           ^
Lawrence.

The construction *as old* is not complete without a second *as*: *as old as . . . the neighboring city of Lawrence.*

Comparisons should be complete so that readers will understand what is being compared.

INCOMPLETE	Depression is more common in adolescent girls.
COMPLETE	Depression is more common in adolescent girls than in adolescent boys.

Also, comparisons should leave no ambiguity for readers. If a sentence lends itself to more than one interpretation, revise the sentence to state clearly which interpretation you intend. In the following ambiguous sentence, two interpretations are possible.

AMBIGUOUS	Ken helped me more than my roommate.
CLEAR	Ken helped me more than *he helped* my roommate.
CLEAR	Ken helped me more than my roommate *did*.

EXERCISE 10–1 Add any words needed for grammatical or logical completeness in the following sentences. Possible revisions appear in the back of the book.

> that
> **The plumber feared the pipes were completely rusted through.**
> ^

a. Oranges are a better source of vitamin C.

b. The golden eagle's wingspan is nearly as wide as the bald eagle.

c. Looking out the family room window, Sarah saw her favorite tree, which she had climbed as a child, was gone.

d. The graphic designers are interested and knowledgeable about producing posters for the balloon race.

e. My town's high school is much larger than the neighboring town.

---

11 Untangle mixed constructions.

A mixed construction contains sentence parts that do not sensibly fit together. The mismatch may be a matter of grammar or of logic.

11a Untangle the grammatical structure.

Do not begin a sentence with one grammatical plan and switch without warning to another. Often you must rethink the purpose of the sentence and revise.

> Most
> ▶ ~~For most~~ drivers who have a blood alcohol content of .05 percent
> ^
> increase their risk of causing an accident.

In the original sentence, the prepositional phrase beginning with *For* is incorrectly made the subject of the verb *increase*. This revision makes *drivers* the subject.

▶ For most drivers who have a blood alcohol content of .05 percent,
  the risk of causing an accident is increased.
  ~~increase their risk of causing an accident.~~

Here, the writer begins with the prepositional phrase and finishes the
sentence with a proper subject and verb (*risk . . . is increased*).

▶ Although Luxembourg is a small nation, ~~but~~ it has a rich cultural

history.

The coordinating conjunction *but* cannot link a subordinate clause (*Although
Luxembourg . . .*) with an independent clause (*it has a rich cultural history*).

For Multilingual Writers

When writing in English, watch out for double subjects, which can happen
when a noun and a pronoun try to serve the same grammatical function in a
sentence. See 29c.

▶ My father ~~he~~ moved to Peru before he met my mother.

11b Straighten out the logical connections.

A sentence's subject and verb should make sense together.

> financial-aid benefits for
▶ Under the revised plan, first-generation college students/
  ~~who now receive financial-aid benefits,~~ will increase.

The benefits, not the students, will increase.

11c Avoid *is when, is where,* and *reason . . . is because* constructions.

Sentences with *is when, is where,* and *reason . . . is because* constructions are
often ungrammatical or illogical.

▶ Anorexia nervosa is ~~where people~~ diet to the point of
a disorder experienced by people who
^

starvation.

Where refers to places. Anorexia nervosa is a disorder, not a place.

▶ The ~~reason the~~ experiment failed ~~is~~ because conditions in the lab

were not sterile.

The writer might have changed *because* to *that* (*The reason the experiment
failed is that conditions in the lab were not sterile*), but the preceding revision is
more concise.

EXERCISE 11–1 Edit the following sentences to untangle mixed
constructions. Possible revisions appear in the back of the book.

Taking
~~By taking~~ the oath of allegiance made Ling a US citizen.
^

a. Using surgical gloves is a precaution now worn by dentists to prevent
   contact with patients' blood and saliva.

b. A physician, the career my brother is pursuing, requires at least ten years
   of challenging work.

c. The reason the pharaohs had bad teeth was because tiny particles of sand
   found their way into Egyptian bread.

d. Recurring bouts of flu among team members set a record for number of
   games forfeited.

e. In this box contains the key to your future.

---

12 Repair misplaced and dangling modifiers.

Modifiers should point clearly to the words they modify. As a rule, related
words should be kept together.

12a Put limiting modifiers in front of the words they modify.

Limiting modifiers such as *only*, *even*, *almost*, *nearly*, and *just* should appear in front of a verb only if they modify the verb. If they limit the meaning of some other word in the sentence, they should be placed in front of that word.

▶ Research shows that students ~~only~~ learn new vocabulary
   only
   words when they are encouraged to read.
   ^

   Only limits the meaning of the *when* clause.

            just
▶ If you ~~just~~ interview chemistry majors, your picture of the student
                ^
   response to the new policies will be incomplete.

   The adverb *just* limits the meaning of *chemistry majors*, not *interview*.

When the limiting modifier *not* is misplaced, the sentence usually suggests a meaning the writer did not intend.

               not
▶ In the United States in 1860, all Black southerners were
                              ^
   ~~not~~ enslaved.

   The original sentence says that no Black southerners were enslaved. The revision is clear and accurate.

12b Place phrases and clauses so that readers can see at a glance what they modify.

Although phrases and clauses can appear at some distance from the words they modify, make sure your meaning is clear.

MISPLACED   The soccer player returned to the clinic where he had undergone
              emergency surgery in 2021 in a limousine sent by Adidas.

REVISED   Traveling in a limousine sent by Adidas, the soccer player
                 returned to the clinic where he had undergone emergency
                 surgery in 2021.

The revision corrects the false impression that the soccer player under-
went emergency surgery in a limousine.

▶ ~~There~~ *On the walls*
  are many pictures of comedians who have performed at
  ^
  Gavin's. ~~on the walls.~~
          ^

The comedians weren't performing on the walls; the pictures were on the
walls.

12c Avoid split infinitives when they are awkward.

An infinitive consists of *to* plus the base form of a verb: *to think, to breathe.*
When a modifier appears between *to* and the verb, the infinitive is said to
be "split": *to completely understand.*

   If a split infinitive is awkward, move the modifier to another position
in the sentence.

▶ Cardiologists encourage their patients to ~~more carefully~~ watch
                                              more carefully.
  their cholesterol levels/
                          ^

   Attempts to avoid split infinitives can result in equally awkward
sentences. When alternative phrasing sounds unnatural, most experts
allow—and even encourage—splitting the infinitive.

AWKWARD   We decided actually to enforce the law.
BETTER   We decided to actually enforce the law.

EXERCISE 12–1 Edit the following sentences to correct misplaced or awk-wardly placed modifiers. Possible revisions appear in the back of the book.

over Zoom
Delivering a group presentation can be difficult. ~~over Zoom.~~
                                                        ∧   ∧

a. The manager asked her employees to if they had time submit their reports on Friday.

b. Many students graduate with debt from college totaling more than fifty thousand dollars.

c. It is a myth that humans only use 10 percent of their brains.

d. Daria found the old nightgown she used to wear to sleep in the closet.

e. All geese do not fly beyond Narragansett for the winter.

12d Repair dangling modifiers.

A dangling modifier fails to refer logically to any word in the sentence. Dangling modifiers are easy to repair, but they can be hard to recognize, especially in your own writing.

Dangling modifiers are usually word groups (such as verbal phrases) that suggest but do not name an actor. When a sentence opens with such a modifier, readers expect the subject of the next clause to name the actor. If it doesn't, the modifier dangles.

> *Upon entering the doctor's office*, a skeleton caught my attention.

> *Deciding to join the navy*, the recruiter enthusiastically pumped Jing-mei's hand.

These dangling modifiers falsely suggest that the skeleton entered the doctor's office and that the recruiter decided to join the navy.

To repair a dangling modifier, you can revise the sentence in one of two ways:

• Name the actor in the subject of the sentence.

• Name the actor in the modifier.

Depending on your sentence, one of these revision strategies may be more appropriate than the other.

ACTOR NAMED IN SUBJECT

I noticed
▶ Upon entering the doctor's office, a skeleton. ~~caught my attention.~~
　　　　　　　　　　　　　　　 ^ 　　　 ^

ACTOR NAMED IN MODIFIER

When Jing-mei decided
▶ ~~Deciding~~ to join the navy, the recruiter enthusiastically
　^ 　　　*his*
pumped ~~Jing-mei's~~ hand.
　　　　 ^

You cannot repair a dangling modifier simply by moving it: *A skeleton caught my attention upon entering the doctor's office.* The sentence still suggests that the skeleton entered the office.

EXERCISE 12–2　Edit the following sentences to correct dangling modifiers. Most sentences can be revised in more than one way. Possible revisions appear in the back of the book.

a student must complete
To graduate, two science courses. ~~must be completed.~~
　　　　　 ^ 　　　　　　　　 ^

a. To complete an online purchase with a credit card, the expiration date and the security code must be entered.

b. Though only sixteen, UCLA accepted Martha's application.

c. Settled in the cockpit, the pounding of the engine was muffled only slightly by my helmet.

d. After studying polymer chemistry, computer games seemed less complex to Letitia.

e. When a young man, my mother enrolled me in tap dance classes.

13　Eliminate distracting shifts.

This section can help you avoid unnecessary shifts that might distract or confuse your readers: shifts in point of view, in verb tense, in mood or voice, or from indirect to direct questions or quotations.

13a Make the point of view consistent in person and number.

The point of view in a piece of writing is the perspective from which it is written: first person (*I* or *we*), second person (*you*), or third person (*he, she, it, one,* or *they*).

The *I* (or *we*) point of view, which emphasizes the writer, is a good choice for informal messages and writing based on personal experience. The *you* point of view, which emphasizes the reader, works well for giving advice or explaining how to do something. The third-person point of view, which emphasizes the subject, is appropriate in academic and professional writing.

Once you have settled on a point of view, stick with it. Shifting points of view within a piece of writing confuses readers.

> ▶ Our class practiced rescuing a victim trapped in a wrecked car.
>
> We learned to dismantle the car with the essential tools. ~~You~~ ᴡᵉ were
>   ^
>   our   our
> graded on ~~your~~ speed and ~~your~~ skill in freeing the victim.
>   ^   ^

The writer should have stayed with the *we* point of view. Avoid using *you* in a vague sense meaning "anyone." (See 24d.)

EXERCISE 13–1   Edit the following paragraph to eliminate distracting shifts in point of view (person and number). Create two versions. First, rewrite it in the first person (using *I* and *we*). Then rewrite the paragraph in the third person (using *people* and *they*). In what contexts would each version be the best choice?

When online dating first became available, many people thought that it would simplify romance. We believed that you could type in a list of criteria—sense of humor, college education, green eyes, good job—and a database would select the perfect mate. Thousands of people signed up for services and filled out their profiles, confident that true love was only a few clicks away. As it turned out, however, virtual dating was no easier than traditional dating—and it has only gotten more complicated over the years. I still have to contact the people I find, exchange messages, and meet him in the real world. Although a dating app might produce a list of possibilities and screen out obviously undesirable people, you can't predict chemistry. More often than not, people who seem perfect for each other online just don't click in person. Dating apps and social media do help a single person expand their pool of potential dates, but they're no substitute for the hard work of romance.

13b Maintain consistent verb tenses.

Consistent verb tenses clearly establish the time of the actions being described. When a passage begins in one tense and then shifts to another tense for no reason, readers are distracted and confused.

> ► Our candidate struggled in the debate. Just as we gave up hope,
> soared
> she ~~soars~~ ahead in the polls.
> ^

The writer thought that the present tense (*soars*) would convey excitement. But having begun in the past tense (*struggled*, *gave up*), the writer should follow through in the past tense.

14 Emphasize key ideas.

Within each sentence, emphasize your point by expressing it in the subject and verb of an independent clause, the words that receive the most attention from readers.

14a Coordinate equal ideas; subordinate minor ideas.

When combining two or more ideas in one sentence, you have two choices: coordination or subordination. Choose coordination to indicate that the ideas are equal or nearly equal in importance. Choose subordination to indicate that one idea is less important than another.

Coordination

Coordination draws attention equally to two or more ideas. To coordinate single words or phrases, join them with a coordinating conjunction or with a pair of correlative conjunctions: bananas **and** strawberries; **not only** a lackluster plot **but also** inferior acting (see 40g).

To coordinate independent clauses—word groups that express a complete thought and that can stand alone as a sentence—join them with a comma and a coordinating conjunction or with a semicolon and a word such as *therefore*. (See the following chart.)

Using coordination to combine sentences of equal importance

1. Consider using a comma and a coordinating conjunction. (See 30a.)

and	but	or	nor
for	so	yet	

▶ In Orthodox Jewish funeral ceremonies, the shroud is a simple
            and the
linen vestment/, ~~The~~ coffin is plain wood.
    ^

2. Consider using a semicolon with a conjunctive adverb or a transitional phrase. (See 32b.)

also	however	next
as a result	in addition	now
besides	in fact	of course
consequently	in other words	otherwise
finally	in the first place	still
for example	meanwhile	then
for instance	moreover	therefore
furthermore	nevertheless	thus

              in addition, she
▶ Alicia scored well on the SAT/; ~~She also~~ had excellent grades and a record
         ^

of community service.

3. Consider using a semicolon alone. (See 32a.)

        in
▶ In youth we learn/; ~~In~~ age we understand.
    ^

Subordination

To give unequal emphasis to two or more ideas, express the major idea in an independent clause and place any minor ideas in subordinate clauses or phrases. (For specific subordination strategies, see the following chart.)

Using subordination to combine sentences of unequal importance

1. Consider putting the less important idea in a subordinate clause beginning with one of the following words. (See 42e.)

after	before	that	which
although	even though	unless	while
as	if	until	who
as if	since	when	whom
because	so that	where	whose

When
▸ Elizabeth Cady Stanton proposed a convention to discuss the status of
   ^
women in America/, Lucretia Mott agreed.
             ^

2. Consider putting the less important idea in an appositive phrase. (See 42c.)

▸ Karate, ~~is~~ a discipline based on the philosophy of nonviolence/,
        ^   ^
~~It~~ teaches the art of self-defense.

3. Consider putting the less important idea in a participial phrase. (See 42b.)

                                                        E
▸ ~~American essayist Cheryl Peck was~~ ⊘ncouraged by friends to write
                              American essayist Cheryl Peck
about her life/, ~~She~~ began combining humor and irony in her essays
             ^
about being overweight.

Let your intended meaning determine which idea you emphasize. Thinking about your purpose and your audience often helps you decide which ideas deserve emphasis.

14b Combine choppy sentences.

Short sentences demand a reader's attention, so you should use them primarily for emphasis. Too many short sentences, one after the other, make for a choppy style.

If an idea is not important enough to deserve its own sentence, try combining it with a sentence close by. Put any minor ideas in subordinate structures such as phrases or subordinate clauses. (See 42.)

▶ Twitter has started to label certain posts by its users/~~The~~ company *because the*
is concerned about the spread of misinformation on its platform.

The writer wanted to emphasize that Twitter has started to label certain posts, so she put the reason in a subordinate clause beginning with *because*.

▶ The Chesapeake and Ohio Canal, ~~is~~ a 184-mile waterway constructed in the 1800s/, ~~It~~ was a major source of transportation for goods during the Civil War.

A minor idea is now expressed in an appositive phrase (*a 184-mile waterway constructed in the 1800s*).

For Multilingual Writers

Unlike some other languages, written English does not repeat objects or adverbs in adjective clauses.

▶ The apartment that we rented ~~it~~ needed repairs.

The pronoun *it* cannot repeat the relative pronoun *that*.

EXERCISE 14–1 Combine the following sentences by subordinating minor ideas or by coordinating ideas of equal importance. You must decide which ideas are minor because the sentences are given out of context. Possible revisions appear in the back of the book.

> **Agnes, ~~was~~ a girl I worked with/, ~~She~~ was a quiet child.**
>   ^   ^

a. The X-Men comic books and Japanese woodcuts of kabuki dancers were part of Marlena's research project on popular culture. They covered the tabletop and the chairs.

b. The students organized a petition. The petition asked to change the school motto. The motto was "A man's greatest strength is his education."

c. Employees can apply for a spot in the leadership program. The program teaches management and communication skills.

d. Shore houses were flooded. Beaches were washed away. Brant's Lighthouse was swallowed by the sea.

e. Laura Thackray was an engineer at Volvo Car Corporation. She addressed women's safety needs. She designed a pregnant crash-test dummy.

14c Avoid ineffective or excessive coordination.

Coordinate structures are appropriate only when you intend to draw readers' attention equally to two or more ideas: *Professor Sakellarios praises loudly, and she criticizes softly.* If one idea is more important than another, or if a coordinating conjunction does not clearly signal the relationship between the ideas, you should subordinate the less important idea.

INEFFECTIVE COORDINATION	Closets were taxed as rooms, and most colonists stored their clothes in chests or clothespresses.
IMPROVED WITH SUBORDINATION	Because closets were taxed as rooms, most colonists stored their clothes in chests or clothespresses.

The revision subordinates the less important idea (*closets were taxed as rooms*). Notice that the subordinating conjunction *Because* signals the relation between the ideas more clearly than the coordinating conjunction *and.*

Because it is so easy to string ideas together with *and*, writers often rely too heavily on coordination in their rough drafts. Look for opportunities to tuck minor ideas into subordinate clauses or phrases.

After four hours,
▶ ~~Four hours went by, and~~ a rescue truck finally arrived, but by that
   ^
time we had been evacuated in a helicopter.

Having three independent clauses was excessive. The least important idea has become a prepositional phrase.

EXERCISE 14-2 The following sentences show coordinated ideas (ideas joined with a coordinating conjunction or a semicolon). Restructure the sentences by subordinating minor ideas. You must decide which ideas are minor because the sentences are given out of context. Possible revisions appear in the back of the book.

                                   where they
   The rowers returned to shore, ~~and~~ had a party on the beach
   to celebrate   ^
   ~~and celebrated~~ the start of the season.
   ^

a. These particles are known as "stealth liposomes," and they can hide in the body for a long time without detection.

b. Irena is a competitive gymnast and majors in biochemistry; her goal is to apply her athletic experience and her science degree to a career in sports medicine.

c. Consumers and workers alike have loudly protested warehouse working conditions, so some politicians have proposed stronger labor regulations for major retailers.

d. IRC (Internet relay chat) was developed in a European university; it was created as a way for a group of graduate students to talk about projects from their dorm rooms.

e. The cafeteria's new menu has an international flavor, and it includes everything from pizza to pad thai.

14d Do not subordinate major ideas.

If a sentence buries its major idea in a subordinate construction, readers may not give the idea enough attention. Make sure to express your major idea in an independent clause and to subordinate any minor ideas.

► I was driving home from my new job, heading down Ranchitos
Road, ~~when~~ my car suddenly overheated.

[handwritten annotation: "As" inserted before "I"; caret "^" before "Road,"]

> The writer wanted to emphasize that the car overheated, not the fact of driving home. The revision expresses the major idea in an independent clause and places the less important idea in an adverb clause (*As I was driving home from my new job*).

15 Provide some variety.

When a rough draft is filled with too many sentences that begin the same way or have the same structure, try injecting some variety — as long as you can do so without sacrificing clarity or ease of reading.

15a Vary your sentence openings.

Most sentences in English begin with the subject, move to the verb, and continue to the object, with modifiers tucked in along the way or put at the end. For the most part, such sentences are fine. Put too many of them in a row, however, and they become monotonous.

Words, phrases, or clauses modifying the verb can often be inserted ahead of the subject.

► Eventually a

▲ few drops of sap ~~eventually~~ began to trickle into the aluminum
^
bucket.

Like most adverbs, *eventually* does not need to appear close to the verb it
modifies (*began*).

Just as the sun was coming up, a
► ▲ pair of black ducks flew over the pond. ~~just as the sun was coming up.~~
^   ^
The adverb clause, which modifies the verb *flew*, is as clear at the beginning
of the sentence as it is at the end.

Adjectives and participial phrases can frequently be moved to the
beginning of a sentence without loss of clarity.

Dejected and down,
► Edward/~~dejected and down,~~ nearly gave up his search for
^
a job.

NOTE: When beginning a sentence with an adjective or a participial
phrase, make sure that the subject of the sentence names the person or
thing described in the introductory phrase. If it doesn't, the phrase will
dangle. (See 12d.)

15b Use a variety of sentence structures.

A writer should not rely too heavily on simple sentences and compound
sentences, as the effect tends to be both monotonous and choppy. (See
14b and 14c.) Too many complex or compound-complex sentences,
however, can be equally monotonous. Try to achieve a mix of sentence
types.

SIMPLE	Lowering the bedroom temperature often leads to better sleep.
COMPOUND	Several factors affect sleep quality, but research has shown that simply lowering the bedroom temperature often leads to better sleep.

COMPLEX   When other factors are taken out of the equation, simply
                 lowering the bedroom temperature has been shown to lead
                 to better sleep.

COMPOUND-   Some people turn to sleep aids for a better night's sleep, but
COMPLEX   often, because core body temperature is a factor in restful
                 sleep, just lowering the bedroom temperature can be equally
                 effective.

For a fuller discussion of sentence types, see section 43.

15c Try inverting sentences occasionally.

A sentence is inverted if it does not follow the normal subject-verb-object
pattern. Many inversions sound artificial and should be avoided, except
in the most formal contexts. If an inversion sounds natural, though, it can
provide a welcome touch of variety.

> *Set at the top two corners of the stage were huge*
> ~~Huge~~ lavender hearts outlined in bright white lights. ~~were set at the~~
> ^   ^
> ~~top two corners of the stage.~~

In the revision, the subject, *hearts*, appears after the verb, *were set*. Notice that
the two parts of the verb are also inverted—and separated from each other
(*Set . . . were*)—without any awkwardness or loss of meaning.

Word Choice

16 Tighten wordy sentences.

Long sentences are not necessarily wordy, nor are short sentences always concise. A sentence is wordy if it can be tightened without loss of meaning.

16a Eliminate redundancies.

Redundancies such as *cooperate together, yellow in color,* or *basic essentials* are a common source of wordiness. There is no need to say the same thing twice.

> ► Daniel ~~is now employed~~ at a private rehabilitation center ~~working~~ *works*
>
> as a registered physical therapist.

Modifiers are redundant when their meanings are suggested by other words in the sentence.

> ► Martina ~~very quickly~~ scribbled her name, address, and phone num-
>
> ber on a greasy napkin.

The word *scribbled* already suggests that Martina wrote *very quickly.*

16b Cut empty or inflated phrases.

An empty phrase can be cut with little or no loss of meaning. Common examples are word groups that weaken the writer's authority by apologizing or hedging: *in my opinion, I think that, it seems that,* and so on.

> ► ~~In my opinion,~~ *O*ur current economic policy is misguided.

Readers understand that they are hearing the writer's opinion.

Inflated phrases can be reduced to a word or two without loss of meaning.

INFLATED	CONCISE
along the lines of	like
as a matter of fact	in fact
at this point in time	now, currently
due to the fact that	because
for the purpose of	for
in order to	to
in spite of the fact that	although, though
in the event that	if

16c Simplify the structure.

Simplifying sentences and using stronger verbs can make writing more direct. Look for opportunities to strengthen verbs.

▶ The analyst claimed that because of volatile market conditions,

she could not ~~make an~~ estimate ~~of~~ the company's future

profits.

The verb *estimate* is more vigorous and concise than *make an estimate of.*

The colorless verbs *is*, *are*, *was*, and *were* frequently generate excess words.

          studied
▶ Investigators ~~were involved in studying~~ the effect of classical music
        ^
on unborn babies.

The action (*studying*), originally appearing in a subordinate structure, has become a strong verb, *studied.*

16d Reduce clauses to phrases, phrases to single words.

Word groups functioning as modifiers can often be made more compact. Look for opportunities to reduce clauses to phrases or phrases to single words.

▶ We took a side trip to Monticello, ~~which was~~ the home of Thomas

Jefferson.

EXERCISE 16–1   Edit the following sentences to reduce wordiness. Possible revisions appear in the back of the book.

>   *even though*
> The Wilsons moved into the house ~~in spite of the fact that~~ the back
>
> door was only ten yards from the train tracks.

a.   Martin Luther King Jr. was a man who set a high standard for future leaders to meet.

b.   Alice has been deeply in love with cooking since she was little and could first peek over the edge of a big kitchen tabletop.

c.   In my opinion, Bloom's race for the governorship is a futile exercise.

d.   It is pretty important in being a successful graphic designer to have technical knowledge and at the same time an eye for color and balance.

e.   Your task will be to set up digital mail communications capabilities for all employees in the company.

17 Choose language that fits your writing situation.

When you are writing, choose the language that best expresses your meaning and is the most effective for your subject, purpose, and context.

17a Choose a suitable level of formality.

In deciding on a level of formality, consider both your subject and your audience. For most college and professional writing, some degree of formality is suitable. In a job application, for example, it is a mistake to sound breezy and informal.

| TOO INFORMAL | I'd like to get that sales job you've got on the website. |
| MORE FORMAL | I would like to apply for the position of sales manager posted on LinkedIn. |

In choosing a level of formality, above all be consistent. When a writer's voice shifts from one level of formality to another, readers receive mixed messages.

> Jorge's pitching lesson ~~commenced~~ ^{began} with his famous curveball, ~~implemented~~ ^{thrown} by tucking the little finger behind the ball. Next he ~~elucidated~~ ^{revealed} the mysteries of the sucker pitch, a slow ball coming behind a fast windup.

Words such as *commenced* and *elucidated* are too formal for the subject matter, and they clash with informal terms such as *sucker pitch* and *fast windup*.

17b Avoid jargon, except in specialized writing situations.

Jargon is specialized language used among members of a trade, discipline, or professional group. Use jargon only when readers will be familiar with it and when plain language will not do as well.

| JARGON | We outsourced the work to an outfit in Ohio because we didn't have the bandwidth to tackle it in-house. |
| REVISED | We hired a company in Ohio because we had too few employees to do the work. |

Sentences with jargon are hard to read and are often wordy.

▶ The CEO should ~~dialogue~~ ^talk^ with investors about ~~partnering~~ ^working^ with
clients to ~~ameliorate~~ ^improve^ profits.

17c Avoid most euphemisms and doublespeak.

Euphemisms—words or phrases substituted for words thought to sound harsh or ugly—are sometimes suitable. We may use euphemisms out of concern for someone's feelings. Telling parents, for example, that their daughter is "unmotivated" is more sensitive than saying she's lazy. Tact or politeness, then, can occasionally justify euphemisms, but use them sparingly. Many euphemisms are needlessly evasive or even deceitful.

EUPHEMISM	PLAIN LANGUAGE
adult beverage	alcohol
correctional facility	prison
preowned automobile	used car
revenue enhancers	taxes

The term *doublespeak* applies to any deliberately evasive or deceptive language, including euphemisms. Doublespeak is especially common in politics and business. Torture is described as *enhanced interrogation*, for example, and *downsizing* really means firing or laying off employees.

17d In most contexts, avoid slang.

Slang is a casual and sometimes private vocabulary that expresses the solidarity of a group such as rock musicians or sports fans. Slang changes rapidly. For example, the slang teenagers use to express approval changes every few years; *cool, groovy, neat, awesome, sick,* and *dope* have replaced one another within the last half century.

Although slang has a certain vitality, it is an informal code that not everyone understands. Avoid using it in academic writing, unless you have a specific purpose for doing so.

▶ Without ~~the receipts,~~ ^evidence,^ we can't move forward with our proposal.

17e Avoid sexist and noninclusive language.

Sexist and noninclusive language stereotypes or demeans people and should be avoided. Using inclusive language and recognizing individuals' chosen pronoun usage shows awareness of others. As you write for different audiences, keep in mind that words matter, and always select words that show respect for your readers.

Recognizing sexist and noninclusive language

Some sexist language is easy to recognize because it reflects genuine contempt for women: referring to a woman as a "babe," for example, or calling a lawyer a "lady lawyer."

Other forms of sexist and noninclusive language are less blatant. The following practices reflect stereotypical thinking: referring to members of one profession as exclusively one gender (teachers as women or engineers as men, for instance) or using different conventions when naming or identifying people of different genders.

STEREOTYPICAL LANGUAGE

After a nursing student graduates, *she* must face a difficult state board examination. [Not all nursing students are women.]

Running for city council are Boris Stotsky, an attorney, and *Mrs.* Cynthia Jones, a professor of English *and mother of three*. [The title *Mrs.* and the phrase *and mother of three* are irrelevant.]

Sometimes noninclusive language arises from the practice of using gendered pronouns to refer generically to persons of all genders, or from using incorrect pronouns to refer to individuals.

GENDERED PRONOUNS

A journalist is motivated by *his* deadline. [Not all journalists are men.]

A good interior designer treats *her* clients' ideas respectfully. [Not all interior designers are women.]

When a student applies for federal financial aid, *he or she* is given an FSA ID. [Not all students identify as *he* or *she*.]

Similarly, terms including *man* and *men* were once used to refer generically to everyone in a particular profession or group. Current usage demands gender-neutral terms.

INAPPROPRIATE	APPROPRIATE
chairman	chairperson, moderator, chair, head
congressman	member of Congress, representative, legislator
fireman	firefighter
to man	to operate, to staff
mankind	people, humans
manpower	personnel, staff

Revising sexist and noninclusive language

When revising sexist language, some writers substitute *he or she* and *his or her*. Others alternate female pronouns with male pronouns. These strategies are wordy, can become awkward or confusing, and are not inclusive of all individuals. Instead, use the plural or revise the sentence. You may also use the singular gender-neutral pronouns *they* and *them* to refer to individuals inclusively.

USING THE PLURAL

Journalists are motivated by *their* deadlines.

REVISING THE SENTENCE

A journalist is motivated by *a* deadline.

USING SINGULAR *THEY*

A journalist is motivated by *their* deadline.

For more examples of these revision strategies, see section 23.

NOTE: When using pronouns to refer to people, choose the pronouns that the individuals themselves would use. Some transgender, nonbinary, and gender-fluid people refer to themselves by new pronouns (*ze/hir*, for example), but if you are unfamiliar with an individual's pronouns, *they* and *them* are acceptable gender-neutral options.

EXERCISE 17–1 Edit the following sentences to eliminate noninclusive language or sexist assumptions. Possible revisions appear in the back of the book.

> Scholarship athletes
> ~~A scholarship athlete~~ must be as concerned about ~~his~~ academic
> ^   they are   their   ^
> performance as ~~he is~~ about ~~his~~ athletic performance.
>   ^   ^

a. Mrs. Geralyn Farmer, who is the mayor's wife, is the chief surgeon at University Hospital. Dr. Paul Green is her assistant.

b. Every applicant wants to know how much he will earn.

c. An elementary school teacher should understand the concept of nurturing if she intends to be effective.

d. Our company is going to hire a new I.T. guy. He will update the server and set up remote desktops.

e. If man does not stop polluting his environment, mankind will perish.

18 Find the exact words.

Two reference works (or their online equivalents) will help you find words to express your meaning exactly: a good dictionary, such as *The American Heritage Dictionary* or *Merriam-Webster* online, and a collection of synonyms and antonyms, such as *Roget's International Thesaurus*.

NOTE: Do not turn to a thesaurus in search of impressive words. Look instead for precise words that express your meaning exactly.

18a Select words with suitable connotations.

In addition to their strict dictionary meanings (or *denotations*), words have *connotations*, emotional colorings that affect how readers respond to them. The word *steel* denotes "commercial iron that contains carbon," but it also calls up images associated with steel. These associations give the word its connotations — cold, hard, smooth, unbending.

If the connotation of a word does not seem to suit your purpose, your audience, or your subject matter, you should change the word. When a more effective synonym does not come quickly to mind, consult a dictionary or a thesaurus.

▶ When American soldiers returned home after World War II, many
women ~~abandoned~~ their jobs in favor of marriage.
      left
      ^

The word *abandoned* is too negative for the context.

18b Prefer specific, concrete nouns.

Unlike general nouns, which refer to broad classes of things, specific nouns point to particular items. *Film*, for example, names a general class, *animated film* names a narrower class, and *Coco* is more specific still. Other examples: *team, football team, Denver Broncos; music, symphony, Beethoven's Ninth*.

Unlike abstract nouns, which refer to qualities and ideas (*justice, beauty, realism*), concrete nouns point to immediate, often sensory experiences and to physical objects (*steeple, lilac, stone*).

Specific, concrete nouns express meaning more vividly than general or abstract ones. Although general and abstract language is sometimes necessary to convey your meaning, use specific, concrete words when possible.

▶ The senator spoke about the challenges of the future:
~~the environment and world peace.~~
  climate change, dwindling resources, and domestic extremism.
  ^

Nouns such as *thing, area, aspect, factor,* and *individual* are especially dull and imprecise.

▶ Toni Morrison's *Beloved* is about slavery, ~~among other things.~~
                            motherhood, and memory.
                            ^

18c Take care with idioms.

Idioms are speech forms that follow no easily specified rules. The English say "Bernice went *to hospital*," an idiom strange to American ears, which are accustomed to hearing *the* in front of *hospital*. Idioms with prepositions (such as *with*, *to*, *at*, and *of*) sometimes cause trouble, especially when they follow certain verbs and adjectives. When in doubt, consult a dictionary.

UNIDIOMATIC	IDIOMATIC
angry at (a person)	angry with (a person)
different than	different from
preferable than	preferable to
think on	think of, about
try and	try to

For Multilingual Writers

Because idioms follow no particular rules, it's best to learn them individually. You may find it helpful to keep a list of idioms that you frequently encounter in conversation and in reading.

18d Do not rely heavily on clichés.

The pioneer who first announced that he had "slept like a log" no doubt amused his companions with a fresh, unlikely comparison. Today, however, that comparison is a cliché, a saying that can no longer add emphasis or surprise.

To see just how dully predictable clichés are, put your hand over the right-hand column in the following list and then finish the phrases on the left.

cool as a	cucumber
busy as a	bee, beaver
light as a	feather
quiet as a	mouse
avoid clichés like the	plague

The solution for clichés is simple: Delete them.

▶ When I received a full scholarship from my second-choice school, I
felt pressured to settle for second best.
~~found myself between a rock and a hard place.~~
∧

18e Use figures of speech with care.

A figure of speech is an expression that uses words imaginatively (rather than literally) to make abstract ideas concrete. Most often, figures of speech compare two seemingly unlike things to reveal surprising similarities.

In a *simile*, the writer makes the comparison explicitly, usually by introducing it with *like* or *as*: *By the time cotton had to be picked, Grandfather's neck was as red as the clay he plowed.* In a *metaphor*, the *like* or *as* is omitted, and the comparison is implied. Historians, economists, and politicians, for example, use metaphors when they compare the economy to a rigged game, describe a historical moment as a new chapter, or debate whether America is a melting pot.

Although figures of speech are useful devices, writers sometimes misuse them if they don't think about the images they evoke. The result is often a *mixed metaphor*, the use of two or more images that don't make sense together.

▶ Our manager decided to put all controversial issues ~~in a holding pattern~~ on a back burner until after the annual meeting.

Here the writer is mixing airplanes and stoves. Simply deleting one of the images corrects the problem.

EXERCISE 18–1　Edit the following sentences to replace worn-out expressions and clarify mixed figures of speech. Possible revisions appear in the back of the book.

When he heard about the accident, ~~he turned white as a sheet.~~ *the color drained from his face.*

a. John stormed into the room like a bull in a china shop.
b. Some people insist that they'll always have your back, even if they haven't been there for you before.
c. The Cubs easily beat the Mets, who were in over their heads early in the game today at Wrigley Field.
d. We ironed out the sticky spots in our relationship.
e. My mother accused me of beating around the bush when in fact I was just talking off the top of my head.

19 Use the right words. (Glossary of usage)

This glossary includes words commonly confused, words commonly misused, and words that are nonstandard. It also lists words that may be suitable for informal speech but are not effective in formal writing.

accept, except *Accept* is a verb meaning "to receive." *Except* is usually a preposition meaning "excluding." *I will accept all the packages except that one. Except* is also a verb meaning "to exclude." *Please except that item from the list.*

advice, advise *Advice* is a noun, *advise* a verb. *We advise you to follow Hector's advice.*

affect, effect *Affect* is usually a verb meaning "to influence." *Effect* is usually a noun meaning "result." *The drug did not affect the disease, and it had adverse side effects. Effect* can also be a verb meaning "to bring about." *Only the president can effect such a dramatic change.*

agree to, agree with *Agree to* means "to give consent to." *Agree with* means "to be in accord with" or "to come to an understanding with." *He agrees with me about the need for change, but he won't agree to my plan.*

all ready, already *All ready* means "completely prepared." *Already* means "previously." *Susan was all ready for the concert, but her friends had already left.*

all together, altogether *All together* means "everyone or everything in one place." *Altogether* means "entirely." *We were not altogether certain that we could bring the family all together for the reunion.*

allude To *allude* to something is to make an indirect reference to it. Do not use *allude* to mean "to refer directly." *In his lecture, the professor referred* (not *alluded*) *to several pre-Socratic philosophers.*

allusion, illusion An *allusion* is an indirect reference. An *illusion* is a misconception or false impression. *Did you catch my allusion to Shakespeare? Mirrors give the room an illusion of depth.*

a lot *A lot* is two words. Do not write *alot. Sam lost a lot of weight.* See also *lots, lots of.*

among, between See *between, among.*

amount, number Use *amount* with quantities that cannot be counted; use *number* with those that can. *This recipe calls for a large amount of sugar. We have a large number of toads in our garden.*

anyone, any one *Anyone*, an indefinite pronoun, means "any person at all." *Any one*, the pronoun *one* preceded by the adjective *any*, refers to a particular person or thing in a group. *Anyone from the winning team may choose any one of the prizes on display.*

anyplace *Anyplace* is informal. In formal writing, use *anywhere.*

as Do not use *as* to mean "because" if there is any chance of ambiguity. *We canceled the picnic because* (not *as*) *it began raining. As* here could mean either "because" or "when." See also *since.*

awhile, a while *Awhile* is an adverb; it can modify a verb, but it cannot be the object of a preposition such as *for.* The two-word form *a while* is a noun preceded by an article and therefore can be the object of a preposition. *Stay awhile. Stay for a while.*

being as, being that *Being as* and *being that* are nonstandard expressions. Write *because* instead. *Because* (not *Being as*) *I slept late, I had to skip breakfast.*

beside, besides *Beside* is a preposition meaning "at the side of" or "next to." *Annie sleeps with a flashlight beside her bed. Besides* is a preposition meaning "except" or "in addition to." *No one besides Terrie can have that ice cream. Besides* is also an adverb meaning "in addition." *I'm not hungry; besides, I don't like ice cream.*

between, among Ordinarily, use *among* with three or more entities, *between* with two. *The prize was divided among several contestants. You have a choice between carrots and beans.*

bring, take Use *bring* when an object is being transported toward you, *take* when it is being moved away. *Please bring me a glass of water. Please take these forms to Mr. Scott.*

can, may *Can* is traditionally reserved for ability, *may* for permission. *Can you speak French? May I help you?*

capital, capitol *Capital* refers to a city, *capitol* to a building where lawmakers meet. *Capital* also refers to wealth or resources. *The residents of the state capital protested plans to close the streets surrounding the capitol.*

cite, site *Cite* means "to quote as an authority or example." *Site* is usually a noun meaning "a particular place." *He cited the zoning law in his argument against the proposed site of the gas station.* Locations on the Internet are usually referred to as *sites* (short for *websites*). *The library's site now includes a chat feature.*

compare to, compare with *Compare to* means "to represent as similar." *She compared him to a wild stallion. Compare with* means "to examine similarities and differences." *The study compared the language ability of apes with that of dolphins.*

complement, compliment *Complement* is a verb meaning "to go with or complete" or a noun meaning "something that completes." As a verb, *compliment* means "to flatter"; as a noun, it means "flattering remark." *Her skill at rushing the net complements his skill at volleying. Min's flower arrangements receive many compliments.*

conscience, conscious *Conscience* is a noun meaning "moral principles." *Conscious* is an adjective meaning "aware or alert." *Let your conscience be your guide. Were you conscious of his love for you?*

continual, continuous *Continual* means "repeated regularly and frequently." *She grew weary of the continual telephone calls. Continuous* means "extended or prolonged without interruption." *The broken siren made a continuous wail.*

council, counsel A *council* is a deliberative body, and a *councilor* is a member of such a body. *Counsel* usually means "advice" and can also mean "lawyer"; a *counselor* is one who gives advice or guidance. *The councilors met to draft the council's position paper. The pastor offered wise counsel to the troubled teenager.*

data *Data* is a plural noun technically meaning "facts or propositions." But *data* is increasingly being accepted as a singular noun. *The new data suggest* (or *suggests) that our theory is correct.* (The singular *datum* is rarely used.)

different from, different than Ordinarily, write *different from. Your sense of style is different from Jim's.* However, *different than* is acceptable to avoid an awkward construction. *Please let me know if your plans are different than* (to avoid *from what) they were six weeks ago.*

disinterested, uninterested *Disinterested* means "impartial, objective"; *uninterested* means "not interested." *We sought the advice of a disinterested counselor to help us solve our problem. Mark was uninterested in anyone's opinion but his own.*

e.g. When writing sentences, replace the Latin abbreviation *e.g.* with its English equivalent: *for example* or *for instance.*

emigrate from, immigrate to *Emigrate* means "to leave one country or region to settle in another." *In 1903, my great-grandfather emigrated from Russia to escape the religious pogroms. Immigrate* means "to enter another country and reside there." *More than fifty thousand Bosnians immigrated to the United States in the 1990s.*

etc. Avoid ending a list with *etc.* It is more emphatic to end with an example, and in most contexts readers will understand that the list is not exhaustive. When you don't wish to end with an example, *and so on* is more graceful than *etc.*

everyone, every one *Everyone* is an indefinite pronoun. *Every one,* the pronoun *one* preceded by the adjective *every,* means "each individual or thing in a particular group." *Every one* is usually followed by *of. Everyone wanted to go. Every one of the missing books was found.*

except See *accept, except.*

explicit, implicit *Explicit* means "expressed directly" or "clearly defined"; *implicit* means "implied, unstated." *I gave him explicit instructions not to go swimming. My mother's silence indicated her implicit approval.*

farther, further *Farther* usually describes distances. *Further* usually suggests quantity or degree. *Chicago is farther from Miami than I thought. I would be grateful for further suggestions.*

fewer, less Use *fewer* for items that can be counted; use *less* for items that cannot be counted. *Fewer people are living in the city. Please put less sugar in my tea.*

firstly *Firstly* sounds pretentious, and it leads to the ungainly series *firstly, secondly, thirdly,* and so on. Write *first, second, third* instead.

further See *farther, further.*

good, well *Good* is an adjective, *well* an adverb. (See 27a, 27b, and 27c.) *He hasn't felt good about his game since he sprained his wrist last season. She performed well on the uneven parallel bars.*

hanged, hung *Hanged* is the past-tense and past-participle form of the verb *hang* meaning "to execute." *The prisoner was hanged at dawn. Hung* is the past-tense and past-participle form of the verb *hang* meaning "to fasten or suspend." *The stockings were hung by the chimney with care.*

hopefully *Hopefully* means "in a hopeful manner." *We looked hopefully to the future.* Some usage experts object to the use of *hopefully* as a sentence adverb on grounds of clarity. To be safe, avoid using *hopefully* in sentences such as the following: *Hopefully, your son will recover soon.* Instead, indicate who is doing the hoping: *I hope that your son will recover soon.*

however It is acceptable to start a sentence with the conjunctive adverb *however*, but be careful to place the word in your sentence according to your intended meaning and emphasis. All of the following sentences are correct. *Pam decided, however, to attend the lecture. However, Pam decided to attend the lecture.* (She had been considering other activities.) *Pam, however, decided to attend the lecture.* (Unlike someone else, Pam chose to attend the lecture.)

hung See *hanged, hung.*

i.e. When writing sentences, use *in other words* or *that is* rather than the Latin abbreviation *i.e.* to introduce a clarifying statement. *Exposure to borax usually causes only mild skin irritation; in other words* (not *i.e.*), *it's not usually toxic.*

if, whether Use *if* to express a condition and *whether* to express alternatives. *If you go on a trip, whether to Idaho or Italy, remember to bring identification.*

illusion See *allusion, illusion.*

immigrate See *emigrate from, immigrate to.*

imply, infer *Imply* means "to suggest or state indirectly"; *infer* means "to draw a conclusion." *Jonathan implied that he knew all about databases, but the interviewer inferred that Jonathan was inexperienced.*

in, into *In* indicates location or condition; *into* indicates movement or a change in condition. *They found the lost letters in a box after moving into the house.*

irregardless *Irregardless* is nonstandard. Use *regardless.*

kind of, sort of Avoid using *kind of* or *sort of* to mean "somewhat." *The movie was somewhat* (not *sort of*) *boring.* Do not put *a* after either phrase. *That kind of* (not *kind of a*) *movie bores me.*

lay, lie See *lie, lay.*

lead, led *Lead* is a metallic element; it is a noun. *Led* is the past tense of the verb *lead. He led me to the treasure.*

less See *fewer, less.*

lie, lay *Lie* is an intransitive verb meaning "to recline or rest on a surface." Its forms are *lie, lay, lain. Lay* is a transitive verb meaning "to put or place." Its forms are *lay, laid, laid. I'm going to lay my phone on the picnic table and lie in the hammock.*

like, as *Like* is a preposition, not a subordinating conjunction. It can be followed only by a noun or a noun phrase. *As* is a subordinating conjunction that introduces a subordinate clause. In casual speech, you may say *She looks like she hasn't slept.* But in academic writing, use *as. She looks as though she hasn't slept.*

loose, lose *Loose* is an adjective meaning "not securely fastened." *Lose* is a verb meaning "to misplace" or "to not win." *Did you lose all your loose change?*

lots, lots of *Lots* and *lots of* are informal substitutes for *many, much,* or *a lot.* Avoid using them in formal writing.

may See *can, may.*

maybe, may be *Maybe* is an adverb meaning "possibly." *Maybe the sun will shine tomorrow. May be* is a verb phrase. *Tomorrow may be brighter.*

number See *amount, number.*

of Use the verb *have,* not the preposition *of,* after the verbs *could, should, would, may, might,* and *must. They must have* (not *must of*) *left early.*

off of *Off* is sufficient. Omit *of. The ball rolled off* (not *off of*) *the table.*

passed, past *Passed* is the past tense of the verb *pass. Ann passed me another slice of cake. Past* usually means "belonging to a former time" or "beyond a time or place." *Our past president spoke until past midnight. The hotel is just past the next intersection.*

precede, proceed *Precede* means "to come before." *Proceed* means "to go forward." *As we proceeded up the mountain path, we noticed fresh tracks in the mud, evidence that a group of hikers had preceded us.*

principal, principle *Principal* is a noun meaning "the head of a school or an organization" or "a sum of money." It is also an adjective meaning "most important." *Principle* is a noun meaning "a basic truth or law." *The principal expelled her for three principal reasons. We believe in the principle of equal justice for all.*

quotation, quote *Quotation* is a noun; *quote* is a verb. Avoid using *quote* as a shortened form of *quotation. Her quotations* (not *Her quotes*) *are appearing in various social media channels.*

raise, rise *Raise* is a transitive verb meaning "to move or cause to move upward." It takes a direct object. *I raised the shades. Rise* is an intransitive verb meaning "to go up." *Heat rises.*

real, really *Real* is an adjective; *really* is an adverb. *Real* is sometimes used informally as an adverb, but avoid this use in formal writing. *She was really* (not *real*) *angry.*

reason why The expression *reason why* is redundant. *The reason* (not *The reason why*) *Jones lost the election is clear.*

respectfully, respectively *Respectfully* means "showing or marked by respect." *Respectively* means "each in the order given." *He respectfully submitted his opinion to the judge. Sofia, Henry, and Jesse were a butcher, a baker, and a lawyer, respectively.*

set, sit *Set* is a transitive verb meaning "to put" or "to place." Its past tense is *set. Sit* is an intransitive verb meaning "to be seated." Its past tense is *sat. She set the dough in a warm corner of the kitchen. The cat sat in the doorway.*

since Do not use *since* to mean "because" if there is any chance of ambiguity. *Because* (not *Since*) *we won the game, we have been celebrating with pizza. Since* here could mean either "because" or "from the time that." See also *as.*

site See *cite, site.*

sometime, some time, sometimes *Sometime* is an adverb meaning "at an indefinite time." *Some time* is the adjective *some* modifying the noun *time* and means "a period of time." *Sometimes* is an adverb meaning "at times" or "now and then." *I'll see you sometime soon. I haven't lived there for some time. Sometimes I see him at work.*

suppose to *Suppose to* is nonstandard for *supposed to. I am supposed to* (not *suppose to*) *be there by noon.*

sure and Write *sure to. We were all taught to be sure to* (not *sure and*) *look both ways before crossing a street.*

take See *bring, take.*

than, then *Than* is a conjunction used in comparisons; *then* is an adverb denoting time. *That pizza is more than I can eat. Tom laughed, and then we recognized him.*

that See *who, which, that.*

there, their, they're *There* is an adverb specifying place; it is also an expletive (placeholder). Adverb: *Sylvia is sitting there patiently.* Expletive: *There are* *two plums left. Their* is a possessive pronoun. *Fred and Jane finally washed their car. They're* is a contraction of *they are. They're later than usual today.*

to, too, two *To* is a preposition; *too* is an adverb; *two* is a number. *Too many of your shots slice to the left, but the last two were just right.*

toward, towards *Toward* and *towards* are generally interchangeable, although *toward* is preferred in American English.

try and *Try and* is nonstandard for *try to. The teacher asked us all to try to* (not *try and*) *write an original haiku.*

wait for, wait on *Wait for* means "to be in readiness for" or "to await." *Wait on* means "to serve." *We're waiting for* (not *waiting on*) *Ruth to take us to the museum.*

weather, whether The noun *weather* refers to the state of the atmosphere. *Whether* is a conjunction referring to a choice between alternatives. *We wondered whether the weather would clear.*

well, good See *good, well.*

which See *who, which, that.*

while Avoid using *while* to mean "although" or "whereas" if there is any chance of ambiguity. *Although* (not *While*) *Gloria lost money in the slot machine, Tanya won money at roulette.* Here *While* could mean either "although" or "at the same time that."

who, which, that Do not use *which* to refer to persons. Use *who* instead. *That,* though generally used to refer to things, may be used to refer to a particular group of people. *The player who* (not *that* or *which*) *made the basket at the buzzer was named MVP. The team that scores the most points in this game will win the tournament.*

who, whom *Who* is used for subjects and subject complements; *whom* is used for objects. *Who are the candidates for this year's scholarship? The candidates, whom I met with yesterday, are impressive.* (See 26.)

who's, whose *Who's* is a contraction of *who is; whose* is a possessive pronoun. *Who's ready for more popcorn? Whose coat is this?* (See 33c and 33e.)

would of *Would of* is nonstandard for *would have. She would have* (not *would of*) *had a chance to play if she had arrived on time.*

your, you're *Your* is a possessive pronoun; *you're* is a contraction of *you are. Is that your new bike? You're in the finals.*

Grammatical Sentences

Language is not static. The rules of grammar change over time, and these rules are not always inclusive of how everyone speaks and writes. The guidelines laid out here are meant to help you make your writing as clear as possible to readers. When your purpose or audience calls for it, you may want to consider putting the rules aside.

20 Repair sentence fragments.

A sentence fragment is a word group that pretends to be a sentence. Sentence fragments are easy to recognize when they appear out of context, like these:

When the cat leaped onto the table.

Running for the bus.

When fragments appear next to related sentences, however, they are harder to spot.

We had just sat down to dinner. When the cat leaped onto the table.

I tripped and twisted my ankle. Running for the bus.

To be a sentence, a word group must consist of at least one independent clause. An independent clause includes a subject and a verb, and it either stands alone or could stand alone.

You can repair most fragments in one of two ways:

- Pull the fragment into a nearby sentence.

- Rewrite the fragment as a complete sentence.

> We had just sat down to dinner/ ~~When~~ the cat leaped onto the table.
>   *when*

> I tripped and sprained my ankle. ~~Running for the bus.~~
>   *Running for the bus,*

For Multilingual Writers

Unlike some other languages, English sentences always have a subject and a verb (except in commands, where the subject *you* is understood but not present: *Sit down*).

▶ Students usually very busy at the end of the semester taking
    are
    ^

  exams and writing papers.

20a Attach fragmented subordinate clauses or turn them into sentences.

A subordinate clause is patterned like a sentence, with both a subject and a verb, but it begins with a word that marks it as subordinate. The following words commonly introduce subordinate clauses: *after, although, because, before, if, so that, though, unless, until, when, where, which,* and *who.* (See 42e for a full list.)

Most fragmented clauses can be pulled into a sentence nearby.

▶ Several US states have adopted ranked-choice voting/ ~~Because~~
                                          because

  advocates believe it creates fairer elections.

If a fragmented clause cannot be attached to a nearby sentence, try turning the clause into a sentence. The simplest way to do this is to delete the opening word or words that mark it as subordinate.

▶ Uncontrolled development is taking a toll on the environment.
   Across
  ~~So that across~~ the globe, fragile ecosystems are collapsing.
  ^

20b Attach fragmented phrases or turn them into sentences.

Like subordinate clauses, phrases function within sentences as adjectives, as adverbs, or as nouns. They cannot stand alone. Fragmented phrases are often prepositional or verbal phrases; sometimes they are appositives, words or word groups that rename nouns or pronouns. (See 42a, 42b, and 42c.)

Often a fragmented phrase may simply be pulled into a nearby sentence.

▶ The archaeologists worked slowly~~/~~ ~~Examining~~ *examining* and labeling every

pottery shard they uncovered.

The word group beginning with *Examining* is a verbal phrase.

▶ The patient displayed symptoms of ALS~~.~~ ~~A~~ *a* neurodegenerative

disease.

A neurodegenerative disease is an appositive renaming the noun *ALS*. (For punctuation of appositives, see 30e.)

If a fragmented phrase cannot be pulled into a nearby sentence effectively, turn the phrase into a sentence. You may need to add a subject, a verb, or both.

▶ Jamie explained how to access our new database. ~~Also~~ *She also taught us* how to

submit expense reports and request vendor payments.

The revision turns the fragmented phrase into a sentence by adding a subject and a verb.

20c Attach other fragmented word groups or turn them into sentences.

Other word groups that are commonly fragmented include parts of compound predicates, lists, and examples introduced by *for example, in addition,* or similar expressions.

► The woodpecker finch of the Galápagos Islands carefully selects a

                      and
twig of a certain size and shape/ ~~And~~ then uses this tool to pry out
                     ^

grubs from trees.

The subject is *finch*, and the compound predicate is *selects . . . and . . . uses.*
(For punctuation of compound predicates, see 31a.)

► It has been said that there are only three indigenous American art

      musical
forms/: ~~Musical~~ comedy, jazz, and soap opera.
   ^

To correct a fragmented list, often you can attach it to a nearby sentence with a colon or a dash. Sometimes a term like *especially, namely, like,* and *such as* introduce a list that is a fragment. Such a fragment can usually be attached to the preceding sentence.

► In the twentieth century, the South produced some great American

       such
writers/ ~~Such~~ as Flannery O'Connor, William Faulkner, Zora Neale
   ^

Hurston, and Tennessee Williams.

Although you may begin a sentence with one of the following words or phrases, make sure that what follows has a subject and a verb.

also	for example	mainly
and	for instance	or
but	in addition	that is

Often the easiest solution is to turn the fragment into a sentence.

► In his memoir, Primo Levi describes the horrors of living in a

                          he worked
concentration camp. For example, ~~working~~ without food and
suffered   ^
~~suffering~~ emotional abuse.
^

EXERCISE 20–1   Repair any fragment by attaching it to a nearby sentence or by rewriting it as a complete sentence. If a word group is correct, write "correct" after it. Possible revisions appear in the back of the book.

> selling
> Adrienne turned her love of baking into a small business/, ~~Selling~~ her
> delicious creations online and mailing them to customers.

a.   Listening to the playlist her sister had created, Mia was overcome with a mix of emotions. Happiness, homesickness, and nostalgia.

b.   Cortés and his soldiers were astonished when they looked down from the mountains and saw Tenochtitlán. The magnificent capital of the Aztecs.

c.   Although my spoken Spanish is not very good. I can read the language with ease.

d.   There are several reasons for not eating meat. One reason being that dangerous chemicals are used throughout the various stages of meat production.

e.   To learn how to sculpt beauty from everyday life. This is my intention in studying art and archaeology.

21   Revise run-on sentences.

Run-on sentences are independent clauses that have not been joined correctly. An independent clause is a word group that can stand alone as a sentence. (See 43a.) When two independent clauses appear in one sentence, they must be joined in one of these ways:

• with a comma and a coordinating conjunction (*and, but, or, nor, for, so, yet*)

• with a semicolon (or occasionally with a colon or a dash)

There are two types of run-on sentences. When a writer puts no mark of punctuation and no coordinating conjunction between independent clauses, the result is called a *fused sentence*.

INDEPENDENT CLAUSE ┐ ┌ INDEPENDENT
CLAUSE

**FUSED
SENTENCE** Air pollution poses risks to all humans it can be deadly for

asthma sufferers.

A far more common type of run-on sentence is the *comma splice*—two or more independent clauses joined with a comma but without a coordinating conjunction. In some comma splices, the comma appears alone.

**COMMA
SPLICE** Air pollution poses risks to all humans, it can be deadly for asthma sufferers.

In other comma splices, the comma is accompanied by a joining word that is *not* a coordinating conjunction.

**COMMA
SPLICE** Air pollution poses risks to all humans, however, it can be deadly for asthma sufferers.

However is a transitional expression, not a coordinating conjunction, and it cannot be used with only a comma to join two independent clauses (see 21b).

To revise a run-on sentence, you have four choices.

1. Use a comma and a coordinating conjunction. See 21a.

2. Use a semicolon (or, if appropriate, a colon or a dash). A semicolon may be used alone; it can also be accompanied by a transitional expression. See 21b.

3. Make the clauses into separate sentences. See 21c.

4. Restructure the sentence, perhaps by subordinating a clause. See 21d.

As you revise, decide which of these revision techniques will work best for a particular sentence.

21a Consider separating the clauses with a comma and a coordinating conjunction.

There are seven coordinating conjunctions in English: *and, but, or, nor, for, so,* and *yet*. When a coordinating conjunction joins independent clauses, it is usually preceded by a comma. (See 30a.)

▶ Many law enforcement officials admit that the polygraph is
  yet
  unreliable, they still use it as an assessment tool.
  ^

21b Consider separating the clauses with a semicolon, a colon, or a dash.

When the independent clauses are closely related and their relation is clear without a coordinating conjunction, a semicolon is one method of revision. (See 32a.)

▶ Tragedy depicts the individual confronted with the fact of death/;

  comedy depicts the adaptability of human nature.
  ^

A semicolon is required between independent clauses that have been linked with a transitional expression such as *however, therefore, moreover, in fact,* or *for example.* For a longer list, see 32b.

▶ In her film adaptation, the director changed key details of the plot/;

  in fact, she added new scenes that do not appear in the novel.
  ^

A colon or a dash may be more appropriate if the first independent clause introduces the second or if the second clause summarizes or explains the first. (See 32e and 36a.) In formal writing, the colon is usually preferred to the dash.

A colon is an appropriate method of revision if the first independent clause introduces a quoted sentence.

▶ Nobel Peace Prize winner Al Gore had this to say about climate

  change/:"The truth is that our circumstances are not only new; they
      ^
  are completely different than they have ever been in all of human

  history."

21c Consider making the clauses into separate sentences.

▶ Why should we spend money on space exploration/?
We
~~we~~ have enough underfunded programs here on Earth.
^

A question and a statement should be separate sentences.

21d Consider restructuring the sentence, perhaps by subordinating one of the clauses.

If one of the independent clauses is less important than the other, turn the less important clause into a subordinate clause or phrase. (For more about subordination, see section 14, especially the chart on p. 105.)

▶ One of the most famous advertising slogans is Wheaties cereal's
which
"Breakfast of Champions," ~~it~~ associated the product with famous
^
athletes.

▶ Mary McLeod Bethune, ~~was~~ the seventeenth child of formerly
^
enslaved parents, ~~she~~ founded the National Council of Negro Women.

Minor ideas in these sentences are now expressed in a subordinate clause or phrase.

EXERCISE 21-1 Revise each of the run-on sentences beginning on the next page using the method of revision suggested in brackets. Possible revisions appear in the back of the book.

When a
A critic commented on Michael Chabon's use of first-person
^
perspective, the author was inspired to write his next novel in

the third person. [*Restructure the sentence.*]

a. Greta recently started working at a new company, it designs and manufactures educational toys. [*Restructure the sentence.*]
b. The building is being renovated, therefore at times we have no heat, water, or electricity. [*Use a comma and a coordinating conjunction.*]
c. I don't think I will buy the new model of smartphone, why spend the money when my current phone works perfectly? [*Make two sentences.*]
d. Walker's coming-of-age novel is set against a gloomy scientific backdrop, the Earth's rotation has begun to slow down. [*Use a semicolon.*]
e. City officials had good reason to fear a major earthquake, most of the business district was built on landfill. [*Use a colon.*]

22 Make subjects and verbs agree.

In the present tense, verbs agree with their subjects in number (singular or plural) and in person (first, second, third): *I sing, you sing, she sings, we sing, they sing.* Even if your ear recognizes the subject-verb combinations in 22a, you will no doubt encounter tricky situations such as those described in 22b–22j.

22a Learn to recognize subject-verb combinations.

The present-tense ending *-s* (or *-es*) is used on a verb if its subject is third-person singular (*he, she, it,* and singular nouns); otherwise the verb takes no ending. Consider, for example, the present-tense forms of the verb *give.*

	SINGULAR	PLURAL
FIRST PERSON	I give	we give
SECOND PERSON	you give	you give
THIRD PERSON	he/she/it gives	they give
	Yolanda gives	parents give

The verb *be* varies from this pattern; it has special forms in both the present and the past tense.

PRESENT-TENSE FORMS OF *BE*		PAST-TENSE FORMS OF *BE*	
I am	we are	I was	we were
you are	you are	you were	you were
he/she/it is	they are	he/she/it was	they were

22b Make the verb agree with its subject, not with a word that comes between.

Word groups often come between the subject and the verb. Such word groups, usually modifying the subject, may contain a noun that at first appears to be the subject. By mentally stripping away such modifiers, you can isolate the noun that is in fact the subject.

▶ High levels of air pollution cause~~s~~ damage to the respiratory tract.

The subject is *levels*, not *pollution*.

▶ The slaughter of pandas for their pelts ~~have~~ has caused the panda population to decline drastically.

The subject is *slaughter*, not *pandas* or *pelts*.

NOTE: Phrases beginning with the prepositions *as well as*, *in addition to*, *accompanied by*, *together with*, and *along with* do not make a singular subject plural: *The governor as well as his press secretary was on the plane.*

22c Treat most subjects joined with *and* as plural.

A subject with two or more parts is said to be compound. If the parts are connected with *and*, the subject is nearly always plural.

▶ Bleach and ammonia create~~s~~ a toxic gas when mixed.

EXCEPTIONS: When the parts of the subject form a single unit or when they refer to the same person or thing, treat the subject as singular: *Fish and chips is always on the menu.* When a compound subject is preceded by *each* or *every,* treat it as singular: *Each tree, shrub, and vine needs to be sprayed.*

22d With subjects joined with *or* or *nor* (or with *either . . . or* or *neither . . . nor*), make the verb agree with the part of the subject nearer to the verb.

▶ If an infant or a child ~~have~~ has a high fever, call a doctor.

▶ Neither the chief financial officer nor the marketing managers ~~was~~ were able to convince the client to reconsider.

The verb must be matched with the part of the subject closer to it: *child has* in the first sentence, *managers were* in the second.

NOTE: If one part of the subject is singular and the other is plural, put the plural part last to avoid awkwardness.

22e Treat most indefinite pronouns as singular.

Indefinite pronouns, those that do not refer to specific persons or things, are singular.

anybody	each	everyone	nobody	somebody
anyone	either	everything	no one	someone
anything	everybody	neither	nothing	something

Many of these words appear to have plural meanings, and they are often treated as plural in casual speech. In more formal writing situations, however, they are nearly always treated as singular.

▶ Each of the essays ~~have~~ has been graded.

▶ Nobody who participated in the clinical trials ~~were~~ given a

was

∧

placebo.

The subjects of these sentences are *Each* and *Nobody*. These indefinite pronouns are third-person singular, so the verbs must be *has* and *was*.

A few indefinite pronouns (*all, any, none, some*) may be singular or plural depending on the noun or pronoun they refer to: *Some of our luggage was lost. Some of the rocks were slippery. None of his advice makes sense. None of the eggs were broken.*

22f Treat collective nouns as singular unless the meaning is clearly plural.

Collective nouns such as *jury, committee, audience, crowd, troop, family,* and *couple* name a class or a group. Collective nouns are nearly always treated as singular, to emphasize the group as a unit.

meets

▶ The board of trustees ~~meet~~ in Denver twice a year.

∧

Occasionally, to draw attention to the individual members of the group, a collective noun may be treated as plural: *The class are debating among themselves.* Many writers prefer to add a clearly plural noun such as *members*: *The class members are debating among themselves.*

NOTE: In general, when a fraction or a unit of measurement is used with a singular noun, treat it as singular; when it is used with a plural noun, treat it as plural: *Three-fourths of the pie has been eaten. One-fourth of the drivers were texting.*

22g Make the verb agree with its subject even when the subject follows the verb.

Verbs ordinarily follow subjects. When this normal order is reversed, it is easy to become confused. Sentences beginning with *there is* or *there are* (or *there was* or *there were*) are inverted; the subject follows the verb. See the example on the next page.

▶ There ~~is~~ *are* surprisingly few honeybees left in southern China.

The subject, *honeybees*, is plural, so the verb must be *are*.

Occasionally you may decide to invert a sentence for variety or effect. When you do so, check to make sure that your subject and verb agree.

▶ Of particular concern ~~is~~ *are* penicillin and tetracycline, antibiotics used to make animals more resistant to disease.

The subject, *penicillin and tetracycline*, is plural, so the verb must be *are*.

22h Make the verb agree with its subject, not with a subject complement.

One basic sentence pattern in English consists of a subject, a linking verb, and a subject complement: *Amir is a lawyer.* Because the subject complement (*lawyer*) names or describes the subject (*Amir*), it is sometimes mistaken for the subject.

▶ A major force in today's economy ~~are~~ *is* children—as consumers, decision makers, and trendspotters.

Force is the subject, not *children*. If the corrected version seems too awkward, make *children* the subject: *Children are a major force in today's economy—as consumers, decision makers, and trendspotters.*

22i Ensure that *who, which,* and *that* take verbs that agree with their antecedents.

Like most pronouns, the relative pronouns *who, which,* and *that* have antecedents, nouns or pronouns to which they refer. A relative pronoun used as the subject of a subordinate clause takes a verb that agrees with its antecedent.

ANT   PN   V

Take a *course that prepares* you for classroom management.

Constructions such as *one of the students who* [or *one of the things that*] cause problems for writers. Do not assume that the antecedent must be *one*. Instead, consider the logic of the sentence.

▶ Our ability to use language is one of the things that set̸ us apart

from animals.

> The antecedent of *that* is *things*, not *one*. Several things set us apart from animals.

When the phrase *the only* comes before *one*, you are safe in assuming that *one* is the antecedent of the relative pronoun.

▶ Veronica was the only one of the first-year Spanish students who
was
~~were~~ fluent enough to apply for the exchange program.
^

> The antecedent of *who* is *one*, not *students*. Only one student was fluent enough.

22j Treat titles of works, company names, and words mentioned as words as singular.

describes
▶ *Lost Cities* ~~describe~~ the discoveries of fifty ancient civilizations.
^

specializes
▶ Delmonico Brothers ~~specialize~~ in organic produce and additive-free
^

meats.

is
▶ *Controlled substances* ~~are~~ a euphemism for illegal drugs.
^

EXERCISE 22–1 Edit the following sentences to eliminate problems with subject-verb agreement. If a sentence is correct, write "correct" after it. Answers appear in the back of the book.

> _were_
> **Jack's first days in the infantry ~~was~~ grueling.**
>   ^

a. One of the main reasons for elephant poaching are the profits received from selling the ivory tusks.

b. Not until my interview with Dr. Hwang were other possibilities opened to me.

c. Most students in the seminar was aware of the importance of joining the discussion.

d. Batik cloth from Bali, blue and white ceramics from Delft, and a bocce ball from Turin has made Angelie's room the talk of the dorm.

e. The board of directors, ignoring the wishes of the neighborhood, has voted to allow further development.

23 Make pronouns and antecedents agree.

Pronouns are words that substitute for nouns. Many pronouns have antecedents, nouns or pronouns to which they refer. A pronoun and its antecedent agree when they are both singular or both plural. (See 23a for advice on using plural _they_ with singular nouns and pronouns in some cases.)

SINGULAR   Dr. _Ava Berto_ finished _her_ rounds.

PLURAL   The hospital _interns_ finished _their_ rounds.

For Multilingual Writers

The pronouns _he, his, she, her, it,_ and _its_ must agree in gender (masculine, feminine, or neutral) with their antecedents, not with the words they modify.

Steve visited _his_ [not _her_] sister in Seattle.

23a Take care with indefinite pronouns (*anybody, everyone*) and generic nouns.

Writers are frequently tempted to use plural pronouns to refer to two kinds of singular antecedents: indefinite pronouns and generic nouns.

Indefinite pronouns

Indefinite pronouns refer to nonspecific persons or things.

anybody	each	everyone	nobody	somebody
anyone	either	everything	no one	someone
anything	everybody	neither	nothing	something

In the past, indefinite pronouns have been treated as singular. However, using a singular pronoun to refer to an indefinite pronoun can result in a sentence that is sexist, and the traditional alternatives (*he or she, he/she*) are wordy and noninclusive. (See 17e.)

SEXIST	*Everyone* performs at *his* own fitness level.
NONINCLUSIVE	*Everyone* performs at *his or her* own fitness level.

It is increasingly acceptable to use the gender-neutral pronoun *they* to refer to indefinite pronouns.

Everyone performs at *their* own fitness level.

The following are your options for revision.

1. Make the antecedent plural.

2. Rewrite the sentence so that no problem of agreement exists.

3. Use the gender-neutral pronoun *they* to refer to the singular antecedent.

▶ When ~~someone travels~~ outside the United States for the
       people travel
       ^
       they need
first time, ~~he needs~~ to apply for a passport.
    ^

▶ ~~When someone~~ travels outside the United States for the first time,⁄
      Anyone who *(inserted above "When someone")*
      ^
~~he~~ needs to apply for a passport.

▶ When someone travels outside the United States for the first time,
    they need
~~he needs~~ to apply for a passport.
  ^

If you change a pronoun in a sentence, check to be sure that the verb agrees with the new pronoun (see 22e).

Generic nouns

A generic noun represents a typical member of a group, such as a typical student, or any member of a group, such as any lawyer. Like indefinite pronouns, generic nouns have previously been considered singular. However, the singular use of *they* is increasingly acceptable with generic nouns. Avoid using *he* to refer to generic nouns, as in *A runner must train if he wants to excel.*

When revising sentences with generic nouns, you will usually have the same three options as for indefinite pronouns.

▶ ~~A medical student~~ must study hard if ~~he wants~~ to succeed.
  Medical students   *they want*
  ^   ^

▶ A medical student must study hard ~~if he wants~~ to succeed.

▶ A medical student must study hard if ~~he wants~~ to succeed.
                                 they want
                                 ^

23b Treat collective nouns as singular unless the meaning is clearly plural.

Collective nouns such as *jury, committee, audience, crowd, class, troop, family, team,* and *couple* name a group. Ordinarily the group functions as a unit, so the noun should be treated as singular; if the members of the group function as individuals, however, the noun should be treated as plural. (See also 22f.)

AS A UNIT   The *committee* granted *its* permission to build.

AS INDIVIDUALS   The *committee* put *their* signatures on the document.

When treating a collective noun as plural, many writers prefer to add a clearly plural antecedent such as *members* to the sentence: *The members of the committee put their signatures on the document.*

its
▶ After only an hour of deliberation, the jury returned ~~their~~ verdict.
                                                          ^

There is no reason to draw attention to the individual members of the jury, so *jury* should be treated as singular.

23c Take care with compound antecedents.

President Obama and Chinese president Xi held a meeting at which *they* formally signed the Paris Agreement.

With compound antecedents joined with *or* or *nor* (or with *either . . . or* or *neither . . . nor*), make the pronoun agree with the nearer antecedent.

Either *Bruce* or *Sebastian* should receive first prize for *his* poem.

Neither the *mouse* nor the *rats* could find *their* way through the maze.

NOTE: If one of the antecedents is singular and the other plural, as in the second example, put the plural antecedent last to avoid awkwardness.

EXCEPTION: If the two antecedents are people of different genders, do not follow the traditional rule. The sentence *Either Bruce or Elizabeth should receive first prize for her short story* makes no sense. The best solution is to recast the sentence: *The prize for best short story should go to either Bruce or Elizabeth.*

EXERCISE 23–1   Edit the following sentences to eliminate problems with pronoun-antecedent agreement. Most of the sentences can be revised in more than one way, so experiment before choosing a solution. If a sentence is correct, write "correct" after it. Possible revisions appear in the back of the book.

> *they choose*
> **Recruiters may tell the truth, but there is much that ~~he chooses~~ not**
>   ^
> **to tell.**

a. Every presidential candidate must appeal to a wide variety of ethnic and social groups if he wants to win the election.

b. Either Tom Hanks or Denzel Washington will win an award for their lifetime achievement in cinema.

c. The aerobics instructor motioned for everyone to move his or her arms in wide, slow circles.

d. The parade committee was unanimous in its decision to allow all groups and organizations to join the festivities.

e. The applicant should be bilingual if she wants to qualify for this position.

24 Make pronoun references clear.

Pronouns substitute for nouns; they are a kind of shorthand. In the sentence *When Andrew returned home, he took a nap*, the noun *Andrew* is the antecedent of the pronoun *he*. A pronoun should refer clearly to its antecedent.

24a Avoid ambiguous pronoun reference.

Ambiguous pronoun reference occurs when a pronoun could refer to two possible antecedents.

The pitcher broke when Gloria set it
▶ ~~When Gloria set the pitcher~~ on the glass-topped table~~/. it broke.~~
  ^   ^

"You have
▶ Andrés told James, ~~that he had~~ won the lottery."
                 ^   ^

What broke—the pitcher or the table? Who won the lottery—Andrés or James? The revisions eliminate the ambiguity.

24b Avoid making broad references with *this*, *that*, *which*, and *it*.

For clarity, the pronouns *this*, *that*, *which*, and *it* should ordinarily refer to specific antecedents rather than to whole ideas or sentences. When a pronoun's reference is needlessly broad, either replace the pronoun with a noun or supply an antecedent to which the pronoun clearly refers.

▶ By advertising on TV, pharmaceutical companies gain exposure
                                                    the ads
  for their prescription drugs. Patients respond to ~~this~~ by requesting
                                                      ^
  drugs they might not need.

The writer substituted the noun *ads* for the pronoun *this*, which referred broadly to the idea expressed in the preceding sentence.

▶ Romeo and Juliet were both too young to have acquired much
              a fact
  wisdom, ~~and~~ that accounts for their rash actions.
           ^

The writer added an antecedent (*fact*) that the pronoun *that* clearly refers to.

24c Do not use a pronoun to refer to an implied antecedent.

A pronoun should refer to a specific antecedent, not to a word that is implied but not present in the sentence.

                                              the braids
▶ After braiding Gemma's hair, Sue decorated ~~them~~ with ribbons.
                                                ^

The pronoun *them* referred to Gemma's braids (implied by the term *braiding*), but the word *braids* did not appear in the sentence.

24d Avoid the indefinite use of *they* and *it*.

The pronoun *they* should refer to a specific antecedent. Do not use *they* to refer to persons who have not been specifically mentioned.

the school board
▶ In June, ~~they~~ voted to charge a fee for students to participate in
　　　^
sports and music programs.

The word *it* should not be used indefinitely in constructions such as *It is said on television . . .* or *In the article, it says that . . .*

The
▶ ~~In the~~ encyclopedia ~~it~~ states that male moths can smell female
　^
moths from several miles away.

24e To refer to persons, use *who, whom,* or *whose,* not *which* or *that.*

In most contexts, use *who, whom,* or *whose* to refer to persons, and use *which* or *that* to refer to animals or things.

▶ During the two-day festival El Día de los Muertos (Day of the
　　　　　　　　　　　　　　　　　　　　　　　　who
Dead), Mexican families celebrate loved ones ~~that~~ have died.
　　　　　　　　　　　　　　　　　　　　　　　　^

EXERCISE 24–1　Edit the following sentences to correct errors in pronoun reference. In some cases, you will need to decide on an antecedent that the pronoun might logically refer to. Possible revisions appear in the back of the book.

Although Apple makes the most widely recognized tablet device,
　　　　　　　　　　　　　　　　　The competition
other companies have gained a share of the market. ~~This~~ has kept
　　　　　　　　　　　　　　　　　　　　　　　^
prices from skyrocketing.

a. They say that engineering students should have hands-on experience with dismantling and reassembling machines.

b. She had decorated her living room with posters from chamber music festivals. This led her date to believe that she was interested in classical music. Actually she preferred rock.

c. The high school principal congratulated the seniors that were graduating later that day.

d. Marianne told Jenny that she was worried about her mother's illness.

e. Though Lewis cried for several minutes after scraping his knee, eventually it subsided.

25 Distinguish between pronouns such as *I* and *me*.

The personal pronouns in the following chart change what is known as *case form* according to their grammatical function in a sentence. Pronouns functioning as subjects or subject complements appear in the *subjective* case; those functioning as objects appear in the *objective* case; and those showing ownership appear in the *possessive* case.

	SUBJECTIVE CASE	OBJECTIVE CASE	POSSESSIVE CASE
SINGULAR	I	me	my
	you	you	your
	he/she/it	him/her/it	his/her/its
PLURAL	we	us	our
	you	you	your
	they	them	their

Pronouns in the subjective and objective cases are frequently confused. Most of the rules in this section specify when to use one or the other of these cases (*I* or *me*, *he* or *him*, and so on). Section 25f explains a special use of pronouns and nouns in the possessive case.

25a Use the subjective case (*I, you, he, she, it, we, they*) for subjects and subject complements.

When personal pronouns are used as subjects, ordinarily your ear will tell you the correct pronoun. Problems sometimes arise, however, with compound word groups containing a pronoun.

▶ Joel left because his stepfather and ~~him~~ ^{he} had argued.

His stepfather and he is the subject of the verb *had argued*. If we strip away the words *his stepfather and*, the correct pronoun becomes clear: *he had argued* (not *him had argued*).

When a pronoun is used as a subject complement (a word following a linking verb), your ear may mislead you, since the incorrect form is frequently used in casual speech.

▶ During the trial, the defendant repeatedly denied that the kidnapper was ~~him.~~ ^{he.}

If *kidnapper was he* seems awkward, rewrite the sentence: *During the trial, the defendant repeatedly denied that he was the kidnapper.*

25b Use the objective case (*me, you, him, her, it, us, them*) for all objects.

When a personal pronoun is used as a direct object, an indirect object, or the object of a preposition, it must be in the objective case.

DIRECT OBJECT	Lin found Tony and brought *him* home.
INDIRECT OBJECT	Alice threw *me* a surprise party.
OBJECT OF A PREPOSITION	Keisha wondered if the call was for *her*.

When in doubt about the correct pronoun, some writers try to avoid making the choice by using a reflexive pronoun such as *myself*. Instead, use the objective case.

▶ Nidra gave my cousin and ~~myself~~ **me** some good tips on traveling in

New Delhi.

My cousin and me is the indirect object of the verb *gave*.

25c Put an appositive and the word to which it refers in the same case.

Appositives are noun phrases that rename nouns or pronouns. A pronoun used as an appositive has the same function (usually subject or object) as the word or words it renames.

▶ The managers, Dr. Bell and ~~me,~~ **I,** could not agree on a plan.

The appositive *Dr. Bell and I* renames the subject, *managers*.
Test: *I could not agree* (not *me could not agree*).

▶ The reporter found only two witnesses, the bicyclist and ~~I.~~ **me.**

The appositive *the bicyclist and me* renames the direct object, *witnesses*.
Test: *found me* (not *found I*).

25d Following *than* or *as*, choose the pronoun that expresses your meaning.

When a comparison begins with *than* or *as*, your choice of a pronoun will depend on your intended meaning. To test for the correct pronoun, mentally complete the sentence.

▶ We respected no other candidate as much as ~~she.~~ **her.**

Test: *as much as* [*we respected*] *her*.

25e Use the objective case for subjects and objects of infinitives.

An infinitive is the word *to* followed by the base form of a verb. (See 42b.) Both subjects and objects of infinitives take the objective case.

> Harriet asked Tamara and ~~I~~ to drive the senator and ~~she~~ to the airport.

me (above I); *her* (above she)

Tamara and me is the subject of the infinitive *to drive*; *senator and her* is the direct object of the infinitive.

25f Use the possessive case to modify a gerund.

A pronoun that modifies a gerund or a gerund phrase should be in the possessive case (*my, our, your, his, her, its, their*). A gerund is a verb form ending in *-ing* that functions as a noun.

> The chances of ~~you~~ being hit by lightning are about two million to one.

your (above you)

Your modifies the gerund phrase *being hit by lightning.*

Nouns as well as pronouns may modify gerunds. To form the possessive case of a noun, use an apostrophe and an *-s* (*victim's*) or just an apostrophe (*victims'*). (See 33a.)

> The old order in France paid a high price for the ~~aristocracy~~

aristocracy's (above aristocracy)

exploiting the lower classes.

The possessive noun *aristocracy's* modifies the gerund phrase *exploiting the lower classes.*

EXERCISE 25–1   Edit the following sentences to eliminate errors in pronoun case. If a sentence is correct, write "correct" after it. Answers appear in the back of the book.

Grandpa mows lawns for neighbors much younger than ~~him.~~

he. (above him.)

a. Rick applied for the job even though he heard that other candidates were more experienced than he.
b. The volleyball team could not believe that the coach was she.
c. She appreciated him telling the truth in such a difficult situation.
d. The director has asked you and I to draft a proposal for a new recycling plan.
e. My roommate and myself dreamed of renting an SUV, packing it with food, and driving two hundred miles to the shore.

26 Distinguish between *who* and *whom*.

The choice between *who* and *whom* (or *whoever* and *whomever*) occurs primarily in subordinate clauses and in questions. *Who* and *whoever*, subjective-case pronouns, are used for subjects and subject complements. *Whom* and *whomever*, objective-case pronouns, are used for objects.

26a Use *who* and *whom* correctly in subordinate clauses.

When *who* and *whom* (or *whoever* and *whomever*) introduce subordinate clauses, their case is determined by their function *within the clause they introduce*.

In the following two examples, the pronouns *who* and *whoever* function as the subjects of the clauses they introduce.

▶ First prize goes to the runner ~~whom~~ who earns the most points.

The subordinate clause is *who earns the most points*. The verb of the clause is *earns*, and its subject is *who*.

▶ Maya Angelou's *I Know Why the Caged Bird Sings* should be read by
whoever
~~whomever~~ is interested in the effects of racial prejudice on children.
∧

The writer selected the pronoun *whomever*, thinking that it was the object of
the preposition *by*. However, the object of the preposition is the entire subordinate clause *whoever is interested in the effects of racial prejudice on children*.
The verb of the clause is *is*, and the subject of the verb is *whoever*.

26b Use *who* and *whom* correctly in questions.

When deciding whether to use *who* or *whom* in a question, check for the
word's function within the question.

Who
▶ ~~Whom~~ was responsible for creating that computer virus?
∧

Who is the subject of the verb *was*.

Whom
▶ ~~Who~~ did the Democratic Party nominate in 2004?
∧

Whom is the direct object of the verb *did nominate*. This becomes clear if you
restructure the question: *The Democratic Party did nominate whom in 2004?*

EXERCISE 26–1   Edit the following sentences to eliminate errors in the use
of *who* and *whom* (or *whoever* and *whomever*). If a sentence is correct, write
"correct" after it. Answers appear in the back of the book.

whom
What is the address of the artist ~~who~~ Antonio hired?
∧

a. Arriving late for rehearsal, we had no idea who was supposed to dance
   with whom.

b. The environmental policy conference featured scholars who I had never
   heard of.

c. Whom did you support in last month's election for student government
   president?

d. Kartik always gives a holiday donation to whomever needs it.

e. The singers who Natalia selected for the choir attended their first
   rehearsal last night.

27 Choose adjectives and adverbs with care.

Adjectives modify nouns or pronouns. Adverbs modify verbs, adjectives, or other adverbs. (See 40d and 40e.)

Many adverbs are formed by adding -*ly* to adjectives (*normal, normally; smooth, smoothly*). But don't assume that all words ending in -*ly* are adverbs or that all adverbs end in -*ly*. Some adjectives end in -*ly* (*lovely, friendly*), and some adverbs don't (*always, here, there*). When in doubt, consult a dictionary.

27a Use adjectives to modify nouns.

Adjectives ordinarily precede the nouns they modify (*tall building*). But they can also function as subject complements or object complements, following the nouns they modify.

> **For Multilingual Writers**
>
> In English, adjectives are not made plural to agree with the words they modify: *The red* [not *reds*] *roses were a surprise.*

Subject complements

A subject complement follows a linking verb and completes the meaning of the subject. (See 41b.) When an adjective functions as a subject complement, it describes the subject.

Justice is *blind*.

Verbs such as *smell, taste, look,* and *feel* may be linking verbs. If the word following one of these verbs describes the subject, use an adjective; if the word following the verb modifies the verb, use an adverb.

| **ADJECTIVE** | The detective looked *cautious.* |
| **ADVERB** | The detective looked *cautiously* for fingerprints. |

The adjective *cautious* describes the detective; the adverb *cautiously* modifies the verb *looked.*

Linking verbs suggest states of being, not actions. Notice, for example, the different meanings of *looked* in the preceding examples. *To look cautious* suggests the state of being cautious; *to look cautiously* suggests performing in a cautious way.

> The lilacs in our backyard smell especially ~~sweetly~~ ^{sweet} this year.

The verb *smell* here suggests a state of being, not an action. Therefore, it should be followed by an adjective, not an adverb.

Object complements

An object complement follows a direct object and completes its meaning. (See 41b.) When an adjective functions as an object complement, it describes the direct object.

Sorrow makes 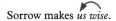 *us wise.*

Object complements occur with verbs such as *call, consider, create, find, keep,* and *make.* When a modifier follows the direct object of one of these verbs, use an adjective to describe the direct object; use an adverb to modify the verb.

| **ADJECTIVE** | The referee called the plays *perfect.* |
| **ADVERB** | The referee called the plays *perfectly.* |

The first sentence means that the referee considered the plays to be perfect; the second means that the referee did an excellent job of calling the plays.

27b Use adverbs to modify verbs, adjectives, and other adverbs.

When adverbs modify verbs (or verbals), they nearly always answer the questions such as the following: When? Where? How? Why? Under what conditions? How often? or To what degree? When adverbs modify adjectives or other adverbs, they usually qualify or intensify the meaning of the word they modify. (See 40e.)

Adjectives are often used incorrectly in place of adverbs in casual speech.

perfectly
▶ The travel arrangement worked out ~~perfect~~ for everyone.
 ^

The adverb *perfectly* modifies the verb *worked out*.

really
▶ The chance of recovering lost property looks ~~real~~ slim.
 ^

Only adverbs can modify adjectives or other adverbs. *Really* intensifies the meaning of the adjective *slim*.

27c Distinguish between *good* and *well, bad* and *badly.*

Good is an adjective (*good performance*). *Well* is an adverb when it modifies a verb (*speak well*).

well
▶ We were glad that Sanya had done ~~good~~ on the CPA exam.
 ^

The adverb *well* modifies the verb *had done*.

Bad is always an adjective and should be used to describe a noun; *badly* is always an adverb and should be used to modify a verb.

bad
▶ The sisters felt ~~badly~~ when they realized they had ignored their
 ^
brother.

27d Use comparatives and superlatives with care.

Most adjectives and adverbs have three forms: the positive, the comparative, and the superlative.

POSITIVE	COMPARATIVE	SUPERLATIVE
fast	faster	fastest
careful	more careful	most careful
bad	worse	worst
good	better	best

Use the comparative to compare two things, the superlative to compare three or more.

▶ Which of these two protein drinks is ~~best?~~ better?

▶ Zhao is the ~~more~~ most qualified of the three candidates running for state senator.

To form comparatives and superlatives of most one- and two-syllable adjectives, use the endings *-er* and *-est*: *smooth, smoother, smoothest; easy, easier, easiest*. With longer adjectives, use *more* and *most* (or *less* and *least* for downward comparisons): *exciting, more exciting, most exciting; considerate, less considerate, least considerate*.

Some one-syllable adverbs take the endings *-er* and *-est* (*fast, faster, fastest*), but longer adverbs and all of those ending in *-ly* form the comparative and superlative with *more* and *most* (or *less* and *least*).

The comparative and superlative forms of some adjectives and adverbs are irregular: *good, better, best; well, better, best; bad, worse, worst; badly, worse, worst*.

▶ According to our projections, sales at brick-and-mortar businesses will be ~~worser~~ worse than those at online retailers this winter.

Do not use double comparatives or superlatives. When you have added *-er* or *-est* to an adjective or adverb, do not also use *more* or *most* (or *less* or *least*).

▶ All the polls indicated that Gore was more ~~likelier~~ to win than Bush.

likely

Avoid expressions such as *less perfect*, *very round*, and *most unique*. Either something is unique or it isn't. It is illogical to suggest that absolute concepts come in degrees.

▶ That is the most ~~unique~~ wedding gown I have ever seen.

unusual

EXERCISE 27–1 Edit the following sentences to eliminate errors in the use of adjectives and adverbs. If a sentence is correct, write "correct" after it. Answers appear in the back of the book.

We weren't surprised by how ~~good~~ the sidecar racing team flowed

well

through the tricky course.

a. Do you expect to perform good on the exam next week?

b. With the budget deadline approaching, our office has been handling routine correspondence more slow than we usually do.

c. When I worked in a flower shop, I learned that some flowers smell surprisingly bad.

d. The customer complained that he hadn't been treated nice by the agent on the phone.

e. Of all the smart people in my family, Uncle Roberto is the most cleverest.

28 Choose the correct verb forms, tenses, and moods.

Except for the verb *be*, all verbs in English have five forms. The following list shows the five forms and provides a sample sentence for each.

BASE FORM	Usually I (*walk, ride*).
PAST TENSE	Yesterday I (*walked, rode*).
PAST PARTICIPLE	I have (*walked, ridden*) many times before.
PRESENT PARTICIPLE	I am (*walking, riding*) right now.
-S FORM	He/she/it (*walks, rides*) regularly.

The verb *be* has eight forms instead of the usual five: *be, am, is, are, was, were, being, been.*

Basic verb forms

	REGULAR (*HELP*)	IRREGULAR (*GIVE*)	IRREGULAR (*BE*)*
BASE FORM	help	give	be
PAST TENSE	helped	gave	was, were
PAST PARTICIPLE	helped	given	been
PRESENT PARTICIPLE	helping	giving	being
-*S* FORM	helps	gives	is

*Be also has the forms *am* and *are*, which are used in the present tense.

28a Choose the correct forms of irregular verbs.

For all regular verbs, the past-tense and past-participle forms are the same (ending in *-ed* or *-d*), so there is no danger of confusion. This is not true, however, for irregular verbs, such as the following.

BASE FORM	PAST TENSE	PAST PARTICIPLE
go	went	gone
break	broke	broken
fly	flew	flown

The past-tense form always occurs alone, without a helping verb. It expresses action that occurred entirely in the past: *I rode to work yesterday. I walked to work last Tuesday.* The past participle is used with a helping verb. It forms the perfect tenses with *has, have,* or *had;* it forms the passive voice with *be, am, is, are, was, were, being,* or *been.* (See 40c for a complete list of helping verbs and 28f for a survey of tenses.)

Common irregular verbs

BASE FORM	PAST TENSE	PAST PARTICIPLE
be	was, were	been
break	broke	broken
bring	brought	brought
choose	chose	chosen
come	came	come
do	did	done
drink	drank	drunk
eat	ate	eaten
find	found	found
go	went	gone
hang (execute)	hanged	hanged
hang (suspend)	hung	hung
have	had	had
know	knew	known
rise	rose	risen
see	saw	seen
sing	sang	sung
take	took	taken
teach	taught	taught
write	wrote	written

28b Distinguish among the forms of *lie* and *lay*.

Writers and speakers frequently confuse the various forms of *lie* (meaning "to recline or rest on a surface") and *lay* (meaning "to put or place something").

BASE FORM	PAST TENSE	PAST PARTICIPLE	PRESENT PARTICIPLE
lie (recline)	lay	lain	lying
lay (put)	laid	laid	laying

               lay
▶ Niko was so exhausted that she ~~laid~~ down for a nap.
                         ^

The past-tense form of *lie* ("to recline") is *lay*.

               laid
▶ The customer gently ~~lay~~ the tablet on the help desk counter.
                 ^

The past-tense form of *lay* ("to place") is *laid*.

               lying
▶ Letters dating from 1915 were ~~laying~~ in a corner of the chest.
                     ^

The present participle of *lie* ("to rest on a surface") is *lying*.

28c Use -s (or -es) endings on present-tense verbs that have third-person singular subjects.

All singular nouns (*child*, *tree*) and the pronouns *he*, *she*, and *it* are third-person singular; indefinite pronouns such as *everyone* and *neither* are also third-person singular. When the subject of a sentence is third-person singular, its verb takes an *-s* or *-es* ending in the present tense, whether the verb is regular or irregular. (See also section 22.)

	SINGULAR		PLURAL	
FIRST PERSON	I	know, have, do	we	know, have, do
SECOND PERSON	you	know, have, do	you	know, have, do
THIRD PERSON	he/she/it	knows, has, does	they	know, have, do
	child	knows, has, does	parents	know, have, do
	everyone	knows, has, does		

          drives
▶ My neighbor ~~drive~~ to Marco Island every weekend.
     ^

          turns   dissolves
▶ Sulfur dioxide ~~turn~~ leaves yellow and ~~dissolve~~ marble.
          ^   ^

The subjects *neighbor* and *sulfur dioxide* are third-person singular, so the verbs must end in *-s*.

NOTE: Do not add the *-s* ending to the verb if the subject is not third-person singular. The writers of the following sentences added *-s* endings where they don't belong.

▶ I prepare**s** system specifications for every installation.

The pronoun *I* is first-person singular, so its verb does not require the *-s*.

▶ The tile floors require**s** continual sweeping.

The *-s* form is used only on present-tense verbs with third-person *singular* subjects.

28d Do not omit *-ed* endings on verbs.

The verb ending *-ed* is sometimes not fully pronounced with words and phrases such as *asked, fixed, pronounced, supposed to,* and *used to.* While the meaning of such words is often clear while speaking, include *-ed* endings in academic writing to avoid confusion.

Past tense

Use the ending *-ed* or *-d* to express the past tense of regular verbs. The past tense is used when the action occurred entirely in the past.

▶ In 2020, author Colson Whitehead ~~receive~~ **received** the Pulitzer Prize for his

novel *The Nickel Boys.*

▶ Last summer, my counselor ~~advise~~ **advised** me to ask my graphic arts

instructor for a recommendation.

Past participles

Past participles are used in three ways: (1) following *have, has,* or *had* to form one of the perfect tenses; (2) following *be, am, is, are, was, were, being,* or *been* to form the passive voice; and (3) as adjectives modifying nouns or pronouns. The perfect tenses are listed in 28f, and the passive voice is discussed in 8a. For a discussion of participles as adjectives, see 42b.

>   *asked*
> Robin has ~~ask~~ for more housing staff for next year.
>   ^

Has asked is the present perfect tense (*have* or *has* followed by a past participle).

> Though it is not a new issue, the environmental effects of mass
>   *discussed*
> production are now ~~discuss~~ more than ever.
>   ^

Are discussed is a verb in the passive voice (a form of *be* followed by a past participle).

28e Do not omit needed verbs.

Linking verbs, used to link subjects to subject complements, are frequently a form of *be*: *be, am, is, are, was, were, being, been.* (See 41b.) While these verbs can sometimes be contracted (*it's* for *it is*, for example), do not omit the verb altogether.

>   *is*
> The city of Venice better protected from flooding thanks to its new
>   ^
> system of dams and gates called MOSE.

Helping verbs, used with main verbs, include forms of *be, do,* and *have* and the modal verbs *can, will, shall, could, would, should, may, might,* and *must.* (See 29a and 40c.) Like linking verbs, some helping verbs may be contracted (*he's leaving, we'll celebrate, they've been told*), but avoid omitting them altogether in your writing.

>   *have*
> Astronomers been studying the skies with the Hubble Telescope
>   ^
> since 1990.

For Multilingual Writers

Some languages do not require a linking verb between a subject and its complement. However, written English sentences always contain a verb.

>   *am*
> Every night, I read to my daughter. When I too busy, her older
>   ^
> brother reads to her.

EXERCISE 28-1 Edit the following sentences to eliminate problems with -s and -ed verb forms and with omitted verbs. If a sentence is correct, write "correct" after it. Answers appear in the back of the book.

covers
The Pell Grant sometimes ~~cover~~ the student's full tuition.
^

a. The glass sculptures of the Swan Boats was prominent in the brightly lit lobby.

b. When I get the urge to exercise, I lay down until it passes.

c. Grandmother had drove our new hybrid to the sunrise church service, so we were left with the van.

d. Christos didn't know about Marlo's promotion because he never listens. He always talking.

e. A pile of dirty rags was laying at the bottom of the stairs.

28f Choose the correct verb tense.

Tenses indicate the time of an action in relation to the time of the speaking or writing about that action.

The most common problem with tenses — confusing shifts from one tense to another — is discussed in section 13. Other problems with tenses are detailed in this section, after the following survey of tenses.

Survey of tenses

Tenses are classified as present, past, and future, with simple, perfect, and progressive forms for each.

Simple tenses (base form or -s form) *For general facts, states of being, and habitual actions*

SIMPLE PRESENT SINGULAR		PLURAL	
I	walk, ride, am	we	walk, ride, are
you	walk, ride, are	you	walk, ride, are
he/she/it	walks, rides, is	they	walk, ride, are

SIMPLE PAST

SINGULAR		PLURAL	
I	walked, rode, was	we	walked, rode, were
you	walked, rode, were	you	walked, rode, were
he/she/it	walked, rode, was	they	walked, rode, were

SIMPLE FUTURE

I, you, he/she/it, we, they   will walk, ride, be

Perfect tenses (a form of *have* plus past participle)   *For an action that was or will be completed at the time of another action*

PRESENT PERFECT

I, you, we, they	have walked, ridden, been
he/she/it	has walked, ridden, been

PAST PERFECT

I, you, he/she/it, we, they   had walked, ridden, been

FUTURE PERFECT

I, you, he/she/it, we, they   will have walked, ridden, been

Progressive forms (a form of *have* plus present participle)   *For actions in progress*

PRESENT PROGRESSIVE

I	am walking, riding, being
he/she/it	is walking, riding, being
you, we, they	are walking, riding, being

PAST PROGRESSIVE

I, he/she/it	was walking, riding, being
you, we, they	were walking, riding, being

FUTURE PROGRESSIVE

I, you, he/she/it, we, they   will be walking, riding, being

PRESENT PERFECT PROGRESSIVE

I, you, we, they	have been walking, riding, being
he/she/it	has been walking, riding, being

PAST PERFECT PROGRESSIVE

I, you, he/she/it, we, they   had been walking, riding, being

FUTURE PERFECT PROGRESSIVE

I, you, he/she/it, we, they   will have been walking, riding, being

NOTE: The progressive forms are not normally used with certain verbs, such as *believe, know,* and *seem.*

Special uses of the present tense

Use the present tense when expressing general truths, when writing about literature, and when quoting, summarizing, or paraphrasing an author's views.

General truths or scientific principles should be stated in the present tense unless such principles have been disproved.

>   *revolves*
> ▶ Galileo taught that the earth ~~revolved~~ around the sun.
>   ^

When writing about a work of literature, you may be tempted to use the past tense. The convention in the humanities, however, is to describe fictional events in the present tense.

>   *reaches*
> ▶ In Masuji Ibuse's *Black Rain,* a child ~~reached~~ for a pomegranate in
>   ^   *is*
> his mother's garden, and a moment later he ~~was~~ dead, killed by the
>   ^
> blast of the atomic bomb.

When you are quoting, summarizing, or paraphrasing the author of a nonliterary work, use present-tense verbs such as *writes, reports,* or *asserts* to introduce the source. This convention is usually followed even when the author is dead (unless a date or the context specifies the time of writing).

EXCEPTION: When you are documenting a paper with the APA (American Psychological Association) style of in-text citations, use past-tense verbs such as *argued* or present perfect verbs such as *has argued* to introduce the source. (See also section 52a.)

The past perfect tense

The past perfect tense (*had* plus past participle) is used for an action already completed by the time of another past action or for an action already completed at some specific past time.

> Everyone *had spoken* by the time I arrived.

<blockquote>
had
► By the time dinner was served, the guest of honor left.
                                                      ^
</blockquote>

The past perfect tense is needed because the action of leaving was already completed at a specific past time (when dinner was served).

Sequence of tenses with infinitives and participles

An infinitive is the base form of a verb preceded by *to*. (See 42b.) Use the present infinitive to show action at the same time as or later than the action of the verb in the sentence.

<blockquote>
pay
► Sonia had hoped to have paid the bill by May 1.
                     ^
</blockquote>

The action expressed in the infinitive (*to pay*) occurred later than the action of the sentence's verb (*had hoped*).

Use the perfect form of an infinitive (*to have* followed by the past participle) for an action occurring earlier than that of the verb in the sentence.

<blockquote>
have joined
► Dan would like to join the Coast Guard, but he could not swim.
                   ^
</blockquote>

The liking occurs in the present; the joining would have occurred in the past.

28g Use the subjunctive mood in the few contexts that require it.

There are three moods in English: the *indicative*, used for facts, opinions, and questions; the *imperative*, used for orders and advice; and the *subjunctive,* used in certain contexts to express wishes, requests, or conditions contrary to fact. For many writers, the subjunctive causes the most problems.

In wishes and *if* clauses expressing conditions contrary to fact, the subjunctive is the past-tense form of the verb; in the case of *be,* it is always *were* (not *was*), even if the subject is singular.

> I wish that Jamal drove more slowly late at night.

> If I were the committee chair, I would allow the policy change.

NOTE: Do not use the subjunctive mood in *if* clauses expressing conditions that exist or may exist: *If Danielle passes* (not *passed*) *the test, she will become a lifeguard.*

In *that* clauses following verbs such as *ask, insist, recommend,* and *request,* the subjunctive is the base form of the verb.

> Dr. Chung insists that her students arrive on time.

EXERCISE 28–2 Edit the following sentences to eliminate errors in verb tense or mood. If a sentence is correct, write "correct" after it. Answers appear in the back of the book.

had been
After the path ~~was~~ plowed, we were able to walk in the park.
  ^

a. The palace of Knossos in Crete is believed to have been destroyed by fire around 1375 BCE.

b. Discovered in 1930, Pluto was an icy dwarf planet that exists at the edge of our solar system.

c. When city planners proposed rezoning the waterfront, did they know that the mayor promised to curb development in that neighborhood?

d. Tonight's lecture begins at 7:30. If it was earlier, I'd consider attending.

e. The math position was filled by the instructor who had been running the tutoring center.

29 Review grammar topics for multilingual writers.

This section offers a brief review of common grammar challenges for multilingual writers.

29a Use modal verbs to express appropriate meaning.

Both native and nonnative speakers of English encounter challenges with verbs. Section 28 provides details about verb forms, tenses, and moods (see also 40c). This section describes the use of modal verbs to express ability, certainty, necessity, permission, obligation, or possibility.

The nine modal verbs — *can, could, may, might, must, shall, should, will*, and *would* — are used with the base forms of verbs. Modals do not change form to indicate tense.

▶ The art museum will ~~launches~~ <u>launch</u> its fundraising campaign next month.

▶ We could ~~spoke~~ <u>speak</u> Portuguese when we were young.

The modal *could* must be followed by the base form *speak*, not the past tense *spoke*.

Modals and their meanings		
can		
• general ability (present)	Ants *can survive* anywhere, even in space. Jorge *can run* a marathon faster than his brother.	
• informal requests or permission	*Can* you *tell* me where the bookstore is?	
	You *can borrow* my calculator until Wednesday.	
could		
• general ability (past)	Lea *could read* when she was only three years old.	
• polite, informal requests or permission	*Could* you *give* me that pen?	

MODALS AND THEIR MEANINGS (cont.)	
may	
• formal requests or permission	*May* I *see* the report? Students *may park* only in the yellow zone.
• possibility	I *may try* to finish my homework tonight, or I *may wake up* early and *finish* it tomorrow.
might	
• possibility	Funding for the language lab *might double* by 2025.
must	
• necessity (present or future)	Employers *must post* a minimum wage poster where employees can view it.
• strong probability or near certainty (present or past)	Amy *must be* nervous. [She is probably nervous.] I *must have left* my wallet at home. [I almost certainly left my wallet at home.]
should	
• suggestions or advice	Diabetics *should drink* plenty of water every day.
• obligations or duties	The government *should protect* citizens' rights.
• expectations	The books *should arrive* soon. [We expect the books to arrive soon.]
will	
• certainty	If you don't leave now, you *will be* late.
• requests	*Will* you *help* me study for my psychology exam?
• promises and offers	Jonah *will arrange* the carpool.
would	
• polite requests	*Would* you *help* me carry these books? I *would like* some coffee. [*Would like* is more polite than *want*.]
• habitual or repeated actions (in the past)	Whenever Elena needed help with sewing, she *would call* her aunt.

EXERCISE 29-1   Edit the following sentences to correct errors in the use of verb forms with modals. If a sentence is correct, write "correct" after it. Answers appear in the back of the book.

We should ~~to~~ order pizza for dinner.

a. A major league pitcher can to throw a baseball more than ninety-five miles per hour.
b. The writing center tutor will helps you revise your essay.
c. A reptile must adjusted its body temperature to its environment.
d. In some states, individuals may renew a driver's license online.
e. My uncle, a cartoonist, could sketched a face in less than a minute.

29b Be familiar with articles and other noun markers.

Articles (*a, an, the*) are part of a category of words known as *noun markers* or *determiners*. Noun markers identify the nouns that follow them. Besides articles, noun markers include possessive nouns (*Elena's, child's*); possessive pronouns/adjectives (*my, your, their*); demonstrative pronouns/adjectives (*this, that*); quantifiers (*all, few, neither, some*); and numbers (*one, twenty-six*).

ART N
Felix is reading a book about mythology.

ART ADJ N
We took an exciting trip to Alaska when I was a child.

When to use *the*

Use *the* with most nouns that the reader can identify specifically. Usually the identity will be clear to the reader for one of the following reasons.

1. The noun has been previously mentioned.

▶   A truck cut in front of our van. When <u>the</u> truck skidded a few seconds
    later, we almost crashed into it.

2. A phrase or clause following the noun restricts its identity.

> the
> ▶ Bryce warned me that radio in his car was not working.
> ⌃

3. A superlative adjective such as *best* or *most intelligent* makes the noun's identity specific. (See also 27d.)

> the
> ▶ Brita had best players on her team.
> ⌃

4. The noun describes a unique person, place, or thing.

> the
> ▶ During an eclipse, one should not look directly at sun.
> ⌃

5. The context or situation makes the noun's identity clear.

> the
> ▶ Please don't slam door when you leave.
> ⌃

6. The noun is singular and refers to a scientific class or category of items (most often animals, musical instruments, or inventions).

> The tin
> ▶ ~~Tin~~ whistle is common in traditional Irish music.
> ⌃

When to use *a* or *an*

Use *a* or *an* with singular count nouns that refer to an unspecific item (not a whole category). *Count nouns* refer to persons, places, things, or ideas that can be counted: *one girl, two girls; one city, three cities; one goose, four geese.*

> a
> ▶ My professor asked me to bring dictionary to class.
> ⌃

> an
> ▶ We want to rent apartment close to the lake.
> ⌃

When not to use articles

Do not use *a* or *an* with noncount nouns. *Noncount nouns* refer to things or abstract ideas that cannot be counted or made plural: *salt, silver, air, furniture, patience, knowledge.* (See the chart below.)

To express an approximate amount of a noncount noun, use a quantifier such as *some* or *more: some water, enough coffee, less violence.* Do not use articles with nouns that refer to all of something or to something in general.

> Kindness
> ▶ ~~The kindness~~ is a virtue.
>   ∧

> ▶ In some places, ~~the~~ rice is preferred to all other grains.

Commonly used noncount nouns

Food and drink

beef, bread, butter, candy, cereal, cheese, cream, meat, milk, pasta, rice, salt, sugar, water, wine

Nonfood substances

air, cement, coal, dirt, gasoline, gold, paper, petroleum, plastic, rain, silver, snow, soap, steel, wood, wool

Abstract nouns

advice, anger, beauty, confidence, courage, employment, fun, happiness, health, honesty, information, intelligence, knowledge, love, poverty, satisfaction, wealth

Other

biology (and other areas of study), clothing, equipment, furniture, homework, jewelry, luggage, machinery, mail, money, news, poetry, pollution, research, scenery, traffic, transportation, violence, weather, work

NOTE: A few noncount nouns (such as *love*) can also be used as count nouns: *He had two loves: music and archery.*

When to use articles with proper nouns

Do not use articles with most singular proper nouns: *Chancellor Merkel, Jamaica, Lake Huron, Ivy Street, Mount Everest.* Use *the* with most plural proper nouns: *the McGregors, the Bahamas, the Finger Lakes, the United States.* Also use *the* with large regions, oceans, rivers, and mountain ranges: *the Sahara, the Indian Ocean, the Amazon River, the Rocky Mountains.* There are, however, many exceptions, especially with geographic names. Note exceptions when you encounter them or consult a native speaker or an ESL dictionary.

29c Overcome certain challenges when writing sentences in English.

Omitted subjects

Some languages do not require a subject in every sentence. Every English sentence, however, needs a subject.

> She seems
> ▶ Your aunt is very energetic. ~~Seems~~ young for her age.
>   ^

EXCEPTION: In a command, the subject *you* is understood but not present in the sentence: *Give me the book.*

The word *it* may be used as the subject of a sentence describing the weather or temperature, stating the time, indicating distance, or suggesting an environmental fact. Do not omit *it* in such sentences.

It is raining in the valley and snowing in the mountains.

It is 9:15 a.m.

It is three hundred miles to Chicago.

In July, it is very hot in Arizona.

In some English sentences, the subject comes after the verb, and a placeholder called an *expletive* (*there* or *it*) comes before the verb.

EXP V ┌── S ──┐   ┌── S ──┐ V
There are many people here today. (Many people are here today.)

EXP V ┌─ S ─┐   ┌─ S ─┐ V
It is important to study daily. (To study daily is important.)

▶ As you know, *there are* many religious sects in India.
            ^

Repeated subjects, objects, and adverbs

Do not repeat a subject in its own clause.

▶ The doctor ~~she~~ advised me to cut down on salt.

Do not add a pronoun even when a word group comes between the subject and the verb.

▶ The car that had been stolen ~~it~~ was found.

Do not repeat an object or an adverb in an adjective clause. Adjective clauses begin with relative pronouns (*who, whom, whose, which, that*) or relative adverbs (*when, where*). Relative pronouns usually serve as subjects or objects in the clauses they introduce; another word in the clause cannot serve the same function.

▶ The cat ran under the car that ~~it~~ was parked on the street.

The relative pronoun *that* is the subject of the adjective clause, so the pronoun *it* cannot be added as a subject.

If the clause begins with a relative adverb, do not use another adverb with the same meaning later in the clause.

▶ The office where I work ~~there~~ is close to home.

The adverb *there* cannot repeat the relative adverb *where*.

29d Become familiar with prepositions that show time and place.

The following chart is limited to three prepositions that show time and place: *at, on,* and *in.* Not every possible use is listed in the chart, so don't be surprised when you encounter exceptions and idiomatic uses that you must learn one at a time. For example, in English a person rides *in* a car but *on* a bus, plane, train, or subway.

At, on, and *in* to show time and place	
Showing time	
AT	*at* a specific time: *at* 7:20, *at* dawn, *at* dinner
ON	*on* a specific day or date: *on* Tuesday, *on* June 4
IN	*in* a part of a 24-hour period: *in* the afternoon, *in* the daytime [but *at* night]
	in a year or month: *in* 2008, *in* July
	in a period of time: finished *in* three hours
Showing place	
AT	*at* a meeting place or location: *at* home, *at* the club
	at the edge of something: sitting *at* the desk
	at the corner of something: turning *at* the intersection
	at a target: throwing the snowball *at* Lucy
ON	*on* a surface: placed *on* the table, hanging *on* the wall
	on a street: the house *on* Spring Street
	on an electronic medium: *on* television, *on* Instagram
IN	*in* an enclosed space: *in* the garage, *in* an envelope
	in a geographic location: *in* San Diego, *in* Texas
	in a print medium: *in* a book, *in* a magazine

EXERCISE 29–2 Edit the following sentences for proper use of articles, nouns, and prepositions and for proper sentence structure. If a sentence is correct, write "correct" after it. Answers appear in the back of the book.

> The play begins ~~on~~ ^{at} 7:30 p.m.

a. Freezing rain causes icy glaze on trees.

b. I don't use the subway because am claustrophobic.

c. Recently have been a number of earthquakes in Turkey.

d. Whenever we eat at the café, we sit at a small table on the corner of the patio.

e. In the 1990s, entrepreneurs created new online business in record numbers.

PART 6

Punctuation

185

30 The comma

The comma was invented to help readers. Without it, sentence parts can collide into one another unexpectedly, causing misreadings.

CONFUSING	If you cook Elmer will do the dishes.
CONFUSING	While we were eating a rattlesnake approached our campsite.

Add commas in the logical places (after *cook* and *eating*), and suddenly all is clear. No longer is Elmer being cooked or the rattlesnake being eaten.

Various rules have evolved to prevent such misreadings and to speed readers along through complex grammatical structures. Those rules are detailed in this section. (Section 31 explains when not to use commas.)

30a Use a comma before a coordinating conjunction joining independent clauses.

When a coordinating conjunction connects two or more independent clauses — word groups that could stand alone as separate sentences — a comma must precede the conjunction. There are seven coordinating conjunctions in English: *and*, *but*, *or*, *nor*, *for*, *so*, and *yet*.

A comma tells readers that one independent clause has come to a close and that another is about to begin.

▶ The department sponsored a seminar on college survival

skills, and it hosted a barbecue for new students.
  ∧

EXCEPTION: If the two independent clauses are short and there is no danger of misreading, the comma may be omitted: *The plane took off and we were on our way.*

NOTE: Do not use a comma with a coordinating conjunction that joins only two words, phrases, or subordinate clauses. (See 31a. See also 30c for commas with coordinating conjunctions joining three or more elements.)

▶ **A good money manager controls expenses/and invests**

surplus dollars to meet future needs.

The word group following *and* is not an independent clause; it is the second half of a compound predicate (*controls . . . and invests*).

30b Use a comma after an introductory clause or phrase.

A comma tells readers that an introductory clause or phrase has come to a close and that the main part of the sentence is about to begin. The most common introductory clauses and phrases function as adverbs. Such word groups usually tell when, where, how, why, or under what conditions the main action of the sentence occurred. (See 42a, 42b, and 42e.)

▶ **When Irwin was ready to iron, his cat tripped on the cord.**
      ∧

Without the comma, readers may think that Irwin is ironing his cat. The comma signals that *his cat* is the subject of a new clause, not part of the introductory one.

EXCEPTION: The comma may be omitted after a short adverb clause or phrase if there is no danger of misreading: *In no time we were at 2,800 feet.*

Sentences also frequently begin with a participial phrase that functions as an adjective, describing the noun or pronoun immediately following it. The comma tells readers that they are about to learn the identity of the person or thing described; therefore, the comma is usually required even when the phrase is short. (See 42b.)

> **Buried under layers of younger rocks, the earth's oldest rocks**
> ^
> **contain no fossils.**

NOTE: Other introductory word groups include transitional expressions and absolute phrases (see 30f).

30c Use a comma between all items in a series.

When three or more items (words, phrases, or clauses) are presented in a series, separate those items from one another with commas.

> **Langston Hughes's poetry is concerned with race, justice, and the**
> ^
> **diversity of the Black American experience.**

Although some writers view the last comma in a series as optional, most experts advise using the comma because its omission can result in ambiguity or misreading.

> **The wildfire destroyed all of our property, barns, and farm equipment.**
> ^
> Did the wildfire destroy the property *and* barns *and* farm equipment—or simply the property, consisting of barns and farm equipment? If the former meaning is intended, a comma is necessary to prevent ambiguity.

30d Use a comma between coordinate adjectives not joined with *and*.

When two or more adjectives each modify a noun separately, they are coordinate.

> Roberto is a *warm, gentle, affectionate* father.

If the adjectives can be joined with *and* (warm *and* gentle *and* affection-ate), the adjectives are coordinate, so you should use commas: *warm, gentle, affectionate.*

NOTE: Do not use a comma between cumulative adjectives, those that do not each modify the noun separately.

> *Three large gray* shapes moved slowly toward us.

Cumulative adjectives cannot be joined with *and* (not *three and large and gray shapes*).

EXERCISE 30–1   Add or delete commas where necessary in the following sentences. If a sentence is correct, write "correct" after it. Answers appear in the back of the book.

We gathered our essentials, took off for the great outdoors, and

ignored the fact that it was Friday the 13th.

a. The cold impersonal atmosphere of the university was unbearable.
b. An ambulance threaded its way through police cars, fire trucks and irate citizens.
c. The *1812 Overture* is a stirring, magnificent piece of music.
d. After two broken arms, three cracked ribs and one concussion, Ken quit the varsity football team.
e. My cat's pupils had constricted to small black shining slits.

30e Use commas to set off nonrestrictive (nonessential) elements, but not restrictive (essential) elements.

Restrictive (essential) elements

A restrictive element defines or limits the meaning of the word it modi-fies; it is therefore essential to the meaning of the sentence and is not set off with commas. If you remove a restrictive modifier from a sentence, the meaning changes significantly, becoming more general than you intended.

RESTRICTIVE (NO COMMAS)

The campers need clothes *that are durable.*

Scientists *who study the earth's structure* are called geologists.

The first sentence does not mean that the campers need clothes in general. The intended meaning is more limited: The campers need durable clothes. The second sentence does not mean that scientists in general are called geologists; only those scientists who specifically study the earth's structure are called geologists. The italicized word groups are essential and are therefore not set off with commas.

Nonrestrictive (nonessential) elements

A nonrestrictive modifier describes a noun or pronoun whose meaning has already been clearly defined or limited. Because the modifier contains nonessential or parenthetical information, it is set off with commas. If you remove a nonrestrictive element from a sentence, some meaning may be lost, but the defining characteristics of the person or thing remain the same.

NONRESTRICTIVE (WITH COMMAS)

The campers need sturdy shoes, *which are expensive.*

The computer scientists, *who represented eight different universities,* met to review applications for the Turing Award.

In the first sentence, the campers need sturdy shoes, and the shoes happen to be expensive. In the second sentence, the computer scientists met to review applications for the award; that they represented eight different universities is informative but not critical to the meaning of the sentence. The nonessential information in both sentences is set off with commas.

NOTE: Often it is difficult to tell whether a word group is restrictive or nonrestrictive without seeing it in context and considering the writer's meaning. Both of the following sentences are grammatically correct, but their meanings differ slightly.

> The dessert made with fresh raspberries was delicious.

> The dessert, made with fresh raspberries, was delicious.

In the first example, the phrase *made with fresh raspberries* tells readers which of two or more desserts the writer is referring to. In the example with commas, the phrase merely adds information about one dessert.

Elements that may be restrictive or nonrestrictive include adjective clauses, adjective phrases, and appositives.

Adjective clauses

Adjective clauses, which usually follow the noun or pronoun they describe, begin with a relative pronoun (*who, whom, whose, which, that*) or with a relative adverb (*when, where*). When an adjective clause is non-restrictive, set it off with commas; when it is restrictive, omit the commas.

NONRESTRICTIVE CLAUSE (WITH COMMAS)

▶ Ed's house, which is located on thirteen acres, was completely furnished with bats in the rafters and mice in the kitchen.

The adjective clause *which is located on thirteen acres* does not restrict the meaning of *Ed's house*; the information is nonessential and is therefore set off with commas.

RESTRICTIVE CLAUSE (NO COMMAS)

▶ The giant panda that was born at the National Zoo in 2013 was sent to China in 2017.

Because the adjective clause *that was born at the National Zoo in 2013* identifies one particular panda out of many, the information is essential and is therefore not set off with commas.

NOTE: Use *that* only with restrictive (essential) clauses. Many writers prefer to use *which* only with nonrestrictive (nonessential) clauses, but usage varies.

Adjective phrases

Prepositional or verbal phrases functioning as adjectives may be restrictive or nonrestrictive. Nonrestrictive phrases are set off with commas; restrictive phrases are not.

NONRESTRICTIVE PHRASE (WITH COMMAS)

▶ The helicopter, with its million-candlepower spotlight illuminating
  ^
  the area, circled above.
  ^

The *with* phrase is nonessential because its purpose is not to specify which of two or more helicopters is being discussed. The phrase is not required for readers to understand the meaning of the sentence.

RESTRICTIVE PHRASE (NO COMMAS)

▶ One corner of the attic was filled with newspapers/ dating from the

  early 1900s.

Dating from the early 1900s restricts the meaning of *newspapers*, so the comma should be omitted.

Appositives

An appositive is a noun or noun phrase that renames a nearby noun. Nonrestrictive appositives are set off with commas; restrictive appositives are not.

NONRESTRICTIVE APPOSITIVE (WITH COMMAS)

▶ Darwin's most important book, *On the Origin of Species*, was the
  ^   ^
  result of many years of research.

Most important restricts the meaning to one book, so the appositive *On the Origin of Species* is nonrestrictive and should be set off with commas.

RESTRICTIVE APPOSITIVE (NO COMMAS)

▶ The song⁄ "Sun Goes Down⁄" was blasted out of huge amplifiers at

the concert.

Once they've read *song*, readers still don't know precisely which song the writer means. The appositive following *song* restricts its meaning, so the appositive should not be set off with commas.

30f Use commas to set off transitional and parenthetical expressions, absolute phrases, and word groups expressing contrast.

Transitional expressions

Transitional expressions serve as bridges between sentences or parts of sentences. They include conjunctive adverbs such as *however, therefore,* and *moreover* and transitional phrases such as *for example, as a matter of fact,* and *in other words*. (For complete lists of these expressions, see 32b.)

When a transitional expression appears between independent clauses in a compound sentence, it is preceded by a semicolon and is usually followed by a comma. (See 32b.)

▶ Minh did not understand the language; moreover, he was unfamiliar
                                                    ∧
with the customs.

When a transitional expression appears at the beginning of a sentence or in the middle of an independent clause, it is usually set off with a comma or commas.

▶ Natural foods are not always salt-free; celery, for example, contains
                                                 ∧   ∧
more sodium than most people think.

Parenthetical expressions

Expressions that provide only supplemental information and interrupt the flow of a sentence should be set off with commas.

▶ Evolution, as far as we know, doesn't work this way.

Absolute phrases

An absolute phrase usually consists of a noun followed by a participle or participial phrase. (See 42d.)

```
┌──────────── ABSOLUTE PHRASE ────────────┐
│   N   PARTICIPLE                          │
```
The sun appearing for the first time in a week, we were at last able to begin the archaeological dig.

▶ Mariah Carey made music industry history in 2020, having become the first artist with a number one song in four different decades.

Word groups expressing contrast

Sharp contrasts beginning with words such as *not, never,* and *unlike* are set off with commas.

▶ Unlike Robert, Celia loved dance contests.

30g Use commas to set off nouns of direct address, the words *yes* and *no*, interrogative tags, and mild interjections.

▶ Forgive me, Angela, for forgetting your birthday.

▶ The film was faithful to the book, wasn't it?

30h Use commas with expressions such as *he said* to set off direct quotations.

▶ In his "Letter from Birmingham Jail," Martin Luther King Jr.

wrote, "We know through painful experience that freedom is never
  ^
voluntarily given by the oppressor; it must be demanded by the

oppressed" (225).

See section 34 on the use of quotation marks and 48c on quoting literary sources.

30i Use commas with dates, addresses, titles, and numbers.

Dates

In dates, set off the year from the rest of the sentence with a pair of commas.

▶ On December 12, 1890, orders were sent out for the arrest of
            ^   ^
Sitting Bull.

EXCEPTIONS: Commas are not needed if the date is inverted or if only the month and year are given: *15 April 2009*; *January 2022*.

Addresses

The elements of an address or a place name are separated with commas. A zip code, however, is not preceded by a comma.

▶ Please send the package to Greg Tarvin at 708 Spring Street,
                                                              ^
Washington, IL 61571.
        ^

Titles

If a title follows a name, set off the title with a pair of commas.

▶ **Ann Hall, MD, has been appointed to the board of trustees.**
∧   ∧

Numbers

In numbers more than four digits long, use commas to separate the numbers into groups of three, starting from the right. In numbers four digits long, a comma is optional.

3,500 [*or* 3500]   100,000   5,000,000

EXERCISE 30–2   This exercise covers the major uses of the comma described in 30a–30e. Add or delete commas where necessary. If a sentence is correct, write "correct" after it. Answers appear in the back of the book.

Even though our brains actually can't focus on two tasks at a time,
∧

many people believe they can multitask.

a. Cricket which originated in England is also popular in Australia, South Africa and India.
b. At the sound of the starting pistol the horses surged forward toward the first obstacle, a sharp incline three feet high.
c. After seeing an exhibition of Western art Gerhard Richter escaped from East Berlin, and smuggled out many of his notebooks.
d. Corrie's new wet suit has an intricate, blue pattern.
e. We replaced the rickety, old, spiral staircase with a sturdy, new ladder.

31 Unnecessary commas

31a Do not use a comma with a coordinating conjunction that joins only two words, phrases, or subordinate clauses.

▶ Ron discovered a leak/ and came back to fix it.

The coordinating conjunction *and* links two verbs in a compound predicate: *discovered* and *came*.

▶ We knew that she had won/ but that the election was close.

The coordinating conjunction *but* links two subordinate clauses, each beginning with *that*.

31b Do not use a comma to separate a verb from its subject or object.

Commas may appear between these major sentence elements only when a specific rule calls for them.

▶ Milk alternatives made from oats or nuts/ have become more

popular over the last decade.

The comma should not separate the subject, *Milk alternatives*, from the verb, *have become*.

31c Do not use a comma before the first or after the last item in a series.

▶ Other causes of asthmatic attacks are/ stress, change in temperature, and cold air.

▶ Even novels that focus on horror, evil, and alienation/ often have themes of spiritual renewal and redemption as well.

31d Do not use a comma between cumulative adjectives, between an adjective and a noun, or between an adverb and an adjective.

▶ In the corner of the closet, we found an old/ maroon hatbox.

▶ It was a senseless, dangerous/ mission.

▶ Deer are often responsible for severely/ damaged crops.

31e Do not use a comma to set off a concluding adverb clause that is essential for meaning.

When adverb clauses introduce a sentence, they are nearly always followed by a comma (see 30b). When they conclude a sentence, however, they are not set off by a comma if their content is essential to the meaning of the earlier part of the sentence. Adverb clauses beginning with *after, as soon as, because, before, if, since, unless, until,* and *when* are usually essential.

▶ Don't try to visit the botanical garden/ unless you have booked a tour in advance.

Without the *unless* clause, the meaning of the sentence might at first seem broader than the writer intended.

When a concluding adverb clause is nonessential, it should be preceded by a comma. Clauses beginning with *although, even though, though,* and *whereas* are usually nonessential.

▶ The lecture seemed to last only a short time, although the clock said
^
it had gone on for more than an hour.

31f Do not use a comma after a phrase that begins an inverted sentence.

Though a comma belongs after most introductory phrases (see 30b), it does not belong after phrases that begin an inverted sentence. In an inverted sentence, the subject follows the verb, and a phrase that ordinarily would follow the verb is moved to the beginning.

▶ At the bottom of the hill / sat the stubborn mule.

31g Avoid other common misuses of the comma.

Do not use a comma in the following situations.

AFTER A COORDINATING CONJUNCTION (*AND, BUT, OR, NOR, FOR, SO, YET*)

▶ Medical schools are beginning to change, but / traditional

dermatology programs have often ignored Black and brown skin.

AFTER *SUCH AS* OR *LIKE*

▶ Shade-loving plants such as / begonias, impatiens, and coleus can

add color to a shady garden.

AFTER *ALTHOUGH*

▶ Although/ the air was balmy, the water was cold.

BEFORE A PARENTHESIS

▶ Jaz knew that her ACT score was low/ (only 22), but she felt

confident about her application essay.

TO SET OFF AN INDIRECT (REPORTED) QUOTATION

▶ Samuel Goldwyn once said/ that a verbal contract isn't worth the

paper it's written on.

WITH A QUESTION MARK OR AN EXCLAMATION POINT

▶ "Why don't you try it?/ " she coaxed. "You can't do any worse than

the rest of us."

EXERCISE 31-1 Delete any unnecessary commas in the following
sentences. If a sentence is correct, write "correct" after it. Answers appear in
the back of the book.

In his Silk Road Project, Yo-Yo Ma incorporates work by musicians such

as/ Kayhan Kalhor and Richard Danielpour.

a. After the morning rains cease, the swimmers emerge from their
   cottages.
b. Tricia's first artwork was a bright, blue, clay dolphin.
c. Some modern musicians, (trumpeter Jon Hassell is an example) blend
   several cultural traditions into a unique sound.
d. Myra liked hot, spicy foods such as, chili, kung pao chicken, and
   buffalo wings.
e. On the display screen, was a soothing pattern of light and
   shadow.

32 The semicolon and the colon

The semicolon is used to connect major sentence elements of equal grammatical rank. The colon is used primarily to call attention to the words that follow it.

32a Use a semicolon between closely related independent clauses not joined with a coordinating conjunction.

When two independent clauses appear in one sentence, they are usually linked with a comma and a coordinating conjunction (*and, but, or, nor, for, so, yet*). If the clauses are closely related and the relation is clear without a conjunction, they may be linked with a semicolon instead.

> In film, a low-angle shot makes the subject look powerful; a high-angle shot does just the opposite.

A semicolon must be used whenever a coordinating conjunction has been omitted between independent clauses. To use merely a comma creates a type of run-on sentence known as a *comma splice*. (See section 21.)

▶ In 1800, a traveler needed six weeks to get from New York to Chicago﹐ in 1860, the trip by train took only two days.
　　　　　　　　　　　　　 ^

32b Use a semicolon between independent clauses linked with a transitional expression.

Transitional expressions include conjunctive adverbs and transitional phrases. A list of transitional phrases begins on the next page.

CONJUNCTIVE ADVERBS

accordingly	furthermore	moreover	still
also	hence	nevertheless	subsequently
anyway	however	next	then
besides	incidentally	nonetheless	therefore
certainly	indeed	now	thus
consequently	instead	otherwise	
conversely	likewise	similarly	
finally	meanwhile	specifically	

TRANSITIONAL PHRASES

after all	even so	in fact
as a matter of fact	for example	in other words
as a result	for instance	in the first place
at any rate	in addition	on the contrary
at the same time	in conclusion	on the other hand

When a transitional expression appears between independent clauses, it is preceded by a semicolon and usually followed by a comma.

▶ **Many corals grow very gradually/; in fact, the creation of a coral**
       ^
reef can take centuries.

When a transitional expression appears in the middle or at the end of the second independent clause, the semicolon goes between the clauses.

▶ **Biologists have observed laughter in primates other than humans/;**
       ^
chimpanzees, however, sound more like they are panting than

laughing.

Transitional expressions should not be confused with the coordinating conjunctions *and, but, or, nor, for, so,* and *yet,* which are preceded by a comma when they link independent clauses. (See 30a.)

32c Use a semicolon between items in a series containing internal punctuation.

▶ Researchers point to key benefits of positive thinking: It leads

to high self-esteem, especially in people who focus on their

achievements; it helps make social interactions, such as those with
                 ^

co-workers, more enjoyable; and, most important, it results in
                    ^

better sleep and overall health.

Without the semicolons, the reader would have to sort out the major groupings, distinguishing between important and less important pauses according to the logic of the sentence. By inserting semicolons at the major breaks, the writer does this work for the reader.

32d Avoid common misuses of the semicolon.

Do not use a semicolon in the following situations.

BETWEEN A SUBORDINATE CLAUSE AND THE REST OF THE SENTENCE

▶ Although children's literature was added to the National Book Awards

in 1969; it has had its own award, the Newbery Medal, since 1922.
      ^

BETWEEN AN APPOSITIVE AND THE WORD IT REFERS TO

▶ The scientists were fascinated by the species *Argyroneta aquatica*;
                                         ^

a spider that lives underwater.

TO INTRODUCE A LIST

▶ Some of my favorite musicians have performed at the Newport Folk

Festival; : Kacey Musgraves, Dolly Parton, and Hozier.
        ^

**BETWEEN INDEPENDENT CLAUSES JOINED BY *AND, BUT, OR, NOR, FOR,
SO,* OR *YET***

▶ Five of the applicants had worked with spreadsheets⸮, but only one
    ^
was familiar with database management.

EXCEPTION: If one or both of the independent clauses contain a comma,
you may use a semicolon with a coordinating conjunction between the
clauses.

32e Use a colon after an independent clause to direct attention to a list, an appositive, a quotation, or a summary or an explanation.

A LIST

The daily routine should include at least the following: ten minutes of
stretching, forty abdominal crunches, and a twenty-minute run.

AN APPOSITIVE

My roommate seems to live on two things: sushi and social media.

A QUOTATION

Consider the words of John Lewis: "Never, ever be afraid to make some
noise and get in good trouble, necessary trouble."

A SUMMARY OR AN EXPLANATION

Faith is like love: It cannot be forced.

TIP: For other ways of introducing quotations, see "Introducing quoted
material" in 34d. When an independent clause follows a colon, MLA recommends using a lowercase letter (see 51a), whereas APA says to begin
with a capital letter (see 53a).

32f Use a colon according to convention.

SALUTATION IN A LETTER Dear Editor:

HOURS AND MINUTES 5:30 p.m.

PROPORTIONS The ratio of students to teachers was 25:1.

TITLE AND SUBTITLE *The Glory of Hera: Greek Mythology and the Greek Family*

CHAPTER AND VERSE IN SACRED TEXT Luke 2:14, Qur'an 67:3

32g Avoid common misuses of the colon.

A colon must be preceded by a full independent clause. Therefore, avoid using it in the following situations.

BETWEEN A VERB AND ITS OBJECT OR COMPLEMENT

▶ Some important vitamins found in vegetables are⫽ vitamin A, thiamine, niacin, and vitamin C.

BETWEEN A PREPOSITION AND ITS OBJECT

▶ The heart's two pumps each consist of⫽ an upper chamber, or atrium, and a lower chamber, or ventricle.

AFTER *SUCH AS, INCLUDING,* OR *FOR EXAMPLE*

▶ The NCAA regulates college athletic sports, including⫽ basketball, baseball, softball, and football.

EXERCISE 32-1 Edit the following sentences to correct errors in the use of the comma, the semicolon, and the colon. If a sentence is correct, write "correct" after it. Answers appear in the back of the book.

Lifting the cover gently, Luca found the source of the odd sound/: a

marble in the gears.

a. We always looked forward to Thanksgiving in Vermont: It was our only chance to see our Grady cousins.

b. If we have come to fight, we are far too few, if we have come to die, we are far too many.

c. Each of the gift baskets included: a greeting card, a coffee mug, and homemade cookies.

d. The news article portrays the land use proposal as reckless; although 62 percent of the town's residents support it.

e. Activist and politician Stacey Abrams tells readers of her book *Lead from the Outside* to ask themselves a powerful question, "How do I banish doubts and get out of my own way?" (xxviii).

33 The apostrophe

33a Use an apostrophe to indicate that a noun is possessive.

Possessive nouns usually indicate ownership, as in *Tim's hat* or *the lawyer's desk*. Frequently, however, ownership is only loosely implied: *the tree's roots, a day's work*. If you are not sure whether a noun is possessive, try turning it into an *of* phrase: *the roots of the tree, the work of a day*. (Pronouns also have possessive forms. See 33b and 33e.)

When to add -'s

1. If the noun does not end in -s, add -'s.

   Luck often propels a rock musician's career.

   The Children's Defense Fund is a nonprofit organization that supports programs for children from low-income families.

2. If the noun is singular and ends in -s or an s sound, add -'s to indicate possession.

   Lois's sister spent last year in India.

   Her article presents an overview of Marx's teachings.

NOTE: To avoid potentially awkward pronunciation, some writers use only the apostrophe with a singular noun ending in -s: *Sophocles'*.

When to add only an apostrophe

If the noun is plural and ends in -s, add only an apostrophe.

   Both diplomats' briefcases were searched by guards.

Joint possession

To show joint possession, use -'s or (-s') with the last noun only; to show individual possession, make all nouns possessive.

   Have you seen Joyce and Greg's new camper?

   Hernando's and Maria's expectations of marriage were quite different.

Joyce and Greg jointly own a camper. Hernando and Maria individually have different expectations.

Compound nouns

If a noun is compound, use -'s (or -s') with the last element.

   My father-in-law's memoir about his childhood in Sri Lanka was published in October.

33b Use an apostrophe and -s to indicate that an indefinite pronoun is possessive.

Indefinite pronouns refer to no specific person or thing: *everyone, someone, no one, something.* (See 40b.)

> Someone's raincoat has been left behind.

33c Use an apostrophe to mark omissions in contractions and numbers.

In a contraction, the apostrophe takes the place of one or more missing letters. *It's* stands for *it is, can't* for *cannot.*

> It's a shame that Frank can't go on the tour.

The apostrophe is also used to mark the omission of the first two digits of a year (*the class of '22*) or years (*the '80s generation*).

33d Do not use an apostrophe in certain situations.

Plural of numbers and abbreviations

Do not use an apostrophe in the plural of any numbers or abbreviations.

> Oksana skated nearly perfect figure 8s.

> The 1920s are known as the Jazz Age.

> Marco earned two PhDs before his 40th birthday.

Plural of letters and words mentioned as words

Usually, letters and words mentioned as words are italicized. In such situations, do not use an apostrophe to form the plural, and set the *-s* ending in roman (regular) type.

> Two large *P*s were painted on the door.

> We've heard enough *maybe*s.

To avoid misreading, you may use an apostrophe to form the plural of some letters: two *A*'s in biology.

Letters and words mentioned as words may also appear in quotation marks. When you choose this option, use the apostrophe.

Two large "P's" were painted on the door.

We've heard enough "maybe's."

33e Avoid common misuses of the apostrophe.

Do not use an apostrophe with nouns that are not possessive or with the possessive pronouns *its, whose, his, hers, ours, yours,* and *theirs.*

▶ Some ~~outpatient's~~ have special parking permits.
    outpatients

▶ Each area has ~~it's~~ own conference room.
    its

It's means "it is." The possessive pronoun *its* contains no apostrophe despite the fact that it is possessive.

▶ We attended a reading by Richard Blanco, ~~who's~~ poetry focuses on
    whose

the experiences of Cuban immigrants.

Who's means "who is." The possessive pronoun is *whose.*

EXERCISE 33–1   Edit the following sentences to correct errors in the use of the apostrophe. If a sentence is correct, write "correct" after it. Answers appear in the back of the book.

Our favorite barbecue restaurant is Poor ~~Richards~~ Ribs.
    Richard's

a. This diet will improve almost anyone's health.

b. The innovative shoe fastener was inspired by the designers young son.

c. Each days menu features a different European country's dish.

d. Lottie worked overtime to increase her families earnings.

e. Ms. Jacobs is unwilling to listen to students complaints about computer failures.

34 Quotation marks

34a Use quotation marks to enclose direct quotations.

Direct quotations of a person's words, whether spoken or written, must be in quotation marks.

> "Twitter," according to social media researcher Jameson Brown, "is the best social network for brand to customer engagement."

Exception: Indirect quotations

Do not use quotation marks around indirect quotations, which report someone's ideas without using that person's exact words. In academic writing, indirect quotation is called *paraphrase* or *summary*. (See 48d.)

> Social media researcher Jameson Brown claims that Twitter is the best social media tool for companies that want to reach their consumers.

Exception: Long quotations

Long quotations of prose or poetry are generally set off from the text by indenting. Quotation marks are not used because the indented format tells readers that the quotation is taken word for word from the source.

> After making an exhaustive study of the historical record, James Horan evaluates Billy the Kid like this:
>> The portrait that emerges of [the Kid] from the thousands of pages of affidavits, reports, trial transcripts, his letters, and his testimony is neither the mythical Robin Hood nor the stereotyped adenoidal moron and pathological killer. Rather Billy appears as a disturbed, lonely young man, honest, loyal to his friends, dedicated to his beliefs, and betrayed by our institutions and the corrupt, ambitious, and compromising politicians in his time. (158)

NOTE: The number in parentheses is a citation in MLA style. MLA and APA have specific guidelines for what constitutes a long quotation and how it should be indented (see 51a and 53a).

34b Use single quotation marks to enclose a quotation within a quotation.

> Megan Marshall notes that Elizabeth Peabody's school focused on "not merely 'teaching' but 'educating children morally and spiritually as well as intellectually from the first' " (107).

34c Use quotation marks around the titles of short works.

Short works include articles, poems, short stories, songs, television and radio episodes, and chapters or subdivisions of long works.

> In James Baldwin's story "Sonny's Blues," two brothers come to understand each other's suffering.

NOTE: Titles of long works such as books, films, and magazines are put in italics. (See 37g.)

34d Use punctuation with quotation marks according to convention.

This section describes the conventions American publishers follow in placing various marks of punctuation inside or outside quotation marks. It also explains how to punctuate when introducing quoted material. (For the use of quotation marks in MLA and APA styles, see 48c and 49b. The examples in this section show MLA style.)

Periods and commas

Place periods and commas inside quotation marks.

> "I'm here as part of my service-learning project," I told the classroom teacher. "I'm hoping to become a reading specialist."

This rule applies to single quotation marks as well as double quotation marks. (See 34b.) It also applies to all uses of quotation marks: for quoted material, for titles of works, and for words used as words.

NOTE: In MLA- and APA-style parenthetical in-text citations, the period follows the citation in parentheses.

> James M. McPherson comments, approvingly, that the Whigs "were not averse to extending the blessings of American liberty, even to Mexicans and Indians" (48).

Colons and semicolons

Put colons and semicolons outside quotation marks.

> Taj wrote, "I regret that I am unable to attend the fundraiser for cancer research"; his letter, however, came with a contribution.

Question marks and exclamation points

Put question marks and exclamation points inside quotation marks unless they apply to the whole sentence.

> Dr. Abram's first question on the first day of class was "What three goals do you have for the course?"

> Have you heard the old proverb "Do not climb the hill until you reach it"?

In the first sentence, the question mark applies only to the quoted question. In the second sentence, the question mark applies to the whole sentence.

NOTE: For a quotation that ends with a question mark or an exclamation point, the parenthetical citation and a period should follow the entire quotation.

> Rosie Thomas asks, "Is nothing in life ever straight and clear, the way children see it?" (77).

Introducing quoted material

After a word group introducing a quotation, choose a colon, a comma, or no punctuation at all, whichever is appropriate in context.

Formal introduction If a quotation is formally introduced, a colon is appropriate. A formal introduction is a full independent clause, not just an expression such as *he said*.

> Thomas Friedman provides a challenging yet optimistic view of the future: "We need to get back to work on our country and on our planet. The hour is late, the stakes couldn't be higher, the project couldn't be harder, the payoff couldn't be greater" (25).

Signal phrase such as *she writes* If a quotation is introduced with an expression such as *he explains* or *she argues*—or if it is followed by such an expression—a comma is needed. (For the use of signal phrases in MLA and APA, see 49c.)

> Mark Twain once declared, "In the spring I have counted one hundred and thirty-six different kinds of weather within four and twenty hours" (55).

Blended quotation When a quotation is blended into the writer's own sentence, either a comma or no punctuation is appropriate, depending on how the quotation fits into the sentence structure.

> The future champion could, as he put it, "float like a butterfly and sting like a bee."

> Virginia Woolf wrote in 1928 that "a woman must have money and a room of her own if she is to write fiction" (4).

Beginning of sentence If a quotation appears at the beginning of a sentence, use a comma after it unless the quotation ends with a question mark or an exclamation point.

> "I've always thought of myself as a reporter," American poet Gwendolyn Brooks has stated (162).

> "What is it?" she asked, bracing herself.

Interrupted quotation If a quoted sentence is interrupted by explanatory words, use commas to set off the explanatory words. If two successive quoted sentences from the same source are interrupted by explanatory words, use a comma before the explanatory words and a period after them.

> "With regard to air travel," Stephen Ambrose notes, "Jefferson was a full century ahead of the curve" (53).

> "Everyone agrees journalists must tell the truth," Bill Kovach and Tom Rosenstiel write. "Yet people are befuddled about what 'the truth' means" (37).

34e Avoid common misuses of quotation marks.

Do not use quotation marks to draw attention to familiar slang, to disown trite expressions, or to justify an attempt at humor.

▶ The economist estimated that 5 percent was only a ⫽ballpark figure.⫽

EXERCISE 34–1 Add or delete quotation marks as needed and make any other necessary changes in punctuation in the following sentences. If a sentence is correct, write "correct" after it. Answers appear in the back of the book.

> Congresswoman Shirley Chisholm famously said, "If they don't give you a seat at the table, bring a folding chair."

a. As for the advertisement "Sailors have more fun", if you consider chipping paint and swabbing decks fun, then you will have plenty of it.

b. Even after forty minutes of discussion, our class could not agree on an interpretation of Robert Frost's poem "The Road Not Taken."

c. After winning the lottery, Juanita said that "she would give half the money to charity."

d. After the film, Vicki said, "The reviewer called this movie "trash of the first order." I guess you can't believe everything you read."

e. "Cleaning your house while your kids are still growing," said Phyllis Diller, "is like shoveling the walk before it stops snowing."

35 End punctuation

35a The period

Use a period to end all sentences except direct questions or genuine exclamations. Also use periods in abbreviations according to convention.

To end most sentences

▶ The professor asked whether talk therapy was more beneficial than

antidepressants~~?~~.
             ^

In some abbreviations

Mr.	i.e.	a.m. (or AM)
Ms.	e.g.	p.m. (or PM)
Dr.	etc.	

NOTE: If a sentence ends with a period marking an abbreviation, do not add a second period.

Periods are not used with most other abbreviations.

CA	NATO	UCLA	BS	BC
NY	IRS	NIH	PhD	BCE

35b The question mark

Use a question mark after a direct question.

What is the horsepower of a 777 engine?

35c The exclamation point

Use an exclamation point after a word group or sentence to express exceptional feeling or to provide special emphasis.

> When Gloria entered the room, we all yelled, "Surprise!"

Do not overuse the exclamation point.

▶ **In the fisherman's memory, the fish lives on, increasing in length**

   and weight with each passing year, until at last it is big enough to

   shade a fishing boat̶.
                          ^
This sentence is emphatic enough without an exclamation point.

36 Other punctuation marks

36a The dash

To use a dash while typing, insert what is called an em-dash using your word processor's tools or type two hyphens (--). (Most word processing and messaging programs will convert the two hyphens to a dash.) Do not put a space before or after the dash.

Use a dash to introduce a list, to signal a restatement or an amplification, or to indicate a shift in tone or thought.

> Peter decided to focus on his priorities—applying to graduate school and getting financial aid.

> Kiere took a few steps back, came running full speed, kicked a mighty kick—and missed the ball.

In the first example, the writer could instead have used a colon. The colon is more formal than the dash and not quite as emphatic.

Use a pair of dashes to set off parenthetical material that deserves special emphasis or to set off an appositive that contains commas.

> Everything in the classroom—from the pencils on the desks to the books on the shelves—was in perfect order.

> In my hometown, people's basic needs—food, clothing, and shelter—are less costly than in a big city like Los Angeles.

36b Parentheses

Use parentheses to enclose supplemental material, minor digressions, and afterthoughts.

> Nurses record patients' vital signs (temperature, pulse, and blood pressure) several times a day.

Use parentheses to enclose letters or numbers labeling items in a series.

> Regulations stipulated that only the following equipment could be used on the survival mission: (1) a knife, (2) thirty feet of parachute line, (3) a book of matches, (4) two ponchos, (5) an E tool, and (6) a signal flare.

Do not overuse parentheses.

> ► Researchers have said that seventeen million (estimates run as high as twenty-three million) Americans have diabetes.

36c Brackets

Use brackets to enclose any words or phrases that you have inserted into an otherwise word-for-word quotation.

> *Audubon* reports that "if there are not enough young to balance deaths, the end of the species [California condor] is inevitable" (4).

The sentence quoted from the *Audubon* article did not contain the words *California condor* (since the context of the full article made clear what species was meant), so the writer needed to add the name in brackets.

The Latin word "sic" in brackets indicates that an error in a quoted sentence appears in the original source.

> According to the review, Lizzo's performance was brilliant, "exceding [sic] the expectations of even her most loyal fans."

Instead of using "sic," the writer could have paraphrased the preceding quotation: *According to the review, even Lizzo's most loyal fans were surprised by the brilliance of her performance.*

NOTE: For advice on using "sic" in MLA and APA styles, see 49b.

36d The ellipsis

The ellipsis consists of three spaced periods. Use an ellipsis to indicate that you have deleted words from an otherwise word-for-word quotation.

> Shute acknowledges that treatment for autism can be expensive: "Sensory integration therapy . . . can cost up to $200 an hour" (82).

If you delete a full sentence or more in the middle of a quoted passage, use a period before the ellipsis.

> "If we don't properly train, teach, or treat our growing prison population," says Luis Rodríguez, "somebody else will. . . . This may well be the safety issue of the new century" (16).

NOTE: Do not use the ellipsis at the beginning or at the end of a quotation. Readers will understand that the quoted material is taken from a longer passage. (If you have cut some words from the end of the final quoted sentence, however, MLA requires an ellipsis.)

36e The slash

Use a slash to separate two or three lines of poetry that have been run into your text. Add a space both before and after the slash.

> In the opening lines of "Jordan," George Herbert pokes gentle fun at popular poems of his time: "Who says that fictions only and false hair / Become a verse? Is there in truth no beauty?" (1–2).

Four or more lines of poetry should be handled as an indented quotation.

The slash may occasionally be used to separate paired terms such as *pass/fail* and *producer/director*. Be sparing in this use of the slash. In particular, avoid the use of *he/she* and *his/her*. Opt for more graceful and inclusive alternatives. (See 17e.)

EXERCISE 36–1   Edit the following sentences to correct errors in punctuation, focusing especially on appropriate use of the dash, parentheses, brackets, the ellipsis, and the slash. If a sentence is correct, write "correct" after it. Answers appear in the back of the book.

> Social insects/—bees, for example/—are able to communicate
>   ^   ^
> complicated messages to one another.

a. A client left his/her cell phone in our conference room after the meeting.

b. The films we made of Kilauea—on our research trip to Hawaii Volcanoes National Park—illustrate a typical spatter cone eruption.

c. Although he was confident in his course selections, Greg chose the pass/fail option for Chemistry 101.

d. Of three engineering fields, chemical, mechanical, and materials, Keegan chose materials engineering for its application to toy manufacturing.

e. The writer Chitra Divakaruni explained her work with other Indian American immigrants: "Many women who came to Maitri [a women's support group in San Francisco] needed to know simple things like opening a bank account or getting citizenship. . . . Many women in Maitri spoke English, but their English was functional rather than emotional. They needed someone who understands their problems and speaks their language."

PART 7

Mechanics

37 Abbreviations, numbers, and italics

37a Use standard abbreviations for titles immediately before and after proper names.

TITLES BEFORE PROPER NAMES	TITLES AFTER PROPER NAMES
Mr. Rafael Zabala	William Albert Sr.
Ms. Nancy Linehan	Thomas Hines Jr.
Dr. Shanice Wallace	Juan López, MD
Rev. John Stone	Margaret Chin, LLD

Do not abbreviate a title if it is not used with a proper name: *My history professor* (not *prof.*) *is an expert on race relations in South Africa.*

Avoid redundant titles such as *Dr. Amy Day, MD.* Choose one title or the other: *Dr. Amy Day* or *Amy Day, MD.*

37b Use abbreviations only when you are sure your readers will understand them.

Familiar abbreviations for the names of organizations, companies, countries, academic degrees, and common terms, written without periods, are generally acceptable.

NBA	CEO	DVD
FBI	NAACP	ESL

My mother went back to school and earned a BA in communications at age fifty.

When using an unfamiliar abbreviation (such as *NASW* for National Association of Social Workers) or a potentially ambiguous abbreviation (such as *AMA*, which can refer to either the American Medical Association or the American Management Association), write the full name followed by the abbreviation in parentheses at the first mention. Then use just the abbreviation throughout the rest of the paper.

37c Units of measurement

Generally, use abbreviations for units when they appear with numerals; spell out the units when they are used alone or when they are used with spelled-out numbers (see also 37f).

METRIC UNITS	US STANDARD UNITS
m, cm, mm	yd, ft, in.
km, kph	mi, mph
kg, g, mg	lb, oz

Results were measured in pounds.

Runners in the 5-km race had to contend with pouring rain.

Use no periods after abbreviations for units of measurement, except the abbreviation for "inch" (*in.*), to distinguish it from the preposition *in*.

37d Plural of abbreviations

To form the plural of most abbreviations, add -*s*, without an apostrophe: *MBAs*. Do not add -*s* to indicate the plural of units of measurement: *mm* (not *mms*), *lb* (not *lbs*), *in.* (not *ins.*).

37e Follow the conventions in your discipline for spelling out or using numerals to express numbers.

Academic styles vary in how they handle numbers in the text of a paper. MLA style uses numerals for numbers that cannot be written in a word or two (*353, 1,020*), or in number-heavy contexts such as lists of data. Spell out numbers that can be written in one or two words: *eleven, thirty-five, fifteen million.*

APA style uses numerals for all but the numbers one through nine. Spell out numbers from one to nine even when they are used with related numerals in a passage.

If a sentence begins with a number, spell out the number or rewrite the sentence.

> One hundred fifty
> ~~150~~ children in our program need expensive dental treatment.
>   ^

Rewriting the sentence may be less awkward if the number is long: *In our program, 150 children need expensive dental treatment.*

37f Use numerals according to convention in dates, addresses, and so on.

DATES July 4, 1776; 56 BC; CE 30

ADDRESSES 77 Latches Lane, 519 West 42nd Street

PERCENTAGES 55 percent (or 55%)

FRACTIONS, DECIMALS 7/8, 0.047

SCORES 7 to 3, 21–18

STATISTICS average age 37, average weight 180

SURVEYS 4 out of 5

EXACT AMOUNTS OF MONEY $105.37, $106,000

DIVISIONS OF BOOKS volume 3, chapter 4, page 189

DIVISIONS OF PLAYS act 3, scene 3 (or act III, scene iii)

TIME OF DAY 4:00 p.m., 1:30 a.m.

37g Italicize the titles of works according to convention.

Titles of the following types of works should be italicized.

BOOKS *The Color Purple*, *The Round House*

MAGAZINES *Time*, *Scientific American*, *Slate*

NEWSPAPERS the *Baltimore Sun,* the *Orlando Sentinel*

LONG POEMS *The Waste Land, Paradise Lost*

PLAYS *The Humans, Hamilton*

FILMS *Casablanca, Moonlight*

TELEVISION PROGRAMS *Squid Game, Frontline*

RADIO PROGRAMS *All Things Considered*

PODCAST SERIES *Embedded*

MUSICAL COMPOSITIONS *Porgy and Bess*

WORKS OF VISUAL ART *American Gothic*

DATABASES OR WEBSITES [MLA] *JSTOR, Salon*

SOFTWARE OR APPS [MLA] *Photoshop, Instagram*

The titles of other works — including short stories, essays, episodes of a podcast or radio or TV program, songs, and short poems — are enclosed in quotation marks. (See 34c.)

NOTE: Do not use italics when referring to the Bible, titles of books in the Bible (Genesis, not *Genesis*), or titles of legal documents (the Constitution, not the *Constitution*).

37h Italicize non-English words used in an English sentence.

My French teacher's *joie de vivre* made learning a new language easy and fun.

EXCEPTION: Do not italicize non-English words that have become a standard part of the English language — "laissez-faire" and "per diem," for example.

38 Spelling and the hyphen

A spell checker is a useful tool, but it has limitations. It won't catch words commonly confused (*accept* for *except*) or some typographical (*won* for *own*) or hyphenation errors. You still need to proofread, and you may need to consult a dictionary.

38a Become familiar with the major spelling rules.

i *before* e *except after* c

In general, use *i* before *e* except after *c* and except when sounded like *ay*, as in *neighbor* and *weigh*.

I BEFORE *E*	relieve, believe, sieve, niece, fierce, frieze
E BEFORE *I*	receive, deceive, sleigh, freight, eight
EXCEPTIONS	seize, either, weird, height, foreign, leisure

Suffixes

Final silent -e   Generally, drop a final silent -*e* when adding a suffix that begins with a vowel. Keep the final -*e* if the suffix begins with a consonant.

combine, combination	achieve, achievement
remove, removable	care, careful
EXCEPTIONS	changeable, judgment, argument, truly

Final -y   When adding -*s* or -*d* to words ending in -*y*, ordinarily change -*y* to -*ie* when the -*y* is preceded by a consonant but not when it is preceded by a vowel.

comedy, comedies	monkey, monkeys
dry, dried	play, played

With proper names ending in -*y*, however, do not change the -*y* to -*ie* even if it is preceded by a consonant: *the Bradys* (the Brady family).

Final consonants If a final consonant is preceded by a single vowel *and* the consonant ends a one-syllable word or a stressed syllable, double the consonant when adding a suffix beginning with a vowel.

bet, betting   occur, occurrence
commit, committed

Plurals

-s or -es Add *-s* to form the plural of most nouns; add *-es* to singular nouns ending in *-s*, *-sh*, *-ch*, and *-x*.

table, tables   church, churches
paper, papers   dish, dishes

Ordinarily, add *-s* to nouns ending in *-o* when the *-o* is preceded by a vowel. Add *-es* when it is preceded by a consonant.

radio, radios   hero, heroes
video, videos   tomato, tomatoes

38b Consult the dictionary to determine how to treat a compound word.

The dictionary indicates whether to treat a compound word as hyphenated (*water-repellent*), as one word (*waterproof*), or as two words (*water table*). If the compound word is not in the dictionary, treat it as two words.

38c Hyphenate two or more words used together as an adjective before a noun.

▶ Today's teachers depend on both traditional textbook material and

web-delivered content.
  ^

▶ Richa Gupta is not yet a well-known candidate.
                                  ^

Generally, do not use a hyphen when such compounds follow the noun.

▶ After our television campaign, Richa Gupta will be well/known.

Do not use a hyphen to connect -*ly* adverbs to the words they modify.

▶ A slowly/moving truck tied up traffic.

38d Hyphenate fractions and certain numbers when they are spelled out.

For numbers written as words, use a hyphen in all fractions (*two-thirds*) and in all forms of compound numbers from twenty-one to ninety-nine (*thirty-five, sixty-seventh*).

38e Use a hyphen with the prefixes *all-*, *ex-* (meaning "former"), and *self-* and with the suffix *-elect*.

▶ The private foundation is funneling more money into self-help
   ^
   projects.

▶ The Student Senate bylaws require the president-elect to attend all
   ^
   senate meetings before the transfer of office.

38f Check for correct word breaks when words must be divided at the end of a line.

Only words that already contain a hyphen should be broken at the end of a line of text. If your word processor automatically breaks words at the ends of lines, disable that setting.

Email addresses, URLs, and DOIs need special attention when they break at the end of a line of text or in bibliographic citations. Do not insert a hyphen. Instead, consult the guidelines for URLs and DOIs in MLA style (51a) and APA style (53a). Break an email address after the @ symbol or before a period.

EXERCISE 38–1 Edit the following sentences to correct errors in spelling and hyphenation. If a sentence is correct, write "correct" after it. Answers appear in the back of the book.

Émile Zola's first readers were scandalized by his slice-of-life novels.
                                                ^ ^

a. The Williams sisters were the heros of my entire high school tennis team.

b. The swiftly-moving tugboat pulled alongside the barge and directed it away from the oil spill in the harbor.

c. We managed to get the most desireable seats in the theater.

d. As a livestock veterinarian, she cares for horses, donkies, cows, and other large farm animals.

e. Road-blocks were set up along all the major highways leading out of the city.

39 Capitalization

39a Capitalize proper nouns and words derived from them; do not capitalize common nouns.

Proper nouns are the names of specific persons, places, and things. All other nouns are common nouns. The following types of words are usually capitalized: names of deities, religions, religious followers, sacred books; words of family relationship used as names; particular places; nationalities and their languages, races, tribes; educational institutions, departments, particular courses; government departments, organizations, political parties; historical movements, periods, events, documents; and trade names.

PROPER NOUNS	COMMON NOUNS
God (used as a name)	a god
Uncle Pedro	my uncle
Father (used as a name)	my father
the South	a southern state
the Democratic Party	a political party
the Enlightenment	the eighteenth century
Advil	a painkiller

Months, holidays, and days of the week are capitalized: *May, Labor Day, Monday.* The seasons and numbers of the days of the month are not: *summer, the fifth of June.*

EXCEPTION: Capitalize Fourth of July (or July Fourth) when referring to the holiday.

Names of school subjects are capitalized only if they are names of languages: *English, French.* Names of particular courses are capitalized: *Geology 101, Principles of Economics.*

39b Capitalize titles of persons when used as part of a proper name but usually not when used alone.

District Attorney Marshall was ruled out of order.

The district attorney was elected for a two-year term.

Usage varies when the title of an important public figure is used alone: *The president* [or *President*] *vetoed the bill.*

39c Capitalize titles according to convention.

In both titles and subtitles of works mentioned in the text of a paper, major words such as nouns, pronouns, verbs, adjectives, and adverbs should be capitalized. Minor words such as articles, prepositions, and coordinating conjunctions are not capitalized unless they are the first or last word of a title or subtitle. (In APA style, capitalize all words of four or more letters. See 53a.)

> *Seizing the Enigma: The Race to Break the German U-Boat Codes*
> *A River Runs through It*

Titles of works are handled differently in the APA reference list. See "Preparing the list of references" in 53a.

39d Capitalize the first word of a sentence or quoted sentence.

The first word of a sentence should be capitalized. Also capitalize the first word of a quoted sentence within a sentence, but not a quoted phrase.

> Loveless writes, "If failing schools are ever to be turned around, much more must be learned about how schools age as institutions" (25).

> Steven Pinker has written that one important element of good writing is "attention to the readers' vantage point" (26).

If a quoted sentence is interrupted by explanatory words, do not capitalize the first word after the interruption. (See also 34d.)

> "If you want to go out," he said, "tell me now."

When a sentence appears within parentheses, capitalize the first word unless the parentheses appear within another sentence.

> Early detection of breast cancer increases survival rates. (See table 2.)

> Early detection of breast cancer increases survival rates (see table 2).

39e Know your options when the first word after a colon begins an independent clause.

When a group of words following a colon can stand on its own as a complete sentence, MLA recommends using lowercase for the first word, except in certain situations, such as if the sentence following the colon is a question (see 51a). APA calls for capitalizing it (see 53a).

MLA STYLE

Clinical trials revealed problems: a high percentage of participants reported severe headaches.

APA STYLE

Clinical trials revealed problems: A high percentage of participants reported severe headaches.

Always use lowercase for a list or an appositive that follows a colon (see 32e).

Students were divided into two groups: residents and commuters.

EXERCISE 39-1 Edit the following sentences to correct errors in capitalization. If a sentence is correct, write "correct" after it. Answers appear in the back of the book.

On our trip to the West, we visited the ~~g~~rand ~~c~~anyon and
G *C*

the ~~g~~reat ~~s~~alt ~~d~~esert.
G *S* *D*

a. Assistant dean Shirin Ahmadi recommended offering more world language courses.

b. We went to the Mark Taper Forum to see a production of *Angels in America*.

c. Kalindi has an ambitious semester, studying differential calculus, classical hebrew, brochure design, and greek literature.

d. Lydia's Aunt and Uncle make modular houses as beautiful as modernist works of art.

e. The labs in Ohio began their research in the Spring, and we expect clinical trials to start at our Cleveland lab next summer.

PART 8

Grammar Basics

40 Parts of speech

Traditional grammar recognizes eight parts of speech: noun, pronoun, verb, adjective, adverb, preposition, conjunction, and interjection. Many words can function as more than one part of speech. For example, the word *paint* can be a noun (*The paint is wet*) or a verb (*Please paint the ceiling*).

40a Nouns

A noun is the name of a person, place, thing, or concept.

> N   N   N
> The *bird* in the *sky* flew down into its *nest*.

Nouns sometimes function as adjectives modifying other nouns. Because of their dual role, nouns used in this manner may be called *noun/ adjectives*.

> N/ADJ   N/ADJ
> The *leather* notebook was tucked in the *student's* backpack.

40b Pronouns

A pronoun is a word used in place of a noun. Usually the pronoun substitutes for a specific noun, known as its *antecedent*.

> ANT   PN
> When the *battery* wears down, we recharge *it*.

Although most pronouns function as substitutes for nouns, some can function as adjectives modifying nouns. Such pronouns may be called *pronoun/adjectives*.

> PN/ADJ
> *That* bird was at the same window yesterday morning.

Pronouns are classified in the following ways.

Personal pronouns Personal pronouns refer to specific persons or things. They always function as substitutes for nouns.

Singular: I, me, you, she, her, he, him, it

Plural: we, us, you, they, them

NOTE: The pronouns *they* and *them* can also be used in singular gender-neutral contexts. (See p. 120.)

Possessive pronouns Possessive pronouns indicate ownership.

Singular: my, mine, your, yours, her, hers, his, its

Plural: our, ours, your, yours, their, theirs

Some of these possessive pronouns function as adjectives modifying nouns: *my, your, her, his, its, our, their.*

Intensive and reflexive pronouns Intensive pronouns emphasize a noun or another pronoun (The senator *herself* met us at the door). Reflexive pronouns name a receiver of an action identical with the doer of the action (Paula nominated *herself*).

Singular: myself, yourself, himself, herself, itself

Plural: ourselves, yourselves, themselves

Relative pronouns Relative pronouns introduce subordinate clauses functioning as adjectives (The writer *who won the award* refused to accept it). The relative pronoun (in this case *who*) also points back to a noun or pronoun that the clause modifies (*writer*). (See 42e.)

who, whom, whose, which, that

The pronouns *whichever, whoever, whomever, what,* and *whatever* are sometimes considered relative pronouns, but they introduce noun clauses and do not point back to a noun or pronoun. (See "Noun clauses" in 42e.)

Interrogative pronouns Interrogative pronouns introduce questions (*Who* is expected to win the election?).

who, whom, whose, which, what

Demonstrative pronouns   Demonstrative pronouns identify or point to nouns. Frequently they function as adjectives (*This* chair is my favorite), but they may also function as substitutes for nouns (*This* is my favorite chair).

this, that, these, those

Indefinite pronouns   Indefinite pronouns (*anybody, anyone, somebody, someone,* etc.) refer to nonspecific persons or things. Most are always singular (*everyone, each*); some are always plural (*both, many*); a few may be singular or plural (see 22e). Most indefinite pronouns function as substitutes for nouns (*Something* is burning), but some can also function as adjectives (*All* campers must check in at the lodge). For a list of indefinite pronouns, see 22e.

Reciprocal pronouns   Reciprocal pronouns (*each other, one another*) refer to individual parts of a plural antecedent (By turns, the penguins fed *one another*).

NOTE: See also pronoun-antecedent agreement (23), pronoun reference (24), distinguishing between pronouns such as *I* and *me* (25), and distinguishing between *who* and *whom* (26).

40c Verbs

The verb of a sentence usually expresses action (*jump, think*) or being (*is, become*). It is composed of a main verb possibly preceded by one or more helping verbs.

> MV
> The horses *exercise* every day.

> HV   MV
> The task force report *was* not *completed* on schedule.

> HV HV   MV
> No one *has been defended* with more passion than our mayor.

Notice that words, usually adverbs, can intervene between the helping verb and the main verb (was *not* completed). (See 40e.)

Helping verbs

There are twenty-three helping verbs in English: forms of *have*, *do*, and *be*, which may also function as main verbs, and nine modals, which function only as helping verbs. *Have*, *do*, and *be* change form to indicate tense; the nine modals do not.

FORMS OF *HAVE*, *DO*, AND *BE*

have, has, had

do, does, did

be, am, is, are, was, were, being, been

MODALS

can, could, may, might, must, shall, should, will, would

The verb phrase *ought to* is often classified as a modal as well.

Main verbs

The main verb of a sentence is always the kind of word that would change form if put into these test sentences:

BASE FORM	Usually I (*cook, drive*).
PAST TENSE	Yesterday I (*cooked, drove*).
PAST PARTICIPLE	I have (*cooked, driven*) many times before.
PRESENT PARTICIPLE	I am (*cooking, driving*) right now.
-S FORM	Usually he/she/it (*cooks, drives*).

If a word doesn't change form when slipped into the test sentences, you can be certain that it is not a main verb. For example, the noun *revolution*, though it may seem to suggest action, can never function as a main verb. Try to make it behave like one (*Today I revolution . . . , Yesterday I revolutioned . . .*) and you'll see why.

When both the past-tense and the past-participle forms of a verb end in *-ed*, the verb is regular (*cooked, cooked*). Otherwise, the verb is irregular (*drove, driven*). (See 28a.)

The verb *be* is highly irregular, having eight forms instead of the usual five: the base form *be*; the present-tense forms *am*, *is*, and *are*; the past-tense forms *was* and *were*; the present participle *being*; and the past participle *been*.

NOTE: Some verbs are followed by words that look like prepositions but are so closely associated with the verb that they are a part of its meaning. These words are known as *particles*. Common verb-particle combinations include *bring up*, *call off*, *drop off*, *give in*, *look up*, *run into*, and *take off*.

TIP: For more information about using verbs, see these sections of the handbook: active verbs (8), subject-verb agreement (22), verb forms (28a), verb tense and mood (28f and 28g), and modal verbs (29a).

40d Adjectives

An adjective is a word used to modify, or describe, a noun or pronoun. An adjective usually answers one of these questions: Which one? What kind? How many?

ADJ
the *broken* window [Which window?]

ADJ   ADJ
cracked old plates [What kind of plates?]

ADJ
nine months [How many months?]

Adjectives usually precede the words they modify. They may also follow linking verbs, in which case they describe the subject. (See 41b.)

ADJ
The decision was *unpopular*.

The definite article *the* and the indefinite articles *a* and *an* are also classified as adjectives.

ART   ART   ART
A defendant should be judged on *the* evidence provided to *the* jury.

Some possessive, demonstrative, and indefinite pronouns can function as adjectives: *their, its, this, all* (see 40b). And nouns can function as adjectives when they modify other nouns: *apple pie* (the noun *apple* modifies the noun *pie*; see 40a).

TIP: You can find more details about using adjectives in 27.

40e Adverbs

An adverb is a word used to modify, or qualify, a verb (or verbal), an adjective, or another adverb. It usually answers one of these questions: When? Where? How? Why? Under what conditions? To what degree?

Pull *firmly* on the emergency handle. [Pull how?]

Read the text *first* and *then* complete the exercises. [Read when? Complete when?]

Adverbs modifying adjectives or other adverbs usually intensify or limit the intensity of the word they modify.

ADV
Be *extremely* kind, and you will have many friends.

ADV
We proceeded *very* cautiously in the dark house.

The words *not* and *never* are classified as adverbs.

40f Prepositions

A preposition is a word placed before a noun or pronoun to form a phrase that modifies another word in the sentence. The prepositional phrase nearly always functions as an adjective or an adverb.

P   P   P

The road *to* the summit travels *past* craters *from* an extinct volcano.

To the summit functions as an adjective modifying the noun *road*; *past craters* functions as an adverb modifying the verb *travels*; *from an extinct volcano* functions as an adjective modifying the noun *craters*. (For more on prepositional phrases, see 42a.)

English has a limited number of prepositions. The most common ones are included in the following list.

about	below	from	outside	underneath
above	beside	in	over	unlike
across	besides	inside	past	until
after	between	into	plus	unto
against	beyond	like	round	up
along	but	near	since	upon
among	by	next	than	with
around	despite	of	through	within
as	down	off	throughout	without
at	during	on	to	
before	except	onto	toward	
behind	for	out	under	

Some prepositions are more than one word long: *along with, as well as, in addition to, next to, rather than.*

40g Conjunctions

Conjunctions join words, phrases, or clauses, and they indicate the relation between the elements joined.

Coordinating conjunctions   A coordinating conjunction is used to connect grammatically equal elements. (See 9b and 14a.) The coordinating conjunctions are *and, but, or, nor, for, so,* and *yet.*

> The sociologist interviewed children *but* not their parents.

> Write clearly, *and* your readers will appreciate your efforts.

In the first sentence, *but* connects two noun phrases; in the second, *and* connects two independent clauses.

Correlative conjunctions   Correlative conjunctions come in pairs; they connect grammatically equal elements.

> both . . . and
>
> either . . . or
>
> neither . . . nor
>
> not only . . . but also
>
> whether . . . or

> *Either* the painting was brilliant *or* it was a forgery.

Subordinating conjunctions   A subordinating conjunction introduces a subordinate clause and indicates the relation of the clause to the rest of the sentence. (See 42e.) The most common subordinating conjunctions are *after, although, as, as if, because, before, if, in order that, once, since, so that, than, that, though, unless, until, when, where, whether,* and *while.*

> *When* the fundraiser ends, we expect to have raised a million dollars.

Conjunctive adverbs   Conjunctive adverbs connect independent clauses and indicate the relation between the clauses. They can be used with a semicolon to join two independent clauses in one sentence, or they can be used alone with an independent clause. The most common conjunctive adverbs are *finally, however, nevertheless, similarly, then, therefore,* and *thus.* (For a complete list, see 32b.)

> The photographer failed to take a light reading; *therefore,* all the pictures were underexposed.

> During the day, the kitten sleeps peacefully. *However,* when night falls, the kitten is ready to play.

Conjunctive adverbs can appear at the beginning or in the middle of a clause.

> When night falls, *however,* the kitten is ready to play.

TIP: The ability to distinguish between conjunctive adverbs and coordinating conjunctions will help you avoid run-on sentences and make punctuation decisions (see 21, 30a, and 30f). The ability to recognize subordinating conjunctions will help you avoid sentence fragments (see 20).

40h Interjections

An interjection is a word used to express surprise or emotion (*Oh! Hey! Wow!*).

EXERCISE 40–1 In the following sentences, identify the part of speech of each underlined word or phrase. Answers appear in the back of the book.

Adjective   Adjective   Noun
Poor road conditions cause **most** bicycle **accidents.**

a. **No one** **had seen** a full-length computer-generated film **before** 1995's *Toy Story.*

b. Runners who **sleep** more than eight hours **nightly** will see their **performance** improve.

c. Wolverines are thought to be **in** the wolf family; **however,** **they** are closely related to weasels.

d. We **might** visit the national museum for **women** artists, **but** our weekend is already busy.

e. **This** building **shakes** **when** a train passes by.

41 Sentence patterns

The vast majority of sentences in English conform to one of these five patterns:

subject/verb/subject complement

subject/verb/direct object

subject/verb/indirect object/direct object

subject/verb/direct object/object complement

subject/verb

Adverbial modifiers (single words, phrases, or clauses) may be added to any of these patterns, and they may appear nearly anywhere — at the beginning, in the middle, or at the end of the sentence.

Predicate is the grammatical term given to the verb plus its objects, complements, and adverbial modifiers.

41a Subjects

The subject of a sentence names whom or what the sentence is about. The simple subject is always a noun or pronoun; the complete subject consists of the simple subject and any words or word groups modifying the simple subject.

The complete subject

To find the complete subject, ask Who? or What?, insert the verb, and finish the question. The answer is the complete subject.

r——— COMPLETE SUBJECT ———┐
The devastating effects of famine can last for many years.

Who or what can last for many years? *The devastating effects of famine.*

```
┌─────────── COMPLETE SUBJECT ───────────┐
```
Adventure novels that contain multiple subplots are often made into successful movies.

Who or what are often made into movies? *Adventure novels that contain multiple subplots.*

```
        ┌─ COMPLETE ─┐
        │  SUBJECT   │
```
In our program, student teachers work full-time for ten months.

Who or what works full-time for ten months? *Student teachers.* Notice that *In our program, student teachers* is not a sensible answer to the question. (It is not safe to assume that the subject must always appear first in a sentence.)

The simple subject

To find the simple subject, strip away all modifiers in the complete subject. This includes single-word modifiers such as *the* and *devastating*, phrases such as *of famine*, and subordinate clauses such as *that contain multiple subplots*.

```
        ┌ SS ┐
```
The devastating effects of famine can last for many years.

```
        ┌ SS ┐
```
Adventure novels that contain multiple subplots are often made into successful movies.

A sentence may have a compound subject containing two or more simple subjects joined with a coordinating conjunction such as *and, but,* or *or.*

```
     ┌─── SS ───┐      ┌SS┐
```
Great commitment and a little luck make a successful actor.

Understood subjects

In imperative sentences, which give advice or issue commands, the subject is understood but not actually present in the sentence. The subject of an imperative sentence is understood to be *you.*

[*You*] Put your hands on the steering wheel.

Subject after the verb

Although the subject ordinarily comes before the verb (*The planes took off*), occasionally it does not. When a sentence begins with *There is* or *There are* (or *There was* or *There were*), the subject follows the verb. In such inverted constructions, the word *There* is an expletive, an empty word serving merely to get the sentence started.

> ⌐ SS ¬
> There are *eight planes waiting to take off.*

Occasionally a writer will invert a sentence for effect.

> ⌐SS¬
> Joyful is *the child whose school closes for snow.*

Joyful is an adjective, so it cannot be the subject. Turn this sentence around and its structure becomes obvious.

> ⌐ SS ¬
> *The child whose school closes for snow* is joyful.

In questions, the subject frequently appears between the helping verb and the main verb.

> HV ⌐—— SS ——¬ MV
> Do *Olympic marathoners* train year-round?

TIP: Recognizing the subject of a sentence will help you edit for fragments (20), subject-verb agreement (22), and pronouns such as *I* and *me* (25).

EXERCISE 41–1   In the following sentences, underline the complete subject(s) and write *SS* above the simple subject(s). If the subject is an understood *you,* insert *you* in parentheses. Answers appear in the back of the book.

> ⌐ SS ¬   ⌐ SS ¬
> <u>Parents and their children</u> often look alike.

a. The hills and mountains seemed endless, and the snow atop them glistened.
b. In foil fencing, points are scored by hitting an electronic target.
c. Do not stand in the aisles or sit on the stairs.
d. There were hundreds of fireflies in the open field.
e. The evidence against the defendant was staggering.

41b Verbs, objects, and complements

Section 40c explains how to find a sentence's verb. A verb is classified as linking, transitive, or intransitive, depending on the kinds of objects or complements the verb can (or cannot) take.

Linking verbs and subject complements

Linking verbs connect the subject to a subject complement, a word or word group that completes the meaning of the subject by renaming or describing it.

┌──────────────── S ──────────────┐ ┌ V ┐ ┌ SC ┐
A phone call requesting personal information may be a scam.

┌────── S ──────┐ V SC
Last month's temperatures were mild.

Whenever they appear as main verbs (rather than helping verbs), the forms of *be* — *be, am, is, are, was, were, being, been* — usually function as linking verbs. In the preceding examples, for instance, the main verbs are *be* and *were*.

Verbs such as *appear, become, feel, grow, look, make, seem, smell, sound,* and *taste* are linking when they are followed by a word or word group that renames or describes the subject.

┌── S ──┐┌ V ┐ SC
As it thickens, the sauce will look unappealing.

Transitive verbs and direct objects

A transitive verb takes a direct object, a word or word group that names a receiver of the action.

┌── S ──┐ V ┌──── DO ────┐
The hungry cat clawed the bag of dry food.

The simple direct object is always a noun or pronoun, in this case *bag*. To find it, simply strip away all modifiers.

Transitive verbs usually appear in the active voice, with the subject doing the action and a direct object receiving the action. Active-voice sentences can be transformed into the passive voice, with the subject receiving the action. (See 8a.)

Transitive verbs, indirect objects, and direct objects

The direct object of a transitive verb is sometimes preceded by an indirect object, a noun or pronoun telling to whom or for whom the action of the sentence is done.

```
    S    V    IO   ┌── DO ──┐    S  ┌─ V ─┐ IO ┌ DO ┐
```
You give Amanda some yarn, and she will knit you a scarf.

The simple indirect object is always a noun or pronoun. To test for an indirect object, insert the word *to* or *for* before the word or word group in question. If the sentence makes sense, the word or word group is an indirect object.

You give [to] *Amanda* some yarn, and she will knit [for] *you* a scarf.

Transitive verbs, direct objects, and object complements

The direct object of a transitive verb is sometimes followed by an object complement, a word or word group that renames or describes the object.

```
     S          V      DO    ┌───── OC ─────┐
```
People often consider chivalry a thing of the past.

```
 ┌─ S ─┐   V    DO  ┌───── OC ─────┐
```
The kiln makes clay firm and strong.

When the object complement renames the direct object, it is a noun or pronoun (such as *thing*). When it describes the direct object, it is an adjective (such as *firm* and *strong*).

Intransitive verbs

Intransitive verbs take no objects or complements.

```
      ┌── S ──┐   V
```
The audience laughed.

```
      ┌── S ──┐   V
```
The driver accelerated in the straightaway.

Nothing receives the actions of laughing and accelerating in these sentences, so the verbs are intransitive. Notice that such verbs may or may not be followed by adverbial modifiers. In the second sentence, *in the straightaway* is an adverbial prepositional phrase modifying *accelerated*.

NOTE: The dictionary will tell you whether a verb is transitive or intransitive. Some verbs can be both transitive and intransitive.

TRANSITIVE	Sandra *flew* her small plane over the canyon.
INTRANSITIVE	A flock of migrating geese *flew* overhead.

In the first example, *flew* has a direct object that receives the action: *her small plane*. In the second example, the verb is followed by an adverb (*overhead*), not by a direct object.

---

42 Subordinate word groups

Subordinate word groups include phrases and clauses. Phrases are subordinate because they lack a subject and a verb; they are classified as prepositional, verbal, appositive, and absolute (see 42a–42d). Subordinate clauses have a subject and a verb, but they begin with a word (such as *although*, *that*, or *when*) that marks them as subordinate (see 42e).

42a Prepositional phrases

A prepositional phrase begins with a preposition such as *at, by, for, from, in, of, on, to,* or *with* (see 40f) and usually ends with a noun or noun equivalent: *on the table, for him, by sleeping late.* The noun or noun equivalent is known as the *object of the preposition.*

Prepositional phrases function as adjectives or as adverbs. As an adjective, a prepositional phrase nearly always appears immediately following the noun or pronoun it modifies.

The hut had *walls of mud.*

Adjective phrases usually answer one or both of the questions *Which one?* and *What kind?* If we ask *Which walls?* or *What kind of walls?* we get a sensible answer: *walls of mud.*

Adverbial prepositional phrases usually modify the verb, but they can also modify adjectives or other adverbs. When a prepositional phrase modifies the verb, it can appear nearly anywhere in a sentence.

James *walked* his dog *on a leash.*

Sabrina *in time adjusted* to life in Ecuador.

During a mudslide, the terrain *can change* drastically.

If a prepositional phrase is movable, you can be certain that it is adverbial.

In the cave, the explorers found well-preserved prehistoric drawings.

The explorers found well-preserved prehistoric drawings *in the cave.*

Adverbial word groups usually answer one of these questions: When? Where? How? Why? Under what conditions? To what degree?

> James walked his dog *how? On a leash.*
>
> Sabrina adjusted to life in Ecuador *when? In time.*
>
> The terrain can change drastically *under what conditions? During a mudslide.*

In questions and subordinate clauses, a preposition may appear after its object.

> *What* are you afraid *of?*
>
> We avoided the bike trail *that* Jun had warned us *about.*

42b Verbal phrases

A verbal is a verb form that does not function as the verb of a clause. Verbals include infinitives (the word *to* plus the base form of the verb), present participles (the *-ing* form of the verb), and past participles (the verb form usually ending in *-d, -ed, -n, -en,* or *-t*). (See 28a and 40c.)

INFINITIVE	PRESENT PARTICIPLE	PAST PARTICIPLE
to dream	dreaming	dreamed
to choose	choosing	chosen
to build	building	built

Instead of functioning as the verb of a clause, a verbal functions as an adjective, a noun, or an adverb.

ADJECTIVE	*Broken* promises cannot be fixed.
NOUN	Constant *complaining* becomes wearisome.
ADVERB	Can you wait *to celebrate?*

Verbals with objects, complements, or modifiers form verbal phrases.

> In my family, *singing loudly* is more appreciated than *singing well.*

Like verbals, verbal phrases function as adjectives, nouns, or adverbs. Verbal phrases are ordinarily classified as participial, gerund, and infinitive.

Participial phrases

Participial phrases always function as adjectives. Their verbals are either present participles (such as *dreaming* or *asking*) or past participles (such as *stolen* or *reached*).

Participial phrases frequently appear immediately following the noun or pronoun they modify.

Congress shall make no *law abridging the freedom of speech or of the press*.

Participial phrases are often movable. They may precede the word they modify.

Being a weight-bearing joint, the *knee* is among the most frequently injured.

They may also appear at some distance from the word they modify.

Last night we saw a *play* that affected us deeply, *written with profound insight into the lives of immigrants*.

Gerund phrases

Gerund phrases are built around present participles (verb forms that end in *-ing*), and they always function as nouns: usually as a subject, a subject complement, a direct object, or the object of a preposition.

S

Rationalizing a fear can eliminate it.

SC

The key to good sauce is browning the mushrooms.

```
          ┌──── DO ────┐
Lizards usually enjoy sunning themselves.
```

```
The American Heart Association has documented the benefits of diet
          ┌─────────── OBJ OF PREP ───────────┐
and exercise in reducing the risk of heart attack.
```

Infinitive phrases

Infinitive phrases, usually constructed around *to* plus the base form of the verb (*to call, to drink*), can function as nouns, as adjectives, or as adverbs. When functioning as a noun, an infinitive phrase may appear in almost any noun slot in a sentence, usually as a subject, subject complement, or direct object.

```
┌─────────────── S ───────────────┐
To hike without a navigation device is risky.
```

```
                    ┌─────────── DO ───────────┐
The orchestra wanted to make its premier season memorable.
```

Infinitive phrases functioning as adjectives usually appear immediately following the noun or pronoun they modify.

```
The Nineteenth Amendment gave women the *right to vote*.
```

The infinitive phrase modifies the noun *right*. Which right? *The right to vote*.

Adverbial infinitive phrases usually qualify the meaning of the verb, telling when, where, how, why, under what conditions, or to what degree an action occurred.

```
Volunteers *rolled up* their pants *to wade through the* floodwaters.
```

NOTE: In some constructions, the infinitive is unmarked; that is, the *to* does not appear.

Graphs and charts can help researchers [*to*] *present complex data*.

42c Appositive phrases

Appositive phrases describe nouns or pronouns. Instead of modifying nouns or pronouns, however, appositive phrases rename them. In form they are nouns or noun equivalents.

Podcasts, *the modern equivalent of radio talk shows,* are increasingly easy to record and produce.

42d Absolute phrases

An absolute phrase modifies a whole clause or sentence, not just one word. It consists of a noun or noun equivalent usually followed by a participial phrase.

Her words reverberating in the hushed arena, the senator urged the crowd to support her former opponent.

42e Subordinate clauses

Subordinate clauses are patterned like sentences, having subjects and verbs and sometimes objects or complements. But they function within sentences as adjectives, adverbs, or nouns. They cannot stand alone as complete sentences.

A subordinate clause usually begins with a subordinating conjunction or a relative pronoun. The chart on page 255 classifies these words according to the kinds of clauses (adjective, adverb, or noun) they introduce.

Adjective clauses

Adjective clauses modify nouns or pronouns, usually answering the question Which one? or What kind? Most adjective clauses begin with a relative pronoun (*who, whom, whose, which,* or *that*). In addition to introducing the clause, the relative pronoun points back to the noun that the clause modifies.

The coach chose *players who would benefit from intense drills.*

A *book that goes unread* is a writer's worst nightmare.

Relative pronouns are sometimes understood rather than appearing in the sentence.

The things [*that*] *we cherish most* are the things [*that*] *we might lose.*

Occasionally an adjective clause is introduced by a relative adverb, usually *when, where,* or *why.*

The aging actor returned to the *stage where he had made his debut as Hamlet half a century earlier.*

The parts of an adjective clause are often arranged as in sentences (subject/verb/object or complement).

                                          S   V   DO
Sometimes it is our closest friends who disappoint us.

Frequently, however, the object or complement appears first, out of the normal order of subject/verb/object.

                                    DO   S   V
They can be the very friends whom we disappoint.

TIP: For punctuation of adjective clauses, see 30e.

> ## Words that introduce subordinate clauses
>
> ### Words introducing adjective clauses
>
> **Relative pronouns:** that, which, who, whom, whose
> **Relative adverbs:** when, where, why
>
> ### Words introducing adverb clauses
>
> **Subordinating conjunctions:** after, although, as, as if, because, before, even though, if, in order that, once, since, so that, than, that, though, unless, until, when, where, whether, while
>
> ### Words introducing noun clauses
>
> **Relative pronouns:** which, who, whom, whose
> **Other pronouns:** what, whatever, whichever, whoever, whomever
> **Other subordinating words:** how, if, that, when, whenever, where, wherever, whether, why

Adverb clauses

Adverb clauses modify verbs, adjectives, or other adverbs, usually answering one of these questions: When? Where? Why? How? Under what conditions? To what degree? They always begin with a subordinating conjunction (such as *after, although, because, that, though, unless,* or *when*). (For a complete list, see the chart above.)

When the sun went down, the bats *hunted* for food.

Noun clauses

A noun clause functions just like a single-word noun, usually as a subject, a subject complement, a direct object, or the object of a preposition. It usually begins with one of the following words: *how, if, that, what, whatever, when, whenever, where, wherever, whether, which, whichever, who, whoever, whom, whomever, whose, why.*

$$\overbrace{\text{Whoever leaves the house last}}^{\text{S}} \text{ must double-lock the door.}$$

$$\text{Copernicus argued } \overbrace{\text{that the sun is the center of the universe.}}^{\text{DO}}$$

The subordinating word introducing the clause may or may not play a significant role in the clause. In the preceding examples, *Whoever* is the subject of its clause, but *that* does not perform a function in its clause.

As with adjective clauses, the parts of a noun clause may appear in normal order (subject/verb/object or complement) or out of their normal order.

$$\text{Loyalty } \overset{\text{S}}{} \text{ is } \overset{\text{V}}{} \text{ what } \overset{\text{DO}}{\text{keeps}} \text{ a friendship } \overset{\text{OC}}{\text{strong.}}$$

$$\text{New Mexico is } \overset{\text{DO}}{\text{where}} \overset{\text{S}}{\text{we}} \overset{\text{V}}{\text{live.}}$$

EXERCISE 42–1   Underline the subordinate clauses in the following sentences. Tell whether each clause is an adjective clause, an adverb clause, or a noun clause and how it is used in the sentence. Answers appear in the back of the book.

Show the committee the latest draft <u>before you print the final report</u>.

(Adverb clause modifying "Show")

a. The city's electoral commission adjusted the voting process so that every vote would count.

b. A marketing campaign that targets baby boomers may not appeal to young professionals.

c. After the Tambora volcano erupted in the southern Pacific in 1815, no one realized that it would contribute to the "year without a summer" in Europe and North America.

d. The concept of peak oil implies that at a certain point there will be no more oil to extract from the earth.

e. Details are easily overlooked when you are rushing.

43 Sentence types

Sentences are classified in two ways: according to their structure (simple, compound, complex, or compound-complex) and according to their purpose (declarative, imperative, interrogative, or exclamatory).

43a Sentence structures

Depending on the number and the types of clauses they contain, sentences are classified as simple, compound, complex, or compound-complex.

Clauses come in two varieties: independent and subordinate. An independent clause contains a subject and a predicate, and it either stands alone or could stand alone as a sentence. A subordinate clause also contains a subject and a predicate, but it functions within a sentence as an adjective, an adverb, or a noun; it cannot stand alone. (See 42e.)

Simple sentences

A simple sentence is one independent clause with no subordinate clauses.

INDEPENDENT CLAUSE

Without a passport, Eva could not visit her grandparents in Hungary.

A simple sentence may contain compound elements — a compound subject, verb, or object, for example — but it does not contain more than one full sentence pattern. The following sentence is simple because its two verbs (*comes in* and *goes out*) share a subject (*Spring*).

┌─────────── INDEPENDENT CLAUSE ───────────┐
Spring comes in like a lion and goes out like a lamb.

Compound sentences

A compound sentence is composed of two or more independent clauses with no subordinate clauses. The independent clauses are usually joined with a comma and a coordinating conjunction (*and, but, or, nor, for, so, yet*) or with a semicolon. (See 14a.)

```
      INDEPENDENT              INDEPENDENT
  ┌──── CLAUSE ────┐       ┌──── CLAUSE ────────┐
```
The car broke down, but a rescue van arrived within minutes.

```
  ┌──── INDEPENDENT CLAUSE ────┐ ┌ INDEPENDENT CLAUSE ┐
```
A shark was spotted near shore; people left immediately.

Complex sentences

A complex sentence is composed of one independent clause with one or more subordinate clauses. (See 42e.)

```
                         SUBORDINATE
                     ┌──── CLAUSE ────┐
```
ADJECTIVE   The pitcher who won the game is a rookie.

```
                      SUBORDINATE
                  ┌──── CLAUSE ────┐
```
ADVERB   If you are too tired to walk, take the bus home.

```
                     SUBORDINATE
                 ┌──── CLAUSE ────┐
```
NOUN   What matters most to us is respect for the land.

Compound-complex sentences

A compound-complex sentence contains at least two independent clauses and at least one subordinate clause. The following sentence contains two independent clauses, each of which contains a subordinate clause.

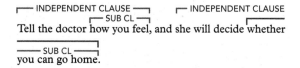

INDEPENDENT CLAUSE   INDEPENDENT CLAUSE
SUB CL
Tell the doctor how you feel, and she will decide whether

SUB CL
you can go home.

43b Sentence purposes

Writers use declarative sentences to make statements, imperative sentences to issue requests or commands, interrogative sentences to ask questions, and exclamatory sentences to make exclamations.

DECLARATIVE	The echo sounded in our ears.
IMPERATIVE	Love your neighbor.
INTERROGATIVE	Did the better team win tonight?
EXCLAMATORY	We're here to save you!

EXERCISE 43–1   Identify the following sentences as simple, compound, complex, or compound-complex. Identify the subordinate clauses and classify them according to their function: adjective, adverb, or noun. (See 42e.) Answers appear in the back of the book.

> **The deli in Courthouse Square was crowded with lawyers at lunchtime.**
>
> (Simple)

a. Fires that are ignited in dry areas spread especially quickly.

b. The early Incas were advanced; they used a calendar and developed a decimal system.

c. Elaine's jacket was too thin to block the wintry air.

d. Before we leave for the station, we always check the Amtrak website.

e. Decide when you want to leave, and I will be there to pick you up.

PART 9

Researched Writing

44 Thinking like a researcher; gathering sources

A college research assignment asks you to pose questions worth exploring, read widely in search of possible answers, interpret what you read, draw reasoned conclusions, and support those conclusions with evidence. In short, it asks you to enter a research conversation by being *in* conversation with other writers and thinkers who have explored and studied your topic. As you listen to and learn from the voices already in the conversation, you'll find entry points where you can add your own insights and ideas.

44a Manage the project.

When you begin a research project, you will need to understand the assignment, choose a direction, and ask questions about your topic. The following strategies will help you manage the beginning phase of research.

Managing time

When you receive your assignment, set a realistic schedule of deadlines. Think about how much time you might need for each step of the assignment. Consider creating a calendar to map out the tasks for your project, keeping in mind that some tasks might overlap or need to be repeated. See the sample research calendar on the opposite page.

Sample calendar for a research assignment

2	3	4	5	6	7	8
	Receive and analyze the assignment.	Pose questions you might explore.	Talk with a reference librarian; plan a → search strategy.		Settle on a topic; narrow the focus.	Revise research questions. Locate → sources.
9	**10**	**11**	**12**	**13**	**14**	**15**
Read, take notes, and → compile a working bibliography. → Locate sources. →			→	Draft a working thesis and an outline.	Draft the paper. →	
16	**17**	**18**	**19**	**20**	**21**	**22**
→ Draft the paper. →			Visit the writing center for feedback.	Do additional → research, if needed.		→
23	**24**	**25**	**26**	**27**	**28**	**29**
Ask peers for feedback. Revise the paper; if necessary, revise the thesis. →				Prepare a list of → works cited.		Proofread the final draft. →
30	**31**					
Proofread the final draft. →	Submit the final draft.					

Getting the big picture

As you consider a possible research topic, take time to read a few sources. Ask yourself questions such as these:

- What aspects of the topic are generating the most debate?
- Why and how are people disagreeing?
- Which arguments and approaches seem worth exploring?

44b Pose questions worth exploring.

Every research project starts with questions. Try using *who, what, when, where, how,* and *why* to form research questions for your project.

- **How** will artificial intelligence solve the Internet's misinformation problems?
- **What** happens to the arts without public funding?
- **Why** are boys diagnosed with attention deficit disorder more often than girls are?

See "How to enter a research conversation" on page 266 for advice on choosing and developing a research question.

Choosing a focused question

If your initial question is too broad, given the length of the essay you plan to write, look for ways to narrow and focus your question.

TOO BROAD	NARROWER
What are the economic effects of a global pandemic such as COVID-19?	**How** has COVID-19 changed the economic circumstances of lower-income women in the United States?

Choosing a debatable question

Your research paper will be more interesting to both you and your audience if you ask a question that is open to debate, not a question that leads to a list of facts. A *why* or *how* question most often leads to a researched argument and engages readers in a debate with multiple perspectives.

TOO FACTUAL	DEBATABLE
What percentage of state police departments use body cameras?	**How** has the widespread use of body cameras changed encounters between officers and civilians?

Choosing a question grounded in evidence

For most college courses, the central argument of a research paper should be grounded in evidence, not in personal preferences or opinions. Your research question should lead you to evidence, not to a defense of your beliefs.

TOO DEPENDENT ON PERSONAL OPINION

Do medical scientists have the right to experiment on animals?

GROUNDED IN EVIDENCE

How have technical breakthroughs made medical experiments on animals increasingly unnecessary?

Writing for an audience

Follow your curiosity, but think about readers, too. Ask yourself: How will my research question engage readers? Why will readers think the question is worth asking? How might my research help readers understand a topic they care about? Frame your research question to show readers why it needs to be asked—and why the answer matters to them.

Testing your research question

Once you have a tentative research question, check to see that it is interesting, debatable, and flexible enough to pursue.

- Does your question allow you to research a topic that interests you?

- Does your question give you (and your readers) an opportunity to think about your topic in a new way?

- Is the question debatable and flexible enough to allow for many possible answers?

- Can you show why the question needs to be asked and why the answer is worth knowing?

Enter a research conversation

A college research project asks you to be in conversation with writers and researchers who have studied your topic or with people who have *lived* your topic—responding to their ideas, experiences, and arguments and contributing your own insights to move the conversation forward. As you ask preliminary research questions, you may wonder where and how to step into a research conversation. The following steps will help you do so.

1 **Identify the experts and ideas in the conversation.** Ask: Who are the major writers and most influential people researching your topic? What are their credentials? What positions have they taken? How and why do the experts disagree?

2 **Identify any gaps in the conversation.** What is missing? Where are the gaps in the existing research? What questions haven't been asked yet? What positions need to be challenged? What perspectives seem to be missing? (See the box on p. 268 for guidance on widening the research conversation.)

3 **Try using sentence starters** to help you find a point of entry.

- *On one side of the debate is position X, and on the other side is Y, but there is a middle position: _____.*

- *The conventional view about the problem needs to be challenged because _____.*

- *Key details in this debate that have been overlooked are _____.*

- *Researchers have drawn conclusion X from the evidence, but one could also draw a different conclusion: _____.*

44c Map out a search strategy.

Before you search for sources, think about what kinds of sources will be appropriate for your project. Considering the kinds of sources you need will help you develop a search strategy—a systematic plan for locating sources.

No single search strategy works for every topic. For some topics, it may be useful to search for information in newspapers, government publications, videos, and websites. For others, the best sources might be scholarly journals and books, research reports, and specialized reference works. Still other topics might be enhanced by field research—interviews, surveys, or observation.

With the help of a librarian, each of the students whose research essays appear in this handbook constructed a search strategy appropriate for her research question.

Researcher   Sophie Harba (See her full paper in 51b.)

Research question   Why should (or why shouldn't) the government enact laws to regulate healthy eating choices?

Search strategy

- Search the web to locate current news, government publications, and information from organizations that focus on government regulation of food.
- Check a library database for current peer-reviewed research articles.
- Use the library catalog to search for a recently published book that was cited by a source.

Researcher   April Bo Wang (See her full paper in 53b.)

Research question   How can technology facilitate a shift from teacher-delivered to student-centered learning?

Search strategy

- Search Google Scholar and *CQ Researcher* to see which aspects of the question are generating debate.
- View a TED talk to deepen understanding of education technology.
- Use specialized databases related to education and technology to search for studies and scholarly articles.

Distinguishing between primary and secondary sources

As you search for sources, determine whether you are looking at a primary or a secondary source.

Primary source letter, diary, film, legislative bill, laboratory study, field research report, speech, eyewitness account, poem, short story, novel

Secondary source commentary on or review or interpretation of a primary source by another writer

Although a primary source is not necessarily more reliable than a secondary source, it has the advantage of being a firsthand account. You can better evaluate what a secondary source says if you have read any primary source it discusses.

44d Search efficiently; master a few shortcuts to finding good sources.

You can save yourself time by becoming an efficient searcher of library databases and the web.

Using the library

The website hosted by your college library links to databases and other references containing articles, studies, and reports written by key researchers. Use your library's resources, designed for academic researchers, to find the most authoritative sources for your project.

Widening the research conversation

Locating sources involves detective work. As you search for sources to answer your research question, note who is in the research conversation, and ask whose voices haven't been represented—and need to be represented. In many research conversations, perspectives become skewed when all the experts are asking the same questions and sharing the same assumptions. As you research a topic, search for voices that might be underrepresented or excluded from

$\rightarrow$

WIDENING THE RESEARCH CONVERSATION (*cont.*)

research conversations and mainstream publications, especially voices whose perspectives question and challenge traditional assumptions.

If, for instance, you are researching the intersection of race and public health, ask whether the voices and perspectives of people of color are included in the research conversation — and if they are not, ask why they are absent and where you will locate them. Or if you are researching the effects of bullying on the mental health of adolescents, seeking out the experiences of specific groups — such as LGBTQ youth — will paint a much more complex picture than researching the topic generally. Even when a topic may not seem related to specific marginalized groups, searching for viewpoints from people of varied backgrounds will result in a far more accurate and representative understanding of the conversation.

As you develop your search strategy, ask questions such as these:

* What sources provide a range of viewpoints, including those that counter mainstream perspectives?

* What assumptions do mainstream sources share? Do those assumptions seem accurate? If not, how might someone challenge them?

* Whose voices are missing from the research conversation — and why might that be?

* Where might you seek out underrepresented voices on your topic? Where have they been published?

The following sources and strategies are good starting points for finding diverse viewpoints.

* **Databases** Many databases, such as the following, feature underrepresented voices and groups: Ethnic NewsWatch, GenderWatch, Latin American Newsstream, allAfrica.com, MideastWire, LGBT Magazine Archive, NPR's Diverse Sources, HAPI (Hispanic American Periodicals Index).

* **Library archives** Most libraries have archives of historical records and primary sources that haven't always been well represented in research conversations.

* **Organizations and groups** Professional and research organizations focus on interest groups. The American Sociology Association, for example, has a first-generation and working-class sociologists section; the U.S. Congress has the Congressional Black Caucus. Seek out publications or other resources from groups relevant to your topic.

Using the web

When conducting searches, use terms that are as specific as possible. Your keywords will determine the quality of the results you see. Use clues in what you find (such as websites of organizations or government agencies that seem informative) to refine your search. When searching for online sources, look for clues about a site's sponsorship. Sometimes a web search brings you to a page that looks useful, but it's difficult to tell whether the site is legitimate. You may find it helpful to shorten a longer URL to its root address—one that ends with .org, .gov, .edu, or .com, for example—so that you can better judge the usefulness of the page's content.

Using bibliographies and citations as shortcuts

Scholarly books and articles list the works the author has cited, usually at the end. Skimming these lists is a useful shortcut for finding additional reliable sources on your topic. Following the trail of citations may lead you to helpful sources and a network of relevant research about your topic.

44e Write a research proposal.

One effective way to manage your project and focus your thinking is to write a research proposal. A proposal gives you an opportunity to look back—to remind yourself why you chose your topic—and to look forward—to predict any difficulties or obstacles that might arise during your project.

The following questions will help you organize your proposal.

- **Research question:** What question will you be exploring? Why does this question need to be asked? What do you hope to learn from the project?

- **Research conversation:** What have you learned so far about the debate or specific research conversation you will enter? What entry point have you found to offer your own insights and ideas?

- **Search strategy:** What kinds of sources will you use to explore your question? What sources will be most useful, and why? How will you locate a variety of sources (primary/secondary, textual/visual)?

- **Research challenges:** What challenges, if any, do you anticipate (locating sufficient sources, managing the project, finding a position to take)? What resources are available to help you meet these challenges?

44f Conduct field research, if appropriate.

Your own field research can enhance or be the focus of a writing project. For a composition class, for example, you might interview a local politician about a current issue, such as the initiation of a city bike-share program. For a sociology class, you might conduct a survey regarding campus trends in community service.

NOTE: Colleges and universities often require researchers to submit projects to an institutional review board (IRB) if the research involves human subjects outside a classroom setting. Before administering a survey or conducting other fieldwork, check with your instructor to see whether IRB approval is required.

Interviewing

Interviews can often shed new light on a topic. Look for an expert who has firsthand knowledge of the subject, or seek out an individual whose personal experience will provide a valuable perspective. Ask open questions that lead to facts, anecdotes, and vivid details that will add a meaningful dimension to your paper.

USING SOURCES RESPONSIBLY: When quoting your source (the interviewee), be accurate and fair. Do not change the meaning of your interviewee's words or take them out of context; do not change the phrasing or dialect of the interviewee's speech. If your interviewee grants permission, record your interview so you can review the accuracy of any quotations and the context in which they were spoken.

Go beyond a Google search

You might start with Google to gain an overview of your topic, but relying on the search engine to choose your sources isn't a research strategy. Good research involves going beyond the information available from a quick Google search. To locate reliable, authoritative sources, be strategic about *how* and *where* to search.

1 **Familiarize yourself with the research conversation.** Identify the current debate about the topic you have chosen and the most influential writers and experts in the debate. Where is the research conversation happening? In scholarly sources? Government agencies? The popular media?

2 **Generate keywords to focus your search.** Use specific words and combinations to search. Add words such as *debate, disagreements, proponents*, or *opponents* to track down the various positions in the research conversation. Use *who, what, when, where, why*, and *how* questions to refine a search.

3 **Search discipline-specific databases available through your school library** to locate carefully chosen scholarly (peer-reviewed) content that doesn't appear in search results on the open web. Use databases such as JSTOR and Academic Search Premier, designed for academic researchers, to locate sources in the most influential publications.

4 **If your topic has been in the news, try *CQ Researcher,*** available through most college libraries. Its brief articles provide pro/con arguments on current controversies in criminal justice, law, environment, technology, health, and education.

5 **Explore the Pew Research Center** (pewresearch.org), which sponsors original research and nonpartisan discussions of findings and trends in a wide range of academic fields.

Conducting a survey

For some topics, you may find it useful to survey opinions or practices through a written questionnaire, a phone or email poll, or questions posted on a social media site. Many people resist long questionnaires, so for a good response rate, limit your questions with your purpose in mind.

Surveys with yes/no questions or multiple-choice options can be completed quickly, and the results are easy to tally, but you may also want to ask a few open-ended questions to invite more individual responses.

45 Managing information; taking notes responsibly

- ► Information to collect for a working bibliography, 274
- ► How to take notes responsibly, 276
- ► How to avoid plagiarizing from the web, 277

An effective researcher is a good record keeper. Whether you decide to keep records on paper or on a computer or mobile device, you will need methods for managing information: maintaining a working bibliography (see 45a), keeping track of source materials (see 45b), and taking notes without plagiarizing your sources (see 45c).

45a Maintain a working bibliography.

Keep a record of sources you read, listen to, or view. This record, called a *working bibliography*, will help you keep track of publication information for the sources you might use so that you can easily refer to them as you write and compile a list of works cited. The format of this list depends on the documentation style you are using (for MLA style, see 51a; for APA style, see 53a). See 46d for advice on using your working bibliography as the basis for an annotated bibliography.

Information to collect for a working bibliography

For an article

- All authors of the article
- Title and subtitle of the article
- Title of the journal, magazine, or newspaper
- Publication date; volume, issue, and page numbers
- Date you accessed the source (for an online article that lists no publication date)

For an article retrieved from a database (in addition to the preceding information)

- Name of the database
- Digital object identifier (DOI), if there is one
- URL to the article or to the journal/database home page, if there is no DOI

For a web source (including visual, audio, and multimedia sources)

- All authors, editors, and/or other key contributors to the source
- Title and subtitle of the source
- Title of the longer work, if the source is contained in a longer work
- Title of the website
- Online page or paragraph numbers or other retrieval information (such as a time stamp or slide number)
- Sponsor or publisher of the site
- Date of online publication or latest update
- Date you accessed the source (for an undated source)
- URL or permalink for the page on which the source appears

INFORMATION TO COLLECT FOR A WORKING BIBLIOGRAPHY (*cont.*)

For an entire book

- All authors; any editors or translators
- Title and subtitle
- Edition, if not the first
- Publication information: publisher and date
- Date you accessed the source (for an undated online book)

45b Keep track of source materials.

Save a copy of each potential source as you conduct your research. Many database services will allow you to email, text, save, or print citations or full texts, and you can easily download, copy, or take screenshots of information from the web. It is always a good idea to use browser bookmarks and make a folder to save sources for your research assignment.

Working with hard copies, screenshots, or files—as opposed to relying on memory or hastily written notes—lets you annotate the source as you read. You also reduce the chances of unintentional plagiarism since you will be able to compare your use of a source in your paper with the actual source, not just with your notes.

45c As you take notes, avoid unintentional plagiarism.

Plagiarism, using someone's words or ideas without giving credit, is often accidental. After spending so much time thinking through your topic and reading sources, it's easy to forget where a helpful idea came from or that the idea wasn't yours to begin with. Even if you half-copy an author's sentences—either by mixing the author's phrases with your own without using quotation marks or by plugging your synonyms into the author's sentence structure—you are plagiarizing. See the boxes beginning on the next page for help with avoiding plagiarism while taking notes and conducting online research.

Take notes responsibly

1 **Understand the ideas in the source.** Start by determining the purpose and meaning of the source. Focus on the overall ideas in the source instead of individual words. Ask: What is the argument? What is the evidence?

2 **Keep the source close by to check for accuracy,** but resist the temptation to look at the source as you take notes—except when you are quoting.

3 **Use quotation marks around any borrowed words or phrases.** Copy the words exactly and keep complete bibliographic information for each source.

4 **Develop an organized system** to distinguish your insights and ideas from those of the source. Some researchers use a color-coding system.

5 **Create a method to label and identify** when you have summarized a text or its data or paraphrased or quoted an author's words.

6 **Record complete bibliographic information for each source** so you can give credit to the source, cite it accurately, and find it again easily.

Avoid plagiarizing from the web

1 **Understand what plagiarism is.** When you use another author's intellectual property (language, visuals, or ideas) in your own writing without giving proper credit, you engage in a kind of academic dishonesty called *plagiarism*.

2 **Treat online sources as someone else's intellectual property.** Language, data, or images that you find on the web must be cited, even if the material is publicly accessible on free sites or social media, is on a government website, or is in the public domain (which includes older works no longer protected by copyright law).

3 **Keep track of words and ideas borrowed from sources.** When you copy and paste passages from online sources, put quotation marks around any text that you have copied. Develop a system for distinguishing your words and ideas from anything you've summarized, paraphrased, or quoted.

4 **Create a complete bibliographic entry for each source to keep track of publication** information. From the start of your research project, maintain accurate records for all online sources you read, listen to, or view.

Summarizing and paraphrasing ideas and quoting exact language are three ways of taking notes without unintentionally plagiarizing.

- **Summarizing:** A summary, written in your own words, condenses information and captures main ideas, reducing a chapter to a short paragraph or a paragraph to a single sentence.

- **Paraphrasing:** Like a summary, a paraphrase is written in your own words, but it restates information in roughly the same number of words as the original source, using different sentence structure.

- **Quoting:** A quotation consists of the exact words from a source. Put all quoted material in quotation marks.

TIP: For more information on how to summarize, paraphrase, and quote effectively, see 48c and 48d.

46 Evaluating sources

You will often locate far more potential sources on your topic than you will have time to read. Your challenge then is to determine what kinds of sources you need—and what you need these sources to do—and to select a reasonable number of trustworthy sources. This kind of decision making is referred to as *evaluating sources*.

46a Evaluate the reliability and usefulness of a source.

Using reliable sources adds to your credibility and authority as a writer. The following questions will help you judge the reliability and usefulness of sources you might use to support your research project.

Relevance   Is the source clearly related to your research topic and your argument? Will your readers understand why you've included the source in your paper? How does it help you answer your research question?

Currency   How recent is the source? Is the information up-to-date? Does your research topic require current information? Will your research benefit from consulting older sources, including primary sources from a historical period?

Credibility   Where does the source come from? What are the author's credentials? How accurate and trustworthy is the information? Who published the source? If the source is authored by an organization, what research has the organization done to support its claims? Are the source's ideas and research cited by other writers?

Bias   Does the author endorse political or religious views that could affect objectivity? Are evidence and counterevidence presented in a fair and objective way? Is the author engaging in a scholarly debate or giving a personal point of view?

Determining whether a source is scholarly

Scholarly sources are written by experts for a knowledgeable audience and usually go into more depth than books and articles written for a general audience. Scholarly sources are sometimes called *refereed* or *peer-reviewed* because the work is evaluated by experts in the field before publication.

To determine whether a source is scholarly, look for the following:

- Formal language and presentation
- Authors who are academics or scientists
- Footnotes or a bibliography documenting the works cited in the source
- Original research and interpretation (rather than a summary of other people's work)

> ## Tips for evaluating sources
>
> ### Check for signs of bias
>
> - Does the author or publisher endorse political or religious views that could affect objectivity?
> - Is the author or publisher associated with a special-interest group, such as People for the Ethical Treatment of Animals (PETA) or the National Rifle Association (NRA), that might emphasize one side of an issue?
> - Are alternative views presented and addressed? How fairly does the author treat opposing views?
> - Does the author's language show signs of bias?
>
> Bias doesn't always render a source unuseful. Acknowledging bias when you see it helps you place the source in the context of the debate and in the context of your own purpose and audience.
>
> ### Assess the writer's (or organization's) argument
>
> - What is the author's central claim or thesis?
> - How does the author support this claim—with relevant and sufficient evidence or with just a few anecdotes or emotional examples?
> - Are statistics consistent with those you encounter in other sources? Does the author explain where the statistics come from?
> - Are any of the author's assumptions questionable? Is the logic flawed?
> - Does the author consider opposing arguments and refute them persuasively?
>
> You want to find sources that both support your argument and present other arguments, but it helps to try to determine whether a source's argument has merit and is based on evidence.

46b Read with an open mind and a critical eye.

As you begin reading the sources you have chosen, keep an open mind. Be curious about the wide range of positions in the research conversation you are entering. Do not let your personal beliefs or an initial working thesis statement prevent you from listening to new ideas and opposing viewpoints.

Assess web sources with special care

46c Assess web sources with special care.

Before using a web source in your paper, make sure you know who created the material and for what purpose. Sources with reliable information can stand up to scrutiny. As you evaluate sources, ask questions about their reliability and purpose.

Evaluating a website: Checking reliability

1 This page on Internet monitoring and workplace privacy appears on a website sponsored by the National Conference of State Legislatures (NCSL). The NCSL is a bipartisan group that functions as a clearinghouse of ideas and research of interest to state lawmakers. It is also a lobby for state issues before the US government. The URL ending .org marks this sponsor as a nonprofit organization.

2 A clear date of publication shows currency.

3 An "About Us" page confirms that this is a credible organization whose credentials can be verified.

Detect false and misleading sources

Sources can distort information or spread misinformation by taking information out of context or by promoting opinions as facts. As you evaluate sources, determine authenticity: Can the information be verified? Is the source reliable? You can verify facts and quotations by reading multiple sources and gathering a variety of perspectives. Because information and misinformation live side by side on the web, you need to read critically to determine the truth.

1 **Consider the source.** Is more than one source covering the topic? Is the author anonymous or named? What can you learn about the author's credentials and the mission of the site from checking the "About Us" tab? Does the site present only one side of an issue? Be skeptical if the source is the only one reporting the story.

2 **Examine the source's language.** Is the language informal? Does the source overuse superlatives such as *most*, *best*, or *worst*? Does it use the second-person pronoun *you*?

3 **Question the seriousness of the source.** Is the source attempting to mimic a reliable source? Is it possible that the source is satirical and humorous and is not intended to be read as factual?

4 **Fact-check the information.** Can the facts be objectively verified? If the conclusions of a research study are cited, find the study to verify; if an authority is quoted, research the original source of the quotation, if possible, to see whether the quotation was taken out of context. Also, be skeptical if a source reports a research study but doesn't quote the study's principal investigator or other respected researchers.

5 **Pay attention to the URL.** Among the more credible sites are those sponsored by higher education (.edu), nonprofit groups (.org), and government agencies (.gov). Established news organizations have standard domain names. Fake sites often use web addresses such as "Newslo" or "com.co" that imitate the addresses of real sites, and they package information with misinformation to make themselves look authentic.

6 **Note your biases.** If an article makes you angry or challenges your beliefs, or if it confirms your beliefs by ignoring evidence to the contrary, take notice, and try to be as objective as possible. Learn about an issue from reliable sources and from multiple perspectives.

Evaluating a website: Checking purpose

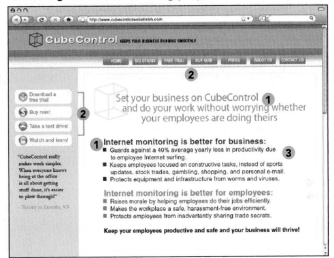

1. The site is sponsored by a company that specializes in employee-monitoring software.

2. Repeated links for trial downloads and purchase suggest the site's intended audience: consumers seeking to purchase software (probably not researchers seeking detailed information about employees' use of the Internet in the workplace).

3. The site appears to provide information and even shows statistics from studies, but ultimately the purpose of the site is to sell a product.

46d Construct an annotated bibliography.

An annotated bibliography is a list of sources with notes about each source. Constructing an annotated bibliography focuses your attention on the most promising sources you've located, providing you with an opportunity to evaluate the usefulness of these sources as you reflect on *how* and *why* they will help you answer your research question. Take the following steps for each source in your annotated bibliography.

RECORD	Using whatever style your assignment requires, record the publication information for your source.
SUMMARIZE	Start by identifying the purpose and thesis of the source and the author's credentials. Summarize the source's main ideas and the evidence used to support these ideas. Summarizing gives you an opportunity to test your understanding of the source's meaning.
EVALUATE	Ask yourself what role a source might play and how it will contribute to your argument. Did it provide key evidence? Lend authority? Offer a counterargument? Evaluate how and why the source can help you answer your research question and support your position.

See the writing guide on page 285 for help.

SAMPLE ANNOTATED BIBLIOGRAPHY ENTRY (MLA STYLE)

Resnik, David. "Trans Fat Bans and Human Freedom." *American Journal of* citation
Bioethics, vol. 10, no. 3, Mar. 2010, pp. 27–32.

Type of source; author's name and credentials

In this scholarly article, bioethicist David Resnik argues that bans on unhealthy foods threaten our personal freedom. He claims that researchers don't have enough evidence to know whether banning trans fats will save lives or money; all we know is that such bans restrict dietary choices. Resnik explains why most Americans oppose food restrictions, noting our multiethnic and regional food traditions as well as our resistance to government limitations on personal freedoms.

Summary presents the author's ideas and shows the student's understanding of the main points.

summary

Evaluation judges the source's reliability and shows how the source contributes to the student's research.

Resnik offers a well-reasoned argument, but he goes too far by insisting that all proposed food restrictions will do more harm than good. This article contributes important perspectives on American resistance to government intervention in food choice and counters arguments in other sources that support the idea of food legislation to advance public health.

evaluation

How to write an annotated bibliography

Creating an **annotated bibliography** gives you an opportunity to summarize, evaluate, and record publication information for your sources before drafting your research paper. You summarize each source to understand its main ideas, and you evaluate each source for accuracy, quality, and relevance. Finally, you reflect, asking yourself how the source will contribute to your research project.

Key features

- **The list of sources, arranged in alphabetical order by author,** includes complete bibliographic information for each source.

- **A brief annotation or note for each source,** typically no longer than one paragraph, contains a summary and an evaluation. The annotation may be written in full sentences or as brief notes; check with your instructor for preferences.

- **The summary** of each source states the work's main ideas and key points briefly and accurately. The summary is written in the present tense, third person, directly and concisely. Summarizing helps you test your understanding of a source and restate its meaning responsibly.

- **The evaluation** of the source's role and usefulness in your project includes an assessment of the source's strengths and limitations, the author's qualifications and expertise, and the function of the source in your project. Evaluating a source helps you analyze how the source fits into your project and separate the source's ideas from your own.

Thinking ahead: Presenting or publishing

If you are asked to submit your annotated bibliography electronically, be sure that any entry for a web source includes a functioning link to the source so that your reader can easily access it.

285

Writing your annotated bibliography

Explore

For each source, begin by brainstorming responses to questions such as the following.

- What is the purpose of the source? Who is the author's intended audience?
- What is the author's thesis? What evidence supports the thesis?
- What qualifications and expertise does the author bring? Does the author have any biases or make any questionable assumptions?
- Why do you think this source is useful for your project?
- How does this source relate to the other sources in your bibliography?

Draft

The following tips can help you draft one or more entries in your annotated bibliography.

- Arrange the sources in alphabetical order by author (or by title for works with no author).
- Provide consistent bibliographic information for each source. For the exact bibliographic format, see 50b (MLA) or 52b (APA).
- Start your summary by identifying the thesis and purpose of the source as well as the credentials of the source's author.
- Keep your research question in mind. How does this source contribute to your project? How does it help you take your place in the research conversation?

Revise

Ask reviewers for specific feedback. Here are some questions to guide their comments.

- Is each source summarized clearly? Have you identified the author's main idea?
- For each source, have you made a clear judgment about how and why the source is useful for your project?

47 Writing a research paper

▸ Testing your thesis statement, **288**
▸ Template for organizing a researched argument, **289**

Once you have read a range of sources, considered your subject from different perspectives, and chosen an entry point in the research conversation, you are ready to focus your research paper by forming a thesis statement and supporting that thesis with well-organized evidence.

47a Form a working thesis statement.

A thesis statement expresses your informed answer to your research question — an answer about which people might disagree. Start by developing a working thesis statement to help you narrow your ideas and clarify your purpose. As your ideas develop, you'll revise your working thesis to make it more specific and focused.

Here, for example, are student writer Sophie Harba's research question and working thesis statement.

RESEARCH QUESTION

Should the government enact laws to regulate healthy eating choices?

Good start; provides an answer to the question — but it doesn't show why the thesis matters.

WORKING THESIS STATEMENT

State governments have the responsibility to regulate healthy eating choices because of the rise of chronic diseases.

REVISED THESIS STATEMENT

In the name of public health and safety, state governments have the responsibility to shape health policies and to regulate healthy eating choices, especially since doing so offers a potentially large social benefit for a relatively small cost.

Revised thesis is sharper, more focused; it announces a clear position and shows readers why the position matters.

In a research paper, readers are accustomed to seeing the thesis statement at the end of the introductory paragraph. To read Harba's thesis in the context of her entire paper, see 51b.

287

Testing your thesis statement

An effective thesis argues for a position in a debate. Keep the following guidelines in mind to develop an effective thesis statement.

● **A thesis should be your answer to a question** and should take a position that needs to be argued and supported. It should not be a statement of fact or a description. Make sure your position is debatable by anticipating opposing viewpoints and counterarguments.

● **A thesis should match the scope of the research project.** If your thesis is too broad, explore a subtopic of your original topic. If your thesis is too narrow, ask a research question that has more than one answer.

● **A thesis should be focused.** Avoid vague words such as *interesting* or *good.* Use concrete language and make sure your thesis lets readers know your position.

● **A thesis should stand up to the "So what?" test** (see p. 10). Ask yourself why readers should be interested in your essay and should care about your thesis.

47b Organize your ideas with an informal plan.

The body of your paper will consist of evidence in support of your thesis. Try sketching an informal plan to focus and organize your ideas. Sophie Harba, for example, used this simple plan to outline the structure of her argument.

INFORMAL OUTLINE

- Debates about the government's role in regulating food have a long history in the United States.

- Some experts argue that we should focus on the dangers of unhealthy eating habits and on preventing chronic diseases linked to diet.

- But food regulations are not a popular solution because many Americans object to government restrictions on personal choice.

- Food regulations designed to prevent chronic disease don't ask Americans to give up their freedom; they ask Americans to see health as a matter of public good.

There is no right or wrong way to organize a researched argument. A fairly typical way for research writers to proceed is shown here, but of course you should consider your own assignment, purpose, and audience as you organize and develop your work.

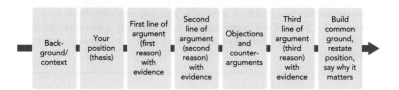

48 Citing sources; avoiding plagiarism

In a research paper, you draw on the work of other writers, and you must document their contributions by citing your sources. As an academic writer, you'll cite sources for two reasons:

1. to tell readers where your information comes from — so that they can assess its reliability and, if interested, find and read the original source

2. to give credit to the writers from whom you have borrowed words and ideas

You must include a citation when you quote from a source, when you summarize or paraphrase, and when you borrow facts that are not common knowledge. Borrowing another writer's language, sentence structure, or ideas without proper acknowledgment is plagiarism. The only exception is common knowledge — information that your readers may know or could easily locate in any number of general sources. When in doubt about whether something is or isn't common knowledge, acknowledge the source.

> ## Writing for an audience
>
> You demonstrate your credibility, your *ethos,* by choosing the most trust-worthy and reliable sources and showing readers how to find them. When your citations guide readers quickly to the sources of quoted, paraphrased, or summarized ideas, you show respect for your audience's interest in your research. Ask yourself two questions: How can I make my documentation useful to my readers? What would readers need to know to find each source themselves?

48a Understand what plagiarism is.

To be fair and responsible, you must document the work of others by citing your sources. When you acknowledge and document your sources, you avoid *plagiarism,* a form of academic dishonesty.

In general, these three acts are considered plagiarism:

1. failing to cite quotations and borrowed ideas
2. failing to enclose borrowed language in quotation marks
3. failing to put summaries and paraphrases in your own words and sentence structure

Definitions of plagiarism vary; it's a good idea to find out how your school defines academic dishonesty.

48b Understand the MLA and APA systems of documentation.

Although various academic disciplines use their own style for citing sources, all disciplines cite sources for the same reasons — to acknowl-edge the contributions of others and to show readers where they can find the sources for themselves.

The Bedford Handbook describes two commonly used documentation styles:

Modern Language Association (MLA) in section 50

American Psychological Association (APA) in section 52

MLA is often used in humanities courses such as composition, literature, and film and media studies. APA is the choice for social science courses such as psychology, sociology, and criminal justice; at times it is used in business, education, and the natural sciences as well.

The MLA and APA styles require you to acknowledge your sources by using in-text citations—citations placed in parentheses within the body of your paper—to indicate the source of a particular quotation, paraphrased or summarized statement, or fact. The in-text citations point readers to a list of works cited or list of references at the end of your paper.

Understand how the MLA system works

In MLA style, you use a parenthetical citation within the text of your paper to credit each source and to refer your readers to a more detailed citation of the source in the works cited list at the end of your paper. There is a direct connection between the in-text citation and the alphabetical entry in your works cited list.

Here, briefly, is how the MLA citation system works.

IN-TEXT CITATION

Signal phrase names the author and gives credentials.

Bioethicist David Resnik emphasizes that such policies "open the door to excessive government control over food, which could restrict dietary choices, interfere with cultural, ethnic, and religious traditions, and exacerbate socioeconomic inequalities" (31).

Writer includes a page number after cited material.

The in-text citation points readers to the list of works cited at the end of the paper.

ENTRY IN THE LIST OF WORKS CITED WITH COMPLETE BIBILIOGRAPHIC INFORMATION

Resnik, David. "Trans Fat Bans and Human Freedom." *The American Journal of Bioethics*, vol. 10, no. 3, Mar. 2010, pp. 27–32.

Be a responsible research writer

Using good citation habits is the best way to avoid plagiarizing sources and to demonstrate that you are a responsible researcher.

1 **Cite your sources as you write drafts.** Don't wait until your final draft is complete to add citations. Include a citation when you quote from a source, when you summarize or paraphrase, and when you borrow facts that are not common knowledge.

2 **Place quotation marks around direct quotations,** both in your notes and in your drafts.

3 **Check each quotation, summary, and paraphrase against the source** to make certain you aren't misrepresenting the source. For a paraphrase, be sure that your language and sentence structure differ from those in the original passage.

4 **Provide a full citation in your list of works cited.** It is not sufficient to cite a source only in the body of your paper; you must also provide complete publication information for each source in a list of works cited.

Understand how the APA system works

APA recommends an author-date system of citations. The date is important because disciplines that use APA style value current research. APA style requires the use of the past tense or the present perfect tense in signal phrases introducing cited material: *Bell (2010) reported, Bell (2010) has argued.*

Here, briefly, is how the APA citation system works.

IN-TEXT CITATION

Signal phrase names the author and gives the date.

Bell (2010) reported that students engaged in this kind of learning performed better on both project-based assessments and standardized texts (pp. 39–40).

Writer includes page numbers for a paginated source.

The in-text citation points readers to the list of references at the end of the paper.

ENTRY IN THE LIST OF REFERENCES WITH COMPLETE PUBLICATION INFORMATION

Bell, S. (2010). Project-based learning for the 21st century: Skills for the future. *The Clearing House, 83*(2), 39–43.

48c Use quotation marks around borrowed language.

To indicate that you are using a source's exact phrases or sentences, you must enclose them in quotation marks unless they have been set off from the text by indenting (see 49b). To omit the quotation marks is to claim—falsely—that the language is your own, as in the following example. Such an omission is plagiarism even if you have cited the source.

ORIGINAL SOURCE

Although these policies may have a positive impact on human health, they open the door to excessive government control over food, which could restrict dietary choices, interfere with cultural, ethnic, and religious traditions, and exacerbate socioeconomic inequalities.

— David Resnik, "Trans Fat Bans and Human Freedom," p. 31

PLAGIARISM

The highlighted words are directly from the original.

Bioethicist David Resnik points out that policies to ban trans fats may protect human health, but they open the door to excessive government control over food, which could restrict dietary choices and interfere with cultural, ethnic, and religious traditions (31).

BORROWED LANGUAGE IN QUOTATION MARKS (MLA STYLE)

Bioethicist David Resnik points out that policies to ban trans fats may protect human health, but "they open the door to excessive government control over food, which could restrict dietary choices [and] interfere with cultural, ethnic, and religious traditions" (31).

48d Put summaries and paraphrases in your own words.

A summary condenses information from a source; a paraphrase conveys the information using roughly the same number of words as the original source. When you summarize or paraphrase, it is not enough to name the source. You must restate the source's meaning using your own words and sentence structure. Half-copying the author's sentences either by using the author's phrases in your own sentences without quotation marks or by plugging synonyms into the author's sentence structure (sometimes called *patchwriting*) is a form of plagiarism.

The first paraphrase of the following source is plagiarized, even though the source is cited, because the paraphrase borrows too much of its language from the original. The highlighted strings of words have been copied exactly (without quotation marks), and the writer has closely echoed the sentence structure of the source, merely substituting some synonyms.

ORIGINAL SOURCE

[A]ntiobesity laws encounter strong opposition from some quarters on the grounds that they constitute paternalistic intervention into lifestyle choices and enfeeble the notion of personal responsibility. Such arguments echo those made in the early days of tobacco regulation.

—Michelle M. Mello et al., "Obesity—the New Frontier of Public Health Law," p. 2602

PLAGIARISM: UNACCEPTABLE BORROWING

Health policy experts Mello and others argue that antiobesity laws encounter strong opposition from some quarters because they interfere with lifestyle choices and decrease the feeling of personal responsibility. These arguments mirror those made in the early days of tobacco regulation (2602).

To avoid plagiarizing an author's language, resist the temptation to look at the source while you are summarizing or paraphrasing. After you have read the passage you want to paraphrase, set the source aside. Ask yourself: What is the author's meaning? In your own words, state your understanding of the author's ideas. Then return to the source and check that you haven't used the author's language or sentence structure or misrepresented the author's ideas.

ACCEPTABLE PARAPHRASE (MLA STYLE)

As health policy experts Mello and others point out, opposition to food and beverage regulation is similar to the opposition to early tobacco legislation: the public views the issue as one of personal responsibility rather than one requiring government intervention (2602).

 Integrating sources

Quotations, summaries, paraphrases, and facts will help you develop your argument, but they cannot speak for you. You need to find a balance between the words of your sources and your own voice so that readers always know who is speaking in your paper. You can use several strategies to integrate sources into your paper while maintaining your voice.

- Use sources as concisely as possible so that your own thinking and voice aren't lost (49a and 49b).

- Use signal phrases to avoid dropping quotations into your paper without indicating the boundary between your words and those of your sources (49c).

- Use language that shows readers how each source supports your argument and how the sources relate to one another (49d).

49a Summarize and paraphrase effectively.

In your academic writing, keep the emphasis on your ideas and your language; use your own words to summarize and paraphrase sources and to explain your points.

Summarizing

When you summarize a source, you express another writer's ideas in your own words, condensing the author's key points and using fewer words than the author.

WHEN TO SUMMARIZE

- When you want to state a source's main ideas simply and briefly in your own words

- When you want to compare arguments or ideas from various sources

- When you want to provide readers with an understanding of a source's argument before you respond to it or launch your own argument

For guidance on summarizing effectively, see the box on page 45.

Paraphrasing

When you paraphrase, you express an author's ideas in your own words and sentence structure, using approximately the same number of words and details as in the source.

WHEN TO PARAPHRASE

- When the ideas and information are important but the author's exact words are not needed
- When you want to restate a source's ideas in your own words
- When you need to simplify and explain a technical or complicated source

The box on page 298 will guide you in paraphrasing effectively.

49b Use quotations effectively.

When you quote a source, you borrow the author's exact words and enclose them in quotation marks. Quotation marks show your readers that both the idea and the words belong to the author. The examples in this section cite sources in MLA style.

WHEN TO USE QUOTATIONS

- When language is especially vivid or expressive
- When exact wording is needed for technical accuracy
- When it is important to let the debaters of an issue explain their positions in their own words
- When the words of an authority lend weight to an argument
- When the language of a source is the topic of your discussion

Paraphrase effectively

A paraphrase shows your readers that you understand a source and can explain it to them. When you choose to paraphrase a passage, you use the source's information and ideas for your own purpose—to provide background information, explain a concept, or advance your argument—while maintaining your voice. It is challenging to write a paraphrase that isn't a word-for-word translation of the original source and doesn't imitate the source's sentence structure. The following strategies will help you paraphrase effectively. The examples in this box are in MLA style.

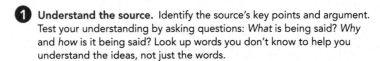 **Understand the source.** Identify the source's key points and argument. Test your understanding by asking questions: *What* is being said? *Why* and *how* is it being said? Look up words you don't know to help you understand the ideas, not just the words.

Original

> People's vision of the world has broadened with the advent of global media such as television and the Internet. Those thinking about going elsewhere can see what the alternatives are and appear to have fewer inhibitions about resettling.
>
> —Darrell M. West, *Brain Gain: Rethinking U.S. Immigration Policy*,
> Brookings Institution Press, 2011, p. 5

Student's notes

— *TV and Internet have opened our eyes, our minds*

— *We can imagine making big moves (country to country) as we never could before; the web offers a preview*

— *"resettling" = moving to a new location, out of the familiar region*

— *Lessens the anxiety about starting over in a new place*

2 **Use your own vocabulary and sentence structure** to convey the source's information. Check to make sure there is no overlap in vocabulary or sentence structure with the original.

> Since TV and the web can offer a preview of life in other places, people feel less uncertainty and anxiety about moving from one area of the world to another.

3 **Use a signal phrase to identify the source** (*According to X,* _____, or *X argues that* _____).

> West argues that since TV and the web can offer a preview of life in other places, people feel less uncertainty and anxiety about moving from one area of the world to another.

4 **Include a citation to give credit to the source.** Even though the words are yours, you need to give credit for the idea. Here, the author's name and the page number on which the original passage appeared are listed.

> West argues that since TV and the web can offer a preview of life in other places, people feel less uncertainty and anxiety about moving from one area of the world to another (5).

NOTE: If you choose to use exact language from the source in a paraphrase, be sure to put quotation marks around any borrowed words or phrases.

> West argues that since TV and the web can offer a preview of life in other places, people "have fewer inhibitions" about moving from one area of the world to another (5).

Limiting your use of quotations

Keep the emphasis on your own ideas, and, as much as possible, keep your ideas in your own voice. It is not always necessary to quote full sentences from a source. Often you can integrate words or phrases from a source into your own sentence structure quite effectively.

> Resnik acknowledges that his argument relies on the "slippery slope" fallacy, but he insists that "social and political pressures" regarding food regulations make his concerns valid (31).

Using the ellipsis

To condense a quoted passage, you can use an ellipsis—a series of three spaced periods—to indicate that you have omitted words. What remains must be grammatically complete.

> In Mississippi, legislators passed "a ban on bans—a law that forbids . . . local restrictions on food or drink" (Conly).

The writer has omitted the words *municipalities to place*, which appear before *local restrictions* in the original source.

If you want to leave out one or more full sentences, use a period before the ellipsis.

> Legal scholars Gostin and Gostin argue that "individuals have limited willpower to defer immediate gratification for longer-term health benefits. . . . A person understands that high-fat foods or a sedentary lifestyle will cause adverse health effects, or that excessive spending or gambling will cause financial hardship, but it is not always easy to refrain" (217).

Ordinarily, do not use an ellipsis at the beginning or at the end of a quotation. Your readers will understand that you have taken the quoted material from a longer passage. The only exception occurs when you have dropped words at the end of the final quoted sentence. In such cases, put the ellipsis before the closing quotation mark and parenthetical citation.

USING SOURCES RESPONSIBLY: Make sure omissions and ellipses do not distort the meaning of your source's words.

Using brackets

Brackets allow you to insert your own words into quoted material to clarify a confusing reference or to keep a sentence grammatical in the context of your writing.

> Neergaard and Agiesta argue that "a new poll finds people are split on how much the government should do to help [find solutions to the national health crisis]— and most draw the line at attempts to force healthier eating."

In this example, the writer inserted words in brackets to clarify the meaning of *help*.

To indicate an error such as a misspelling within a quotation, insert the word "sic" in brackets right after the error.

Setting off long quotations

When you quote more than four typed lines of prose or more than three lines of poetry, set off the quotation by indenting it one-half inch from the left margin, and use the normal right margin.

Long quotations should be introduced by an informative sentence, usually followed by a colon. Quotation marks are unnecessary because the indented format tells readers that the passage is taken word for word from the source.

> The Centers for Disease Control and Prevention explains one source of poor nutrition for children and recommends limiting such sources:
>
>> Although sodas are prohibited in an increasing number of schools, other sugar drinks that may not be commonly perceived as sources of added sugar and excess calories may be available, such as sports drinks and fruit flavored drinks that are not 100% juice. Schools should consider adopting policies that limit access to all sugar drinks in vending machines and school stores. (3)

NOTE: At the end of an indented quotation, the parenthetical citation goes outside the final mark of punctuation.

Quotation marks with other punctuation

Integrating sources smoothly into your own sentences is easier when you follow guidelines about using periods, commas, and question marks with quotation marks.

Quotation with no page number, author mentioned in sentence

The ban, according to MacMillan, "gave consumers a healthier default option."

The ban "gave consumers a healthier default option," according to MacMillan.

NOTE: Place periods and commas inside quotation marks.

Quotation with no page number, author name in parentheses

The ban "gave consumers a healthier default option" (MacMillan).

Quotation with page number

Fortin notes that instead of a ban, the FDA "took a more moderate approach" (113).

Quotation within a writer's own question

Why did the FDA choose "a more moderate approach" (Fortin 113)?

Quotation that is itself a question

Fortin begins with a key question: "Why do we have food laws?" (3).

Long quotation

Hilts argues that Americans have faith in the FDA:

> The Roper Organization has tracked the FDA and government issues consistently, and found that among all government agencies, the FDA has been among the most popular, and routinely number one among regulatory agencies. (295)

NOTE: For a quotation of more than four typed lines, indent the quoted words, do not use quotation marks, and place the parenthetical citation outside of the final punctuation.

49c Use signal phrases to integrate sources.

When you include a paraphrase, summary, or direct quotation of another writer's work in your paper, prepare your readers for it with introductory words called a *signal phrase*. A signal phrase usually names the author of the source, provides some context for the source material — such as the author's credentials — and helps readers distinguish your ideas from those of the source.

When you write a signal phrase, choose a verb that fits with the way you are using the source. Are you, for example, using the source to support a claim or refute an argument? The signal phrase you choose shows readers how you want them to think about the source.

WEAK VERB	Lorine Goodwin, a food historian, says, "..."
STRONGER VERB (MLA)	Lorine Goodwin, a food historian, rejects the claim: "..."
STRONGER VERB (APA)	Lorine Goodwin, a food historian, has rejected the claim: "..."

NOTE: MLA style calls for verbs in the present or present perfect tense (*argues*, *has argued*) to introduce source material unless you include a date that specifies the time of the original author's writing. APA style calls for using verbs in the past tense or present perfect tense (*explained*, *has explained*) to introduce source material. In APA style, use the present tense only for discussing the applications or effects of your own results (*the data suggest*) or knowledge that has been clearly established (*researchers agree*). The examples in this section are in MLA style.

Using signal phrases in MLA papers

To avoid monotony, try to vary both the language and the placement of your signal phrases.

Model signal phrases

Michael Pollan, who has written extensively about Americans' unhealthy eating habits, emphasizes that . . .

As health policy experts Mello and colleagues point out, ". . ."

Marion Nestle, New York University professor of nutrition and public health, notes, ". . ."

Bioethicist David Resnik acknowledges that his argument . . .

In response to critics, Conly offers a persuasive counterargument: ". . ."

Verbs in signal phrases

acknowledges	comments	endorses	points out
adds	compares	explains	reasons
admits	confirms	grants	refutes
agrees	contends	illustrates	rejects
argues	declares	implies	reports
asserts	denies	insists	responds
believes	disputes	notes	suggests
claims	emphasizes	observes	writes

Using signal phrases in APA papers

To avoid monotony, try to vary both the language and the placement of your signal phrases.

Model signal phrases

In the words of Mitra (2013), ". . ."

Bell (2010) has noted that . . .

USING SIGNAL PHRASES IN APA PAPERS (*cont.*)

Donista-Schmidt and Zuzovsky (2014) pointed out that . . .

". . . ," claimed Çubukçu (2012, Introduction section).

Horn and Staker (2011) have offered a compelling argument for this view: ". . ."

In a recent study, Sharon et al. (2019) found that ". . ."

Verbs in signal phrases

admitted	contended	pointed out
agreed	declared	reasoned
argued	denied	refuted
asserted	emphasized	rejected
believed	explained	reported
claimed	insisted	responded
compared	noted	suggested
confirmed	observed	wrote

Marking boundaries

Readers need to move smoothly from your words to the words of a source. Avoid dropping a quotation into the text without warning. Provide a clear signal phrase, including at least the author's name, to indicate the boundary between your words and the source's words. The signal phrase is highlighted in the second example.

DROPPED QUOTATION

Laws designed to prevent chronic disease by promoting healthier food and beverage consumption also have potential economic benefits. "[A] 1% reduction in the intake of saturated fat across the population would prevent more than 30,000 cases of coronary heart disease annually and would save more than a billion dollars in health care costs" (Nestle 7).

QUOTATION WITH SIGNAL PHRASE

Laws designed to prevent chronic disease by promoting healthier food and beverage consumption also have potential economic benefits. Marion Nestle, New York University professor of nutrition and public health, notes that "a 1% reduction in the intake of saturated fat across the population would prevent more than 30,000 cases of coronary heart disease annually and would save more than a billion dollars in health care costs" (7).

Establishing authority

The first time you mention a source, include in the signal phrase the author's title, credentials, or experience to help your readers recognize the source's authority and your own credibility (*ethos*) as a responsible researcher who has located reliable sources. The signal phrases are highlighted in the examples below.

SOURCE WITH NO CREDENTIALS

Michael Pollan notes that "[t]he Centers for Disease Control estimates that fully three quarters of US health care spending goes to treat chronic diseases, most of which are preventable and linked to diet: heart disease, stroke, type 2 diabetes, and at least a third of all cancers."

SOURCE WITH CREDENTIALS

Journalist Michael Pollan, who has written extensively about Americans' unhealthy eating habits, notes that "[t]he Centers for Disease Control estimates that fully three quarters of US health care spending goes to treat chronic diseases, most of which are preventable and linked to diet: heart disease, stroke, type 2 diabetes, and at least a third of all cancers."

Introducing summaries and paraphrases

Introduce most summaries and paraphrases with a signal phrase that names the author and places the material in the context of your argument. Readers will then understand that everything between the signal phrase and the parenthetical citation summarizes or paraphrases the cited source. Without the signal phrase, readers might think that only the quotation at the end is being cited, when the whole paragraph is based on the source.

> To improve public health, advocates such as Bowdoin College philosophy professor Sarah Conly contend that it is the government's duty to prevent people from making harmful choices whenever feasible and whenever public benefits outweigh the costs. In response to critics who claim that laws aimed at stopping us from eating whatever we want are an assault on our freedom of choice, Conly asserts that "laws aren't designed for each one of us individually."

There are times, however, when a summary or a paraphrase does not require a signal phrase naming the author. When the context makes clear where the cited material begins, you may omit the signal phrase and include the author's last name in parentheses.

> According to a nationwide poll, seventy-five percent of Americans are opposed to laws that restrict or put limitations on access to healthy foods (Neergaard and Agiesta).

Integrating statistics and other facts

When you cite a statistic or another specific fact, a signal phrase is often not necessary. Readers usually will understand that the citation refers to the statistic or fact and not the whole paragraph.

> Seat belt use saved an average of more than fourteen thousand lives per year in the United States between 2000 and 2010 (United States, Department of Transportation 231).

Putting source material in context

Readers should not have to guess why source material appears in your paper. A signal phrase can help you connect your own ideas and those of another writer by clarifying how the source will contribute to your paper.

If you use another writer's words, you must explain how they relate to your argument. Quotations don't speak for themselves; you must create a context for readers. Sandwich each quotation between sentences of your own, introducing the quotation with a signal phrase and following it with comments that link the quotation to your paper's argument.

QUOTATION WITH EFFECTIVE CONTEXT (QUOTATION SANDWICH)

Quotation is introduced with a signal phrase naming the author.

Long quotation is set off from the text; quotation marks are omitted.

Analysis connects the source to the student's argument.

>   In response to critics who claim that laws aimed at stopping us from eating whatever we want are an assault on our freedom of choice, Conly offers a persuasive counterargument
>
>   [L]aws aren't designed for each one of us individually. Some of us can drive safely at 90 miles per hour, but we're bound by the same laws as the people who can't, because individual speeding laws aren't practical. Giving up a little liberty is something we agree to when we agree to live in a democratic society that is governed by laws.
>
>   As Conly suggests, it's important to move from either/or thinking (either we have complete freedom of choice *or* we have government regulations and lose our freedom) to seeing health as a matter of public good, not individual liberty.

Using sentence guides to integrate sources

You build your credibility (*ethos*) by accurately representing the views of others and by integrating their ideas into your paper. An important way to present the views of others before agreeing or disagreeing with them is to use sentence guides. These guides act as academic sentence starters; they show you how to use signal phrases in sentences to make clear to your reader whose ideas you're presenting—your own or those you have encountered in a source.

Presenting others' ideas. The following language will help you demonstrate your understanding of a source by summarizing the views or arguments of its author:

X argues that _____.

X and Y emphasize the need for _____.

$\rightarrow$

USING SENTENCE GUIDES TO INTEGRATE SOURCES (*cont.*)

Presenting direct quotations. To introduce the exact words of a source because their accuracy and authority are important for your argument, you might try phrases like these:

X describes the problem this way: "_____."

Y argues in favor of the policy, pointing out that "_____."

Presenting alternative ideas. At times you will have to synthesize the ideas of multiple sources before you introduce your own ideas:

While X and Y have asked an important question, Z suggests that we should be asking a different question: _____.

X has argued that Y's research findings rest upon the questionable assumption that _____.

Presenting your own ideas by agreeing or extending. You may agree with the author of a source but want to add your own voice to extend the point or go deeper:

X's argument is convincing because _____.

Y claimed that _____. But isn't it also true that _____?

Presenting your own ideas by disagreeing and questioning. College writing assignments encourage you to show your understanding of a subject but also to question or challenge ideas and conclusions about the subject:

X's claims about _____ are misguided.

Y insists that _____, but perhaps she is asking the wrong question.

NOTE: The examples in this box are shown in MLA style. If you were writing in APA style, you would include the year of publication after the source's name and typically use past tense or present perfect tense (*emphasized* or *has emphasized*).

Presenting and countering objections to your argument. To anticipate objections that readers might make, try the following sentence guides:

Not everyone will endorse this argument; some may argue instead that

_____.

Some will object to this proposal on the grounds that _____.

49d Synthesize sources.

When you synthesize multiple sources in a research paper, you create a conversation about your research topic. You show readers that your argument is based on your analysis and integration of ideas and is not just a series of quotations and paraphrases strung together. Your synthesis will show how your sources relate to one another; one source may support, extend, or counter the ideas of another. Not every source has to "speak" to another in a research paper, but readers should understand how each source functions in your argument.

Considering how sources relate to your argument

Before you integrate sources and show readers how they relate to one another, consider how each source might contribute to your argument. As student writer Sophie Harba became more informed about her research topic, she asked herself these questions:

- What have I learned from my sources?
- Which sources might support my ideas or illustrate the points I want to make?
- What counterarguments do I need to address to strengthen my position?

She annotated a passage from one of her sources—a nonprofit group's assertion that our choices about food are skewed by marketing messages.

Could use this to counter the point about personal choice in Mello.

STUDENT NOTES ON THE ORIGINAL SOURCE

The food and beverage industry spends approximately $2 billion per year marketing to children.

—"Facts on Junk Food"

Placing sources in conversation

You can show readers how the ideas of one source relate to those of another by connecting and analyzing the ideas in your own voice. After all, you've done the research and thought through the issues, so you should control the conversation. The thread of your argument should be easy to identify and to understand, with or without your sources.

SAMPLE SYNTHESIS (MLA STYLE)

Student writer Sophie Harba sets up her synthesis with a question.

Signal phrase indicates how the source contributes to Harba's argument and shows that the idea that follows is not her own.

Harba interprets a paraphrased source.

Harba uses a source to support her counter-argument.

Why is the public largely resistant to laws that would limit unhealthy choices or penalize those choices with so-called fat taxes? Many consumers and civil rights advocates find such laws to be an unreasonable restriction on individual freedom of choice. As health policy experts Mello and others point out, opposition to food and beverage regulation is similar to the opposition to early tobacco legislation: the public views the issue as one of personal responsibility rather than one requiring government intervention (2602). In other words, if a person eats unhealthy food and becomes ill as a result, that is his or her choice. But those who favor legislation claim that freedom of choice is a myth because of the strong influence of food and beverage industry marketing on consumers' dietary habits. According to one nonprofit health advocacy group, food and beverage companies spend roughly two billion dollars per year marketing directly to children. As a result, kids see nearly four thousand ads per year encouraging them to eat unhealthy food and drinks ("Facts"). As was the case with antismoking laws passed in recent decades, taxes and legal restrictions on junk food sales could help to counter the strong marketing messages that promote unhealthy products.

Student writer

Source 1

Student writer

Source 2

Student writer

Harba extends the argument and follows it with an interpretive comment.

The United States has a history of state and local public health laws that have successfully promoted a particular behavior by punishing an undesirable behavior. The decline in tobacco use as a result of antismoking taxes and laws is perhaps the most obvious example. Another example is legislation requiring the use of seat belts, which have significantly reduced fatalities in car crashes.

→

SAMPLE SYNTHESIS (MLA STYLE) *(cont.)*

One government agency reports that seat belt use saved | Source 3
an average of more than fourteen thousand lives per year in
the United States between 2000 and 2010 (United States,
Department of Transportation 231). Perhaps seat belt laws
have public support because the cost of wearing a seat | Student writer
belt is small, especially when compared with the benefit
of saving fourteen thousand lives per year.

In this synthesis, Harba uses her own analysis to shape the conversation among her sources. She does not simply string quotations together or allow them to overwhelm her writing. She guides readers through a conversation about laws that could promote and have promoted public health. She finds points of intersection among her sources, acknowledges the contributions of others, and shows readers, in her own voice, how the sources support her argument.

To see an example of a synthesis paragraph in an APA paper, see page 408. Look for the marginal annotation that includes the words "synthesis paragraph."

When synthesizing sources, use the following guidelines:

- Be sure your sources address your research question.

- Think about how your sources converse with each other. How do they support, extend, contextualize, or counter each other?

- Be sure that your synthesis is more than a series of quotations and paraphrases strung together. You can do this by connecting and analyzing sources in your own voice.

- Ask: Is my argument easy to identify and to understand, with or without my sources? The answer should be yes.

50 Documenting sources in MLA style

In English and other humanities classes, you may be asked to use the MLA (Modern Language Association) system for documenting sources, which is set forth in the *MLA Handbook*, 9th edition (MLA, 2021).

MLA recommends in-text citations that refer readers to a list of works cited. A typical in-text citation names the author of the source, often in a signal phrase, and gives a page number in parentheses. At the end of the paper, the list of works cited provides publication information for each cited source; the list is alphabetized by authors' last names (or by titles for works without authors). There is a direct connection between the in-text citation and the alphabetical listing. In the following example, that connection is underlined.

IN-TEXT CITATION

Bioethicist David Resnik emphasizes that such policies, despite their potential to make our society healthier, "open the door to excessive government control over food, which could restrict dietary choices, interfere with cultural, ethnic, and religious traditions, and exacerbate socioeconomic inequalities" (31).

ENTRY IN THE LIST OF WORKS CITED

Resnik, David. "Trans Fat Bans and Human Freedom." *The American Journal of Bioethics*, vol. 10, no. 3, Mar. 2010, pp. 27–32.

For a list of works cited that includes this entry, see 51b.

50a MLA in-text citations

MLA in-text citations are made with a combination of signal phrases and parenthetical references. A signal phrase introduces information taken from a source (a quotation, summary, paraphrase, or fact); usually the signal phrase includes the author's name. The parenthetical citation comes after the cited material, often at the end of the sentence. It includes at least a page number (except for unpaginated sources, such as those found on the web, or sources only one page long). In the models in this section, certain elements of the citation are underlined.

IN-TEXT CITATION

Resnik acknowledges that his argument relies on "slippery slope" thinking, but he insists that "social and political pressures" regarding food regulation make his concerns valid (31).

List of MLA in-text citation models

List of MLA works cited models

List of MLA works cited models (*cont.*)

Readers can look up the author's last name in the alphabetized list of works cited, where they will learn the work's title and other publication information. If readers decide to consult the source, the page number will take them straight to the cited passage.

General guidelines for signal phrases and page numbers

Items 1–5 explain how the MLA system usually works for all sources — in print, on the web, in other media, and with or without authors and page numbers. Items 6–25 give variations on the basic guidelines.

1. Author named in a signal phrase   Ordinarily, introduce the material being cited with a signal phrase that includes the author's name. The first time you cite a source, include the author's full name in the signal phrase. In addition to preparing readers for the source, the signal phrase allows you to keep the parenthetical citation with the quotation's page number brief.

> According to Lorine Goodwin, a food historian, nineteenth-century reformers who sought to purify the food supply were called "fanatics" and "radicals" by critics who argued that consumers should be free to buy and eat what they want (77).

Notice that the period follows the parenthetical citation. When a quotation ends with a question mark or an exclamation point, leave the end punctuation inside the quotation mark and add a period after the parenthetical citation.

> Burgess asks a critical question: "How can we think differently about food labeling?" (51).

2. Author named in parentheses   If you do not give the author's name in a signal phrase, put the last name in parentheses with the page number (if the source has one). Use no punctuation between the name and the page number: (Moran 351).

> According to a nationwide poll, seventy-five percent of Americans are opposed to laws that restrict or put limitations on access to unhealthy foods (Neergaard and Agiesta).

3. Author unknown   If a source has no author, the works cited entry will begin with the title. In your in-text citation, either use the complete title in a signal phrase or use a short form of the title in parentheses. Titles of books and other long works are italicized; titles of articles and other short works are put in quotation marks.

> As a result, kids see nearly four thousand ads per year encouraging them to eat unhealthy food and drinks ("Facts").

NOTE: If the author is a corporation or a government agency, see items 8 and 16.

4. Source with no page numbers   Do not include a page number if a source does not provide page numbers. (When the pages of a web source are stable, as in PDF files, supply a page number in your in-text citation.)

> Michael Pollan points out that "cheap food" actually has "significant costs — to the environment, to public health, to the public purse, even to the culture."

If a source has numbered paragraphs or sections, use "par." (or "pars.") or "sec." (or "secs.") in the parentheses: (Smith, par. 4). Notice that a comma follows the author's name. If you cite an audiovisual source (such as an online video), include a time stamp for the material you have quoted or paraphrased: (00:08:31–40).

5. One-page source   If a source is only one page long, do not include the page number in your in-text citation. You should, however, include the page number in your works cited list entry.

IN-TEXT CITATION FOR ONE-PAGE SOURCE

> Sarah Conly uses John Stuart Mill's "harm principle" to argue that citizens need their government to intervene to prevent them from taking harmful actions — such as driving too fast or buying unhealthy foods — out of ignorance of the harm they can do.

ENTRY IN THE WORKS CITED LIST

> Conly, Sarah. "Three Cheers for the Nanny State." *The New York Times*, 25 Mar. 2013, p. A23.

Variations on the general guidelines

This section describes the MLA guidelines for handling a variety of situations not covered in items 1–5.

6. Two authors Name both authors in a signal phrase, as in the following example, or include their last names in the parenthetical citation: (Gostin and Gostin 214).

> As legal scholars Gostin and Gostin explain, "[I]nterventions that do not pose a truly significant burden on individual liberty" are justified if they "go a long way towards safeguarding the health and well-being of the populace" (214).

7. Three or more authors In a parenthetical citation, give the first author's name followed by "et al." (Latin for "and others"). In a signal phrase, give the first author's name followed by a phrase such as "and colleagues."

> The clinical trials were extended for two years, and only after results were reviewed by an independent panel did the researchers publish their findings (Blaine et al. 35).

> Researchers Blaine and colleagues note that clinical trial results were reviewed by an independent panel (35).

8. Organization as author When the author is a corporation or an organization, name that author either in the signal phrase or in the parenthetical citation. (For a government agency as author, see item 16.)

> The American Diabetes Association estimates that the cost of diagnosed diabetes in the United States in 2012 was $245 billion.

In the list of works cited, the American Diabetes Association is treated as the author and alphabetized under *A*. When you give the organization name in the text, spell out the full name; when you use it in parentheses, shorten the name to the first noun and any preceding adjectives, removing any articles (*A, An, The*).

> The cost of diagnosed diabetes in the United States in 2012 has been estimated at $245 billion (American Diabetes).

9. Authors with the same last name If your list of works cited includes works by two or more authors with the same last name, include the author's first name in the signal phrase or first initial in the parentheses.

> One approach to the problem is to introduce nutrition literacy at the elementary level in public schools (E. Chen 15).

10. Two or more works by the same author In addition to the author's name, mention the title of the work in the signal phrase or include a short version of the title in the parentheses.

> The American Diabetes Association tracks trends in diabetes across age groups. In 2012, more than 200,000 children and adolescents had diabetes ("Fast Facts"). Because of an expected dramatic increase in diabetes in young people over the next forty years, the association encourages "strategies for implementing child-hood obesity prevention programs and primary prevention programs for youth at risk of developing type 2 diabetes" ("Number").

Titles of articles and other short works are placed in quotation marks; titles of books and other long works are italicized.

In the rare case when both the author's name and a short title must be given in parentheses, separate them with a comma.

> Researchers have estimated that "the number of youth with type 2 [diabetes] could quadruple and the number with type 1 could triple" by 2050 (American Diabetes, "Number").

11. Two or more works in one citation To cite more than one source in the parentheses, list the authors (or titles) in alphabetical order and separate them with semicolons.

> The prevalence of early-onset type 2 diabetes has been well documented (Finn 68; Sharma 2037; Whitaker 118).

12. Repeated citations from the same source If you cite a source more than once in a paragraph, you may omit the author's name after the first mention as long as it is clear that you are still referring to the same source. Later citations may include only the page number.

> Family expectations are at the heart of *Everything I Never Told You*, a debut novel in which a daughter shrinks from a mother who forces her to read books on science and medicine "to inspire her, to show her what she could accomplish" (Ng 73). But teenage Lydia commits herself to standing up to her overbearing mother, promising that "she will tell her mother: enough" (274).

13. Encyclopedia or dictionary entry When an encyclopedia or dictionary entry does not have an author, include the entry and give the page number on which the entry may be found.

> The word *crocodile* has a complex etymology ("Crocodile" 139).

14. Entire work Use the author's name in a signal phrase or a parenthetical citation. There is no need to use a page number.

> Pollan explores the issues surrounding food production and consumption from a political angle.

15. Selection in an anthology or a collection Put the name of the author of the selection (not the editor of the anthology) in the signal phrase or the parentheses.

> In "How to Write Iranian-America, or the Last Essay," Khakpour details degrading experiences with English language instructors "who look to you with the shine of love but the stench of pity" (3).

In the list of works cited, the work is alphabetized under Khakpour, the author of the essay, not under the name of the editor of the anthology. (See item 27 in 50b.)

16. Government document In a signal phrase, include the name of the agency or governing body as given in the works cited list. In a parenthetical citation, <u>shorten the name</u>.

> In fact, the amount of money the United States spends to treat chronic illnesses is increasing so rapidly that the Centers for Disease Control has labeled chronic disease "the public health challenge of the 21st century" (<u>National Center</u> 1).

If you cite more than one agency or department from the same government in your essay, you may choose to standardize the names by beginning with the name of the government (see item 55 in 50b). In that case, when shortening the names, give enough of each one to differentiate the authors: (United States, Department of Transportation); (United States, Environmental Protection). See 51b for an essay that uses standardized government author names.

17. Historical document For a historical document such as a constitution, provide the <u>document title</u>, neither italicized nor in quotation marks, along with relevant <u>article and section numbers</u>. In parenthetical citations, use abbreviations such as "art." and "sec."

> While the <u>Constitution</u> provides for the formation of new states (<u>art. 4, sec. 3</u>), it does not explicitly allow or prohibit the secession of states.

Constitutions are treated differently in the works cited list. See item 56 in 50b.

18. Legal source For a legislative act (law) or court case, name the <u>act or case</u> either in a signal phrase or in parentheses. Italicize the names of cases but not the names of acts. (See also items 57 and 58 in 50b.)

> The <u>CARES Act</u> of 2020 provided loans for small businesses.

> *Dred Scott v. Sandford*, which concluded that both free and enslaved Black people could not be citizens of the United States, may have been the US Supreme Court's worst decision.

19. Visual such as a table, a chart, or another graphic To cite a visual that has a figure number in the original source, use the abbreviation "fig." and the number in place of a page number in your parenthetical citation: (Manning, fig. 4). If you refer to the figure in your text, spell out the word "figure."

To cite a visual that appears in a print source without a figure number, use the visual's title or a description in your text and cite the author and page number as for any other source. For a visual not in a print source, identify the visual in your text and then in parentheses use the first element in the works cited entry: the artist's or photographer's name or the title of the work. (See items 49–53 in 50b.)

> Photographs such as *Woman Aircraft Worker* (Bransby) and *Women Welders* (Parks) demonstrate the US government's attempt to document the contributions of women during World War II.

20. Personal communication and social media Cite a personal letter, a personal interview, an email message, or a social media post by the name listed in the works cited entry, as you would for any other source. Identify the type of source in your text if you think it is necessary for clarity. (See items 11 and 59–61 in 50b.)

21. Web source Your in-text citation for a source from the web should follow the same guidelines as for other sources. If the source lacks page numbers but has numbered paragraphs, sections, or divisions, use those numbers with the appropriate abbreviation in your parenthetical citation: "par.," "sec.," "ch.," "pt.," and so on. Do not add such numbers if the source itself does not use them; simply give the author or title in your in-text citation.

> Sanjay Gupta, CNN chief medical correspondent, explains that "limited access to fresh, affordable, healthy food" is one of America's most pressing health problems.

22. Indirect source (source quoted in another source) When a writer's or a speaker's quoted words appear in a source written by someone else, begin the parenthetical citation with the abbreviation "qtd. in." In the following example, Gostin and Gostin are the authors of the source given in the works cited list; their work contains a quotation by Beauchamp.

> Public health researcher Dan Beauchamp has said that "public health practices are communal in nature, and concerned with the well-being of the community as a whole and not just the well-being of any particular person" (qtd. in Gostin and Gostin 217).

Literary works and sacred texts

Literary works and sacred texts are usually available in a variety of editions. Your list of works cited will specify which edition you are using, and your in-text citation will usually consist of a page number from the edition you consulted as for any other work. When possible, give additional information — such as book parts, play divisions, or line numbers — so that readers can locate the cited passage in any edition of the work.

23. Literary work or play without line numbers   If a literary work has numbered divisions, include the page number followed by a semicolon and the section, part, or chapter number(s). For a play without line numbers, include the act and/or scene numbers after the page number: (37; sc. 1).

> In utter despair, Dostoyevsky's character Mitya wonders aloud about the "terrible tragedies realism inflicts on people" (376; bk. 8, ch. 2).

24. Verse play or poem   For verse plays, give act, scene, and line numbers that can be located in any edition of the work. Use Arabic numerals and separate the numbers with periods.

> In Shakespeare's *King Lear*, Gloucester learns a profound lesson from a tragic experience: "A man may see how this world goes / with no eyes" (4.2.148–49).

For a poem, cite the part, stanza, and line numbers, if it has them, separated by periods.

> The Green Knight claims to approach King Arthur's court "because the praise of you, prince, is puffed so high, / And your manor and your men are considered so magnificent" (1.12.258–59).

24. Verse play or poem (*cont.*)

For poems that are not divided into numbered parts or stanzas, use line numbers. For the first citation, use the word "lines": (lines 5–8). Thereafter use just the numbers: (12–13).

25. Sacred text The first time you cite the work, give the title of the work as in the works cited entry, followed by the book and then the chapter and verse (or their equivalent), separated with periods. Common abbreviations for books of the Bible are acceptable in a parenthetical citation. Omit the work's title from the parentheses in all citations after the first.

> Consider the words of Solomon: "If your enemy is hungry, give him bread to eat; and if he is thirsty, give him water to drink" (*Oxford Annotated Bible*, Prov. 25.21).

The title of a sacred work is italicized when it refers to a specific edition of the work, as in the preceding example. If you refer to the book in a general sense in your text, neither italicize it nor put it in quotation marks.

> The Bible and the Qur'an provide allegories that help readers understand how to lead a moral life.

50b MLA list of works cited

Your list of works cited, which you will place at the end of your paper, guides readers to the sources you have quoted, summarized, and paraphrased. Usually, you will provide basic information common to most sources, such as author, title, publisher, publication date, and location (page numbers or URL, for example).

Throughout this section of the book, you'll find models organized by type (article, book, website, multimedia source, and so on). But even if you aren't sure exactly what type of source you have (*Is this a blog post or an article?*), you can follow two general principles:

Gather key publication information about the source — the citation elements.

Organize the basic information about the source using what MLA calls "containers."

The author's name and the title of the work are needed for many (though not all) sources and are the first two pieces of information to gather. For the remaining pieces of information, you might find it helpful to think about whether the work is contained within one or more larger works. Some sources are self-contained. Others are nested in larger containers. The chart below illustrates different kinds of sources and their containers.

☐	**SELF-CONTAINED**	a *book* a *film*
☐	**ONE CONTAINER**	an *article* in a scholarly journal a *poem* in a collection of poetry a *video* posted to YouTube a *fact sheet* on a government website
☐	**TWO CONTAINERS**	an *article* in a journal within a database (JSTOR etc.) an *episode* from a TV series within a streaming service (Netflix etc.)

Keep in mind that most sources won't include all of the following pieces of information, so gather only that information that is relevant to and available for your source.

Author.

Title of source.

Title of container,

Contributors,

Version (or edition),

Number(s),

Publisher,

Date,

Location (page numbers, URL, DOI, etc.).

If there is a second container, gather the same information for it (if available).

Title of container 2,

Contributors,

Version (or edition),

Number(s),

Publisher,

Date,

Location.

WORKS CITED ENTRY, ONE CONTAINER (SELECTION IN AN ANTHOLOGY)

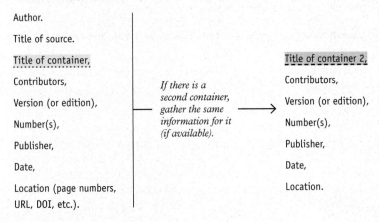

·················· container 1 ··············

author   title of selection   title of collection

Smith, Zadie. "Speaking in Tongues." *The Glorious American Essay: One*

Hundred Essays from Colonial Times to the Present, edited by

contributor   publisher   year   location (pages)

Phillip Lopate, Pantheon, 2020, pp. 886–900.

WORKS CITED ENTRY, TWO CONTAINERS (ARTICLE IN A JOURNAL IN A DATABASE)

author   title of article

Carey, Craig. "Realism and Recording: Remixing Literary and Media History."

·················· container 1 ··················

journal title   volume, issue   date   location (pages)

American Literary Realism, vol. 53, no. 3, spring 2021, pp. 198–203.

·············· container 2 ··············

database title   location (DOI)

JSTOR, https://doi.org/10.5406/amerlitereal.53.3.0198.

Once you've gathered the relevant and available information about a source, you will organize the elements using the list on the previous page as your guideline. Note the punctuation after each element in that list. In this section you will find many examples of how elements and containers are combined to create works cited entries.

General guidelines for the works cited list

In the list of works cited, include only sources that you have quoted, summarized, or paraphrased in your paper. MLA's guidelines apply to a wide variety of sources. You can adapt the guidelines and models in this section to source types you encounter in your research.

Gathering information and organizing entries

A works cited entry typically includes the following elements:

- The author (if a work has one)
- The title of the source
- The title of the larger work in which the source is located, if it is contained in a larger work (MLA calls the larger work a "container"—a collection, a journal, a magazine, a website, and so on)
- As much of the following information as is available about the source and the container:

  Contributor(s), such as editor, translator, director, or performer

  Version or edition

  Number(s), such as issue or episode

  Publisher

  Date of publication

  Location of the source, such as page numbers, URL, or DOI

Not all sources will require every element. See specific models in this section for more details.

GENERAL GUIDELINES FOR THE WORKS CITED LIST (*cont.*)

Authors

- Arrange the list alphabetically either by authors' last names or by titles for works with no authors.

- For the first author in a works cited entry, list the last name first, followed by a comma and the first name. Put a second author's name in typical order (first name followed by last name); separate the two authors' names with "and." For three or more authors, use "et al." after the first author's name.

- For organization authors, list the name in the normal order. If the name begins with an article (*A, An*, or *The*), omit it.

- Spell out "editor," "translator," "edited by," and so on.

Titles

- In titles of works, capitalize all words except articles (*a, an, the*), prepositions, coordinating conjunctions, and the *to* in infinitives — unless the word is first or last in the title or subtitle.

- Use quotation marks for titles of articles and other short works. Place single quotation marks around a quoted term or a title of a short work that appears within an article title; italicize a term or title that is normally italicized.

- Italicize titles of books and other long works, including websites. If a book title contains another title that is normally italicized, neither italicize the internal title nor place it in quotation marks. If the title within the title is normally put in quotation marks, retain the quotation marks and italicize the entire book title.

Publication information

- Use the complete version of publishers' names, except for terms such as *Inc.* and *Co.*; retain terms such as *Books* and *Press*. For university publishers, use *U* and *P* for *University* and *Press*.

- For a book, take the name of the publisher from the title page (or from the copyright page if it is not on the title page). For a website, the publisher might be at the bottom of a page or on the "About" page. If a work has two or more publishers, separate the names with a forward slash.

- If the title of a website and the publisher's name are the same or similar, give the title of the site and omit the publisher.

GENERAL GUIDELINES FOR THE WORKS CITED LIST (*cont.*)

Dates

- For a book, give the most recent year found on the title page or the copyright page.

- For an article from a periodical such as a newspaper or a journal, use the most specific date given, whether it is a month and year, a full date, or a season (*spring 2022*).

- For a web source, use the posting date, the copyright date, or the most recent update date. Use the complete date as listed in the source. If a web source has no date, give your date of access at the end: Accessed 24 Feb. 2022.

- Abbreviate all months except May, June, and July, and give the date in inverted form: 13 Sept. 2020.

Page numbers

- For most articles and other short works, give page numbers when they are available, preceded by "pp." (or "p." for only one page).

- Do not use the page numbers from a printout of a web source.

- If a short work appears on nonconsecutive pages, give the number of the first page followed by a plus sign: 35+.

URLs and DOIs

- Give a DOI (digital object identifier) if a source has one. Include the protocol and host (*https://doi.org/*).

- If a source does not have a DOI, include a permalink if possible. Copy the permalink provided by the website.

- If a source does not have a permalink or a DOI, include the full URL for the source. Copy the URL directly from your browser. You may remove the protocol (*http://* or *https://*) if you do not need to provide live links for your readers. Do not insert any line breaks or hyphens into the URL.

- If a URL is longer than three lines in the list of works cited, you may shorten it, leaving at least the website host (for example, *cnn.com* or *www.usda.gov*) in the entry.

General guidelines for listing authors

The formatting of authors' names in items 1–11 applies to all sources — books, articles, websites — in print, on the web, or in other media. For more models of specific source types, see items 12–62.

1. Single author

Wilkerson, Isabel. *Caste: The Origins of Our Discontents*. Random House, 2020.

2. Two authors
Put the first author's last name first; present the second author's name in typical order.

Gourevitch, Philip, and Errol Morris. *Standard Operating Procedure*. Penguin Books, 2008.

3. Three or more authors
Name the first author followed by "et al." (Latin for "and others"). For in-text citations, see item 7 in 50a.

Cunningham, Stewart, et al. *Media Economics*. Palgrave Macmillan, 2015.

4. Organization or company as author
Begin with the organization name, omitting any initial article (*A*, *An*, or *The*). Your in-text citation also should treat the organization as the author (see item 8 in 50a).

Human Rights Watch. *World Report of 2015: Events of 2014*. Seven Stories Press, 2015.

5. No author listed
Begin the entry with the work's title. Alphabetize by the first word in the title (ignoring, but not omitting, the articles *The*, *A*, or *An*).

"CEO Activism in America Is Risky Business." *The Economist*, 17 Apr. 2021, www.economist.com/business/2021/04/14/ceo-activism-in-america-is-risky -business.

NOTE: In web sources, often the author's name is available but is not easy to find. It may appear at the end of a web page, in tiny print, or on another page of the site, such as the home page. Also, an organization or a government may be the author (see items 4 and 55).

6. Two or more works by the same author or group of authors Alphabetize the works by title (ignoring the article *A*, *An*, or *The* at the beginning of a title). Use the author's name or authors' names for the first entry; for subsequent entries, use three hyphens or dashes and a period. The hyphens or dashes must stand for exactly the same name or names, in the same order, that appear in the first entry.

Coates, Ta-Nehisi. *Between the World and Me*. Spiegel and Grau, 2015.

---. *We Were Eight Years in Power: An American Tragedy*. One World, 2018.

Eaton-Robb, Pat, and Susan Haigh. "Pandemic May Lead to Long-Term Changes
  in School Calendar." *AP News*, 15 Apr. 2021, apnews.com/article
  /pandemics-connecticut-ned-lamont-975d41076ae6b985030c133614685f33.

---. "Rock Star Van Zandt Helping Connecticut Students Re-engage." *AP News*,
  20 Apr. 2021, apnews.com/article/health-music-education-arts-and
  -entertainment-entertainment-5b038c218b30863d76031134db46fa5d.

7. Editor or translator Begin with the editor's or translator's name. After the name, add "editor" or "translator." Use "editors" or "translators" for two or more (see also items 2 and 3 for how to handle multiple contributors).

Horner, Avril, and Anne Rowe, editors. *Living on Paper: Letters from Iris Murdoch,*
  1934–1995. Princeton UP, 2016.

8. Author with editor or translator Begin with the name of the author. Place the editor's or translator's name after the title.

Ullmann, Regina. *The Country Road: Stories*. Translated by Kurt Beals, New Directions
  Publishing, 2015.

9. Graphic narrative or other illustrated work   If a work has both an author and an illustrator, the order in your citation will depend on which contributor's work you emphasize in your paper. If there are multiple contributors but you are not discussing a specific contributor's work in your essay, you may begin with the title. If the author and illustrator are the same person, cite as you would a book with one author (see items 1 and 23).

Gaiman, Neil. *The Sandman: Overture*. Illustrated by J. H. William III, DC Comics, 2015.

Martínez, Hugo, illustrator. *Wake: The Hidden History of Women-Led Slave Revolts*.
    By Rebecca Hall, Simon and Schuster, 2021.

10. Author using a pseudonym (pen name)   Use the author's name as it appears in the source, followed by the author's real name in brackets, if you know it. Alternatively, if the author's real name is more well-known, you may start with that name, followed by *published as*, italicized, and the pen name in brackets.

North, Claire [Catherine Webb]. *The Pursuit of William Abbey*. Orbit, 2019.

Franklin, Benjamin [*published as* Richard Saunders]. "Poor Richard, 1773." 1773.
    Founders Online, National Archives, founders.archives.gov/documents
    /Franklin/01-01-02-0093.

11. Screen name or social media account   Start with the account display name, followed by the screen name or handle (if available) in brackets. If the account name is a first and last name, as in the first example, invert it. If the account name and handle are very similar (for example, ACLU SoCal and @ACLU_SoCal), you may omit the handle.

Gay, Roxane [@rgay]. "The shortness of cultural memory is always astonishing."
    Twitter, 25 Apr. 2021, twitter.com/rgay/status/1386507940601995274?.

Partlycloudy. Comment on "Is This the End?" by James Atlas. *The New York Times*,
    25 Nov. 2012, nyti.ms/3nPkY5j#permid=7726753.

Answer the basic question "Who is the author?"

Problem: Sometimes when you need to cite a source, it's not clear who the author is. This is especially true for sources on the web and other nonprint sources, which may have been created by one person and uploaded by a different person or an organization. Whom do you cite as the author in such a case? How do you determine who *is* the author?

Example: The video "Surfing the Web on the Job" (see below) was uploaded to YouTube by CBSNewsOnline. Is the person or organization that uploads the video the author of the video? Not necessarily.

Surfing the Web on The Job

CBSNewsOnline · 42,491 videos

▶ Subscribe 85,736

Uploaded on Nov 12, 2009
As the Internet continues to emerge as a critical facet of everyday life, CBS News' Daniel Sieberg reports that companies are cracking down on employees' personal Web use.

Strategy: After you view or listen to the source a few times, ask yourself whether you can tell who is chiefly responsible for creating the content in the source. It could be an organization. It could be an identifiable individual. This video consists entirely of reporting by Daniel Sieberg, so the author is Sieberg.

Citation: To cite the source, you would use the basic MLA guidelines for a video found on the web (item 41).

author: last name first — title of video — website title — upload information

Sieberg, Daniel. "Surfing the Web on the Job." *YouTube*, uploaded by CBSNewsOnline,

upload date — URL

12 Nov. 2009, www.youtube.com/watch?v=1wLhNwY-enY.

Articles and other short works

12. Basic format for an article or other short work   After the author's name, provide the title of the article, followed by the title of the publication and other publication information.

a. Print

Tilman, David. "Food and Health of a Full Earth." *Daedalus*, vol. 144, no. 4, fall 2015,
   pp. 5–7.

b. Web   Include the article's online location (such as the DOI, permalink, or URL).

Florez, Nina. "Chicago Rally Held in Support of Colombian Protesters."
   NBC 5 Chicago, 9 May 2021, www.nbcchicago.com/news/local/ikiped
   -rallies-held-in-support-of-colombian-protesters/2505612.

c. Database   Include the database title at the end of your citation. If the database provides a DOI or a permalink, use that after the title. Otherwise, provide the URL to the article in the database.

Harris, Ashleigh May, and Nicklas Hållén. "African Street Literature: A Method for
   an Emergent Form beyond World Literature." *Research in African Literatures*,
   vol. 51, no. 2, summer 2020, pp. 1–26. *JSTOR*, https://doi.org/10.2979
   /reseafrilite.51.2.01.

13. Article in a journal   Provide the volume and issue numbers.

a. Print

Matchie, Thomas. "Law versus Love in *The Round House*." *The Midwest Quarterly*,
   vol. 56, no. 4, summer 2015, pp. 353–64.

b. Online journal

McGuire, Meg. "Women, Healing, and Social Community: Cyberfeminist Activities on
   Reddit." *Kairos*, vol. 25, no. 2, spring 2021, ikipe.technorhetoric.net/25.2/topoi
   /mcguire/index.html.

Citation at a glance

Article in an online journal MLA

To cite an article in an online journal in MLA style, include the following elements:

1 Author(s) of article
2 Title and subtitle of article
3 Title of journal
4 Volume and issue numbers

5 Date of publication (including month or season, if any)
6 Page number(s) of article, if given
7 DOI or permalink, if available; otherwise, URL to article

ONLINE JOURNAL ARTICLE

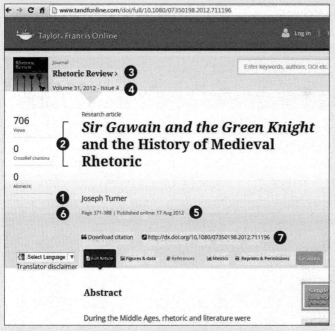

WORKS CITED ENTRY FOR AN ARTICLE IN AN ONLINE JOURNAL

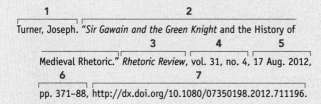

Turner, Joseph. "*Sir Gawain and the Green Knight* and the History of Medieval Rhetoric." *Rhetoric Review*, vol. 31, no. 4, 17 Aug. 2012, pp. 371–88, http://dx.doi.org/10.1080/07350198.2012.711196.

For more on citing online articles in MLA style, see items 12–15.

Citation at a glance

Article from a database MLA

To cite an article from a database in MLA style, include the following elements:

1 Author(s) of article
2 Title and subtitle of article
3 Title of journal, magazine, or newspaper
4 Volume and issue numbers (for journal)
5 Date of publication (including month or season, if any)
6 Page number(s) of article, if any
7 Name of database
8 DOI or permalink, if available; otherwise, URL to article

DATABASE RECORD

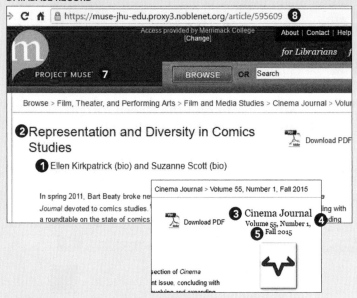

WORKS CITED ENTRY FOR AN ARTICLE FROM A DATABASE

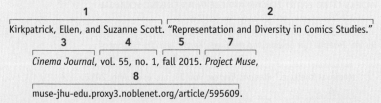

Kirkpatrick, Ellen, and Suzanne Scott. "Representation and Diversity in Comics Studies."
Cinema Journal, vol. 55, no. 1, fall 2015. Project Muse,
muse-jhu-edu.proxy3.noblenet.org/article/595609.

For more on citing articles from a database in MLA style, see items 12 and 13.

13. Article in a journal (*cont.*)

c. Database

Maier, Jessica. "A 'True Likeness': The Renaissance City Portrait." *Renaissance Quarterly*,
vol. 65, no. 3, fall 2012, pp. 711–52. *JSTOR*, https://doi.org/10.1086/668300.

14. Article in a magazine   Include the full publication date given in the
magazine.

Owusu, Nadia. "Head Wraps." *The New York Times Magazine*, 7 Mar. 2021, p. 20.

Stuart, Tessa. "New Study Suggests Burning Fossil Fuels Contributed to 1 in 5 Deaths in
2018." *Rolling Stone*, 17 Feb. 2021, www.rollingstone.com/politics/politics-news
/fossil-fuels-air-pollution-premature-deaths-statistics-1127586/.

15. Article in a newspaper   Include the full publication date and the section and page number, if available.

Corasaniti, Nick, and Jim Rutenberg. "Record Turnout Hints at Future of Vote in U.S."
The New York Times, 6 Dec. 2020, pp. A1+.

Jones, Ayana. "Chamber of Commerce Program to Boost Black-Owned Businesses."
The Philadelphia Tribune, 21 Apr. 2021, www.phillytrib.com/news/business
/chamber-of-commerce-program-to-boost-black-owned-businesses
/article_6b14ae2f-5db2-5a59-8a67-8bbf974da451.html.

16. Editorial or opinion   List the author as it appears in the source. You
may add the word "Editorial" or "Op-ed" to the end of the entry if it is
not clear from the author or title of the source.

Kansas City Star Editorial Board. "Kansas Considers Lowering Concealed Carry Age to 18.
Why It's Wrong for Many Reasons." *The Kansas City Star*, 9 Mar. 2021,
www.kansascity.com/opinion/editorials/article249793143.html.

17. Letter to the editor   Use the label "Letter" as the title if the letter has
no title or headline; otherwise, cite as an article.

Carasso, Roger. Letter. *The New York Times*, 4 Apr. 2021, Sunday Book Review sec., p. 5.

18. Comment on an online article   List the author's name as it appears on the comment (see item 11). After the name, include "Comment on" followed by the article's publication information. Include the URL directly to the comment, if possible; otherwise, use the URL for the article.

satch. Comment on "No Compassion," by Roy Edroso. *Alicublog*, 20 Mar. 2021, 9:50 a.m., disq.us/p/2fu0ulk.

19. Review (book, film, performance, etc.)   If the review is untitled, use the label "Review of" and the title and author or director of the work reviewed. Then add information for the publication in which the review appears. Otherwise, cite as an article, as in the second example.

Jopanda, Wayne Silao. Review of *America Is Not the Heart*, by Elaine Castillo. *Alon: Journal for Filipinx American and Diasporic Studies*, vol. 1, no. 1, Mar. 2021, pp. 106–08. *eScholarship*, https://escholarship.org/uc/item/0d44t8wx.

Bramesco, Charles. "*Honeyland* Couches an Apocalyptic Warning in a Beekeeping Documentary." *The A.V. Club*, G/O Media, 23 July 2019, film.avclub.com /honeyland-couches-an-apocalyptic-warning-in-a-beekeepin-1836624795.

20. Interview   Begin with the person interviewed. Include the name of the interviewer after the title (or after the interviewee if the interview is untitled). For an interview that you conducted, use "the author" as the interviewer.

Harjo, Joy. "The First Native American U.S. Poet Laureate on How Poetry Can Counter Hate." Interview by Olivia B. Waxman. *Time*, 22 Aug. 2019, time.com/5658443 /joy-harjo-poet-interview/.

Kendi, Ibram X. Interview by Eric Deggans. *Life Kit*, NPR, 24 Oct. 2020.

Akufo, Rosa. Interview with the author. 10 Nov. 2020.

21. Article in a dictionary or an encyclopedia (including a wiki)   List the author of the entry (if there is one), the title of the entry, and publication information for the reference work. For an online source that is continually updated, such as a wiki entry, use the most recent update date.

Robinson, Lisa Clayton. "Harlem Writers Guild." *Africana: The Encyclopedia of the African and African American Experience*, edited by Kwame Anthony Appiah and Henry Louis Gates Jr., 2nd ed., Oxford UP, 2005, p. 163.

"House Music." *Wikipedia: The Free Encyclopedia*, Wikimedia Foundation, 8 Apr. 2021, en.wikipedia.org/wiki/House_music.

22. Letter in a collection List the title as it appears in the collection (or, if untitled, "Letter to" and the recipient), followed by the date of the letter. End with the title and publication information for the collection.

Murdoch, Iris. Letter to Raymond Queneau. 7 Aug. 1946. *Living on Paper: Letters from Iris Murdoch, 1934–1995*, edited by Avril Horner and Anne Rowe, Princeton UP, 2016, pp. 76–78.

Oblinger, Maggie. "Letter from Maggie Oblinger to Charlie Thomas, March 31, 1895." 31 Mar. 1895. *Prairie Settlement: Nebraska Photographs and Family Letters, 1862–1912*, Library of Congress / American Memory, memory.loc.gov/cgi-bin /query/r?ammem/ps:@field(DOCID+l306)#l3060001.

Books and other long works

▶ Citation at a glance: Book, 341
▶ Citation at a glance: Selection from an anthology or a collection, 343

23. Basic format for a book

a. Print

Porter, Max. *Lanny*. Graywolf Press, 2019.

b. E-book

Cabral, Amber. *Allies and Advocates: Creating an Inclusive and Equitable Culture*. E-book ed., Wiley, 2021.

c. Web Give whatever print publication information is available for the work, followed by the title of the website and the URL. If the book's original publication date is not available, include the date of online publication.

Piketty, Thomas. *Capital in the Twenty-First Century*. Translated by Arthur Goldhammer, Harvard UP, 2014. *Google Books*, books.google.com/books?isbn=0674369556.

23. Basic format for a book (*cont.*)

d. Audiobook After the title, include the phrase "Narrated by" followed by the narrator's full name. If the author and narrator are the same, include only the last name. Then include "audiobook ed.," the publisher, and the date of release.

de Hart, Jane Sherron. *Ruth Bader Ginsburg: A Life.* Narrated by Suzanne Toren,
audiobook ed., Random House Audio, 2018.

24. Parts of a book (foreword, introduction, preface, or afterword)

Coates, Ta-Nehisi. Foreword. *The Origin of Others,* by Toni Morrison, Harvard UP, 2017,
pp. vii–xvii.

Sullivan, John Jeremiah. "The Ill-Defined Plot." Introduction. *The Best American Essays
2014,* edited by Sullivan, Houghton Mifflin Harcourt, 2014, pp. xvii–xxvi.

25. Book in a language other than English
Capitalize the title according to the conventions of the book's language and include a translation of the title in brackets.

Vargas Llosa, Mario. *El sueño del celta* [*The Dream of the Celt*]. Alfaguara Ediciones, 2010.

26. Entire anthology or collection
An anthology is a collection of works on a common theme, often with different authors for the selections and usually with an editor for the entire volume.

Marcus, Ben, editor. *New American Stories.* Vintage Books, 2015.

27. One selection from an anthology or a collection

Sayrafiezadeh, Saïd. "Paranoia." *New American Stories,* edited by Ben Marcus,
Vintage Books, 2015, pp. 3–29.

28. Two or more selections from an anthology or a collection
Provide an entry for the entire anthology (see item 26) and a shortened entry for each selection. Alphabetize the entries by authors' or editors' last names. In the example on page 342, the Eisenberg and Sayrafiezadeh selections appear in Marcus's anthology, *New American Stories.*

Citation at a glance

Book MLA

To cite a print book in MLA style, include the following elements:

1 Author(s)
2 Title and subtitle
3 Publisher
4 Year of publication (latest year)

TITLE PAGE

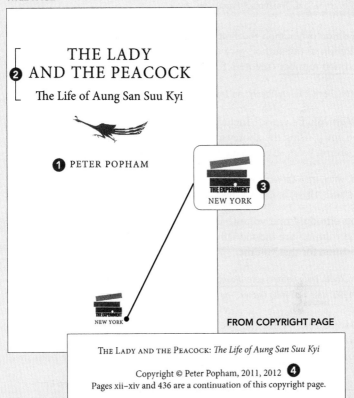

THE LADY
2 AND THE PEACOCK
The Life of Aung San Suu Kyi

1 PETER POPHAM

THE EXPERIMENT **3**
NEW YORK

FROM COPYRIGHT PAGE

THE LADY AND THE PEACOCK: *The Life of Aung San Suu Kyi*

Copyright © Peter Popham, 2011, 2012 **4**
Pages xii–xiv and 436 are a continuation of this copyright page.

WORKS CITED ENTRY FOR A PRINT BOOK

    1   **2**

Popham, Peter. *The Lady and the Peacock: The Life of Aung San Suu Kyi*.

    3   **4**

The Experiment, 2012.

For more on citing books in MLA style, see items 23–30.

28. Two or more selections from an anthology or a collection (*cont.*)

Eisenberg, Deborah. "Some Other, Better Otto." Marcus, pp. 94–136.

Marcus, Ben, editor. *New American Stories*. Vintage Books, 2015.

Sayrafiezadeh, Saïd. "Paranoia." Marcus, pp. 3–29.

29. Edition other than the first   If the book has a translator or an editor in addition to the author, give the name of the translator or editor before the edition number (see item 8 for a book with an editor or a translator).

Eagleton, Terry. *Literary Theory: An Introduction*. 3rd ed., U of Minnesota P, 2008.

30. Multivolume work   Include the total number of volumes at the end of the entry, using the abbreviation "vols." If the volumes were published over several years, give the inclusive dates of publication.

Cather, Willa. *Willa Cather: The Complete Fiction and Other Writings*. Edited by Sharon
 O'Brien, Library of America, 1987–92. 3 vols.

If you cite only one volume in your paper, include the volume's title (if the volumes are individually titled) and number and give the date of publication for that volume.

Cather, Willa. *Willa Cather: Later Novels*. Edited by Sharon O'Brien, Library of America,
 1990. Vol. 2 of *Willa Cather: The Complete Fiction and Other Writings*.

31. Sacred text   Give the title of the edition (taken from the title page), italicized; the editor's or translator's name (if any); and publication information. Add the name of the version, if there is one, before the publisher.

The Oxford Annotated Bible with the Apocrypha. Edited by Herbert G. May and Bruce
 M. Metzger, Revised Standard Version, Oxford UP, 1965.

Quran: The Final Testament. Translated by Rashad Khalifa, Authorized English Version
 with Arabic Text, Universal Unity, 2000.

Citation at a glance

Selection from an anthology or a collection MLA

To cite a selection from an anthology in MLA style, include the following elements:

1 Author(s) of selection
2 Title and subtitle of selection
3 Title and subtitle of anthology
4 Editor(s) of anthology
5 Publisher
6 Year of publication
7 Page number(s) of selection

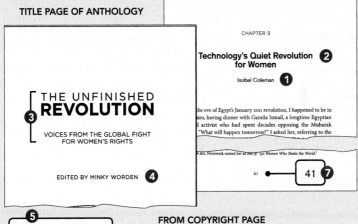

TITLE PAGE OF ANTHOLOGY

FIRST PAGE OF SELECTION

THE UNFINISHED
REVOLUTION

VOICES FROM THE GLOBAL FIGHT
FOR WOMEN'S RIGHTS

EDITED BY MINKY WORDEN

CHAPTER 3

**Technology's Quiet Revolution
for Women**

Isobel Coleman

he eve of Egypt's January 2011 revolution, I happened to be in
iro, having dinner with Gamila Ismail, a longtime Egyptian
l activist who had spent decades opposing the Mubarak
"What will happen tomorrow?" I asked her, referring to the

2011, Newsweek named her as one of 150 Women Who Shake the World."

41   41

Seven Stories Press
NEW YORK

Seven Stories Press
NEW YORK

FROM COPYRIGHT PAGE

Copyright © 2012 by Minky Worden
Individual chapters © 2012 by each author

WORKS CITED ENTRY FOR A SELECTION FROM AN ANTHOLOGY

        1   2   3
Coleman, Isobel. "Technology's Quiet Revolution for Women." *The Unfinished Revolution*:

                                              4
    Voices from the Global Fight for Women's Rights, edited by Minky Worden,

        5   6   7
    Seven Stories Press, 2012, pp. 41–49.

For more on citing selections from anthologies in MLA style, see items 26–28.

32. Dissertation

Kabugi, Magana J. *The Souls of Black Colleges: Cultural Production, Ideology, and Identity at Historically Black Colleges and Universities.* 2020. Vanderbilt U, PhD dissertation. *Vanderbilt University Institutional Repository*, hdl.handle.net/1803/16103.

Web sources

▸ Citation at a glance: Work from a website, 346

33. An entire website Include the website's sponsor or publisher and the update date. If the website name is the same as or similar to the publisher's name, do not include it; if no date is provided, include the date you accessed the source, as in the second example in item 34a.

Lift Every Voice. Library of America / Schomburg Center for Research in Black Culture, 2020, africanamericanpoetry.org/.

The Newton Project. 2022, www.newtonproject.ox.ac.uk/.

34. Work from a website

a. Short work (article, individual web page) Place the title in quotation marks. If there is no posting date or update date, include the date you accessed the source.

Enzinna, Wes. "Syria's Unknown Revolution." *Pulitzer Center*, 24 Nov. 2015, pulitzercenter.org/projects/middle-east-syria-enzinna-war-rojava.

Bali, Karan. "Shashikala." *Upperstall*, upperstall.com/profile/shashikala/. Accessed 22 Apr. 2022.

b. Long work (book, report) Italicize the title. If a book's original publication date is not available, include the date of online publication.

Euripides. *The Trojan Women.* Translated by Gilbert Murray, Oxford UP, 1915. *Internet Sacred Text Archive*, www.sacred-texts.com/cla/eurip/trojan.htm.

35. Blog post Cite a blog post as you would a work from a website (see item 34), with the title of the post in quotation marks. (To cite a comment on a blog, follow the guidelines in item 18.)

Horgan, John. "My Quantum Experiment." *Cross-Check*, Scientific American, 5 June 2020, blogs.scientificamerican.com/cross-check/my-quantum-experiment/.

Edroso, Roy. "No Compassion." *Alicublog*, 18 Mar. 2021, alicublog.blogspot.com /2021/03/no-compassion.html.

36. Social media post Cite as a work from a website (see item 34). Begin with the author (see item 11 for citing screen names). Use the caption or full text of the post as the title, if it is brief; if the post is long, use the first few words followed by an ellipsis. If the post has no text, or if you focus on a visual element in your paper, provide a description of the post, as in the last example.

Abdurraqib, Hanif [@NifMuhammad]. "Tracy Chapman really one of the greatest Ohio writers." *Twitter*, 30 Mar. 2021, twitter.com/NifMuhammad/status /1377086355667320836.

ACLU. "Public officials have . . ." *Facebook*, 10 May 2021, www.facebook.com/aclu /photos/a.74134381812/10157852911711813.

Rosa, Camila [camixvx]. Illustration of nurses in masks with fists raised. *Instagram*, 28 Apr. 2020, www.instagram.com/p/B_h62W9pJaQ/.

Audio, visual, and multimedia sources

37. Podcast series or episode Include the distributor or production company and the site or service where you accessed the podcast.

"Childish Gambino: *Because the Internet*." *Dissect*, hosted by Cole Cuchna, season 7, episode 1, Spotify, Sep. 2020. *Spotify* app.

Dolly Parton's America. Hosted by Jad Abumrad, produced and reported by Shima Oliaee, WNYC Studios, 2019, www.wnycstudios.org/podcasts/dolly-partons-america.

Citation at a glance

Work from a website MLA

To cite a work from a website in MLA style, include the following elements:

1. Author(s) of work, if any
2. Title and subtitle
3. Title of website
4. Publisher of website (unless it is the same as the title of site)
5. Update date
6. URL of page
7. Date of access (if no update date on site)

INTERNAL PAGE FROM A WEBSITE

WORKS CITED ENTRY FOR A WORK FROM A WEBSITE

```
     1                                    2
┌──┐ ┌───────────────────────────────────────────────────────┐
Knop, Brian. "Despite the Internet, Kids Still Involved in Extracurricular Activities."
            3                  5              6
    ┌───────────────────┐ ┌──────────┐ ┌──────────────────────┐
    United States Census Bureau, 6 Nov. 2018, www.census.gov/library/stories

    /2018/11/despite-internet-kids-still-involved-extracurricular-activities.html.
```

For more on citing sources from websites in MLA style, see item 34.

38. Stand-alone audio segment

"The Past Returns to Gdańsk." Written and narrated by Michael Segalov, *BBC*, 26 Apr.
2021, www.bbc.co.uk/sounds/play/m000vh4f.

39. Film Generally, begin the entry with the title, followed by the director, as in the first example. If your paper emphasizes one or more people involved with the film, you may begin with those names, as in the second example. If you viewed the film on a streaming service, include the app or website name and URL.

Judas and the Black Messiah. Directed by Shaka King, Warner Bros., 2021.

Kubrick, Stanley, director. *A Clockwork Orange.* Hawk Films / Warner Bros., 1971.
Netflix, www.netflix.com.

40. Supplementary material accompanying a film Begin with the title of the supplementary material, in quotation marks, and the names of any important contributors. End with information about the film, as in item 39, and about the location of the supplementary material.

"Sweeney's London." Produced by Eric Young. *Sweeney Todd: The Demon Barber of Fleet Street,* directed by Tim Burton, DreamWorks Pictures, 2007, disc 2. DVD.

41. Video from the web If the video is viewed on a video-sharing site such as *YouTube* or *Vimeo*, put the name of the uploader after the name of the website. If the video emphasizes a single speaker or presenter, list that person as the author.

"The Art of Single Stroke Painting in Japan." *YouTube,* uploaded by National Geographic,
13 July 2018, www.youtube.com/watch?v=g7H8IhGZnpM.

Kundu, Anindya. "The 'Opportunity Gap' in US Public Education—and How to Close It."
TED, May 2019, www.ted.com/talks/anindya_kundu_the_opportunity_gap_in_us
_public_education_and_how_to_close_it.

42. Video game List the developer or author of the game (if any); the title, italicized; the version, if there is one; and the distributor and date of publication. If the game can be played on the web, add information as for a work from a website (see item 34).

Gearbox Software. *Borderlands 3: Deluxe Edition*. 2K Games, 2019.

43. Computer software or app Give any available information about the version, distributor, and date.

NYT Cooking. Version 4.36, The New York Times, 2021.

44. TV or radio episode or program After the episode and/or series title, provide relevant information about the program, such as contributors; the episode number (if any); the network, distributor, or production company; and the date of broadcast or upload. If you viewed the program on a website or in an app, include that information.

"Umbrellas Down." *This American Life*, hosted by Ira Glass, WBEZ, 10 July 2020.

"The Super Producers." *Hip-Hop Evolution*, hosted by Shad Kabango, season 4, episode 3, Banger Films / Netflix, 2020. *Netflix*, www.netflix.com.

Hillary. Directed by Nanette Burstein, Propagate Content / Hulu, 2020. *Hulu* app.

45. Transcript Cite the source (interview, radio or television program, video, and so on), and add the label "Transcript" at the end of the entry.

Kundu, Anindya. "The 'Opportunity Gap' in US Public Education—and How to Close It." *TED*, May 2019, www.ted.com/talks/anindya_kundu_the_opportunity_gap_in_us _public_education_and_how_to_close_it/transcript. Transcript.

46. Live performance Begin with either the title of the work performed or, if relevant, the author, composer, or main performer. Include relevant contributors; the theater, ballet, or opera company, if any; the date of performance; and the location.

Beethoven, Ludwig van. *Piano Concerto No. 3*. Conducted by Andris Nelsons, performed by Paul Lewis and Boston Symphony Orchestra, 9 Oct. 2015, Symphony Hall, Boston.

Schreck, Heidi. *What the Constitution Means to Me*. Directed by Oliver Butler, 16 June 2019, Helen Hayes Theater, New York City.

Cite a source reposted from another source

Problem: Some sources that you find on the web, particularly on blogs or on video-sharing sites, did not originate with the person who uploaded or published the source online. In such a case, how do you give proper credit to the source?

Example: Say you need to cite President John F. Kennedy's inaugural address. You have found a video on YouTube that provides footage of the address (see image). The video was uploaded by PaddyIrishMan2 on October 29, 2006. But clearly, PaddyIrishMan2 is not the author of the video or of the address.

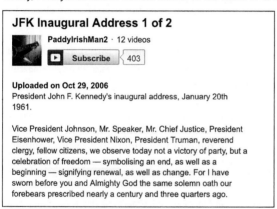

JFK Inaugural Address 1 of 2

PaddyIrishMan2 · 12 videos

▶ Subscribe ⟨ 403

Uploaded on Oct 29, 2006
President John F. Kennedy's inaugural address, January 20th 1961.

Vice President Johnson, Mr. Speaker, Mr. Chief Justice, President Eisenhower, Vice President Nixon, President Truman, reverend clergy, fellow citizens, we observe today not a victory of party, but a celebration of freedom — symbolising an end, as well as a beginning — signifying renewal, as well as change. For I have sworn before you and Almighty God the same solemn oath our forebears prescribed nearly a century and three quarters ago.

Strategy: Start with what you know. The source is a video that you viewed on the web. For this particular video, John F. Kennedy is the speaker and the author of the inaugural address. PaddyIrishMan2 is identified as the person who uploaded the source to YouTube.

Citation: To cite the source, you can follow the basic MLA guidelines for a video found on the web (see item 41).

author/speaker: website   upload
last name first   title of video   title   information

Kennedy, John F. "JFK Inaugural Address: 1 of 2." *YouTube*, uploaded by PaddyIrishMan2,

upload date   URL

29 Oct. 2006, www.youtube.com/watch?v=xE0iPY7XGBo.

NOTE: If your work calls for a primary source, you should try to find the original source of the video; a reference librarian can help.

47. Lecture or public address   Begin with the speaker's name, the title of the lecture, the <u>sponsoring organization</u>, the date, and the <u>location</u>. If you viewed the lecture on the web, cite as you would an online video (see item 41). If the lecture or address has no title, use the label "Lecture" or "Address" after the speaker's name.

Gay, Roxane. "Difficult Women, Bad Feminists and Unruly Bodies." <u>Beatty Lecture Series,</u>
18 Oct. 2018, <u>McGill University</u>.

48. Musical score   Begin with the composer's name; the title of the work, italicized; and the <u>date of composition</u>. For a print source, give the publisher and date. For an online source, give the title of the website, the publisher, the date, and the URL.

Beethoven, Ludwig van. *Symphony No. 5 in C Minor, Opus 67.* <u>1807.</u> *Center for*
Computer Assisted Research in the Humanities, 2008, scores.ccarh.org/beethoven
/sym/beethoven-sym5-1.pdf.

49. Music recording   Begin with the name of the person you want to emphasize: the composer, conductor, or performer. After the song and/or album title, give the names of relevant performers, the <u>record company</u>, and the date. If you accessed the recording on a <u>website or app</u>, include that information.

Bach, Johann Sebastian. *Bach: Violin Concertos.* Performances by Itzhak Perlman,
Pinchas Zukerman, and English Chamber Orchestra, <u>EMI</u>, 2002.

Bad Bunny. "Vete." *YHLQMDLG,* <u>Rimas,</u> 2020. *Apple Music* app.

50. Artwork, photograph, or other visual art   Begin with the artist and the title of the work, italicized. If you viewed the original work, give the date of composition followed by a comma and the <u>location</u>. If you viewed the work online, give the date of composition followed by a period and the <u>website title</u>, publisher (if any), and URL. If you viewed the work reproduced in a book, cite as a work in an anthology or a collection (item 27), giving the date of composition after the title of the work.

Bradford, Mark. *Let's Walk to the Middle of the Ocean*. 2015, Museum of Modern Art, New York.

Lange, Dorothea. *Migrant Mother, Nipomo, California*. Mar. 1936. *MOMA*, www.moma.org/collection/works/50989.

Kertész, André. *Meudon*. 1928. *Street Photography: From Atget to Cartier-Bresson*, by Clive Scott, Tauris, 2011, p. 61.

51. Visual such as a table, a chart, or another graphic   Cite a visual as you would a short work within a longer work. Add a descriptive label at the end if the type of visual is not clear from the title or if it is important for your work.

"New COVID-19 Cases Worldwide." *Coronavirus Resource Center*, Johns Hopkins U of Medicine, 3 May 2021, coronavirus.jhu.edu/data/new-cases. Chart.

"Number of Measles Cases Reported by Year 2010–2019." *Centers for Disease Control and Prevention*, 22 Feb. 2019, www.cdc.gov/measles/cases-outbreaks.html. Table.

52. Cartoon or comic strip   Give the cartoonist's name; the title of the cartoon, if it has one, in quotation marks, or the label "Cartoon" or "Comic Strip" without quotation marks in place of a title; and publication information. Cite an online cartoon as a work from a website (item 34).

Shiell, Mike. Cartoon. *The Saturday Evening Post*, Jan.–Feb. 2021, p. 8.

Munroe, Randall. "Heartbleed Explanation." *xkcd*, xkcd.com/1354/. Accessed 10 Oct. 2020.

53. Advertisement   If the advertisement has no title, begin with the label "Advertisement for" and what is being advertised, followed by the publication information for the source in which the advertisement appears. For some special advertisement formats, you may want to end with a label describing it, such as "Billboard."

Advertisement for Better World Club. *Mother Jones*, Mar.–Apr. 2021, p. 2.

"The Whole Working-from-Home Thing—Apple." *YouTube*, uploaded by Apple, 13 July 2020, www.youtube.com/watch?v=6_pru8U2RmM.

54. Map Cite a map as you would a short work within a longer work. If the map is published on its own, cite it as a book or another long work. Use the label "Map" at the end if it is not clear from the title.

"Map of Sudan." *Global Citizen*, Citizens for Global Solutions, 2011, globalsolutions.org
   /blog/bashir#.VthzNMfi_FI.

"Vote on Secession, 1861." *Perry-Castañeda Library Map Collection*, U of Texas at Austin,
   1976, www.lib.utexas.edu/maps/atlas_texas/texas_vote_secession_1861.jpg. Map.

Government and legal documents

55. Government document Treat the government agency as the author. In most situations, give the name of the publishing agency as presented by the source, as in the first example. If you are using several government sources, you may want to standardize your list of works cited by listing the name of the government, spelled out, followed by the name of any agencies and subagencies, as in the second example.

U.S. Bureau of Labor Statistics. "Consumer Expenditures Report 2019." *BLS Reports*,
   Dec. 2020, www.bls.gov/opub/reports/consumer-expenditures/2019/home.htm.

United States, Department of Transportation, Federal Highway Administration.
   Environmental Justice Analysis in Transportation Planning and Programming:
   State of the Practice. Feb. 2019, www.fhwa.dot.gov/environment
   /environmental_justice/publications/tpp/fhwahep19022.pdf.

56. Historical document The titles of most historical documents, such as treaties and bills, are neither italicized nor put in quotation marks, and their original publication date is provided. Constitutions, however, are treated as longer works, with titles italicized and followed by the publication information for the version referenced.

Magna Carta. 1215. *Britannia History*, www.britannia.com/history/docs/magna2.html.

The Constitution of the United States: A Transcription. 2020. *America's Founding*
   Documents, U.S. National Archives and Records Administration, www.archives.gov
   /founding-docs/constitution-transcript.

57. Legislative act (law) Begin with the name of the legislative body and the act's Public Law number. Then give the publication information for the source in which you found the act.

United States, Congress. Public Law 116–136. *United States Statutes at Large*, vol. 134, 2019, pp. 281–615. *U.S. Government Publishing Office*, www.govinfo.gov /content/pkg/PLAW-116publ136/uslm/PLAW-116publ136.xml.

58. Court case List the name of the court. Then provide the title of the case, the date of the decision, and publication information.

United States, Supreme Court. *Utah v. Evans*. 20 June 2002. *Legal Information Institute*, Cornell Law School, www.law.cornell.edu/supremecourt/text/536/452.

Personal communication and course materials

59. Personal letter Include the letter's format.

Nadir, Abdul. Letter to the author. 6 May 2021. Typescript.

60. Email message

Lewis-Truth, Antoine. Email to the Office of Student Financial Assistance. 30 Aug. 2020.

61. Text message

Primak, Shoshana. Text message to the author. 6 May 2021.

62. Course materials For materials posted to an online learning management system, include as much information as is available about the source (author, title or description, and any publication information); then give the course, instructor, platform, institution name, date of posting, and URL. For materials delivered in a print or PDF course pack, include author and title of the work; the words "Course pack for" with the course number and name; "compiled by" with the instructor's name; the term; and the institution name.

Rose, Mike. "Blue-Collar Brilliance." Introduction to College Writing, taught by Melanie Li. *Blackboard*, Merrimack College, 9 Sept. 2020, blackboard.merrimack.edu/ultra /courses/_25745_1/cl/readings.

50c MLA information notes (optional)

Researchers who use the MLA system of parenthetical documentation may also use information notes for one of two purposes:

1. to provide additional material that is important but might interrupt the flow of the paper

2. to refer to several sources that support a single point or to provide comments on sources

Information notes may be either footnotes or endnotes. Footnotes appear at the foot of the page; endnotes appear on a separate page at the end of the paper, just before the list of works cited. For either style, the notes are numbered consecutively throughout the paper. The text of the paper contains a raised arabic numeral that corresponds to the number of the note.

TEXT

In the past several years, employees have filed a number of lawsuits against employers because of online monitoring practices.[1]

NOTE

    [1] For a discussion of federal law applicable to electronic surveillance in the workplace, see Kesan 293.

51 MLA format; sample research paper

The following guidelines are consistent with advice given in the *MLA Handbook*, 9th edition (MLA, 2021), and with typical requirements for student papers. For a sample MLA research paper, see 51b.

51a MLA format

Formatting the paper: The basics

Papers written in MLA style should be formatted as shown below.

Student's last name and the **page number** appear in the right-hand corner of every page.

Heading includes the student's name, instructor's name, course, and date.

Sophie Harba

Professor Baros-Moon

Engl 1101

9 November 2017

Center the **title**. Add no extra space above or below it, and use no quotation marks or italics.

What's for Dinner? Personal Choices vs. Public Health

Should the government enact laws to regulate healthy eating choices? Many Americans would answer an emphatic "No," arguing that what and how much we eat should be left to individual choice rather than unreasonable laws. Others might argue that it would be unreasonable for the government not to enact legislation, given the rise of chronic diseases that result from harmful diets. In this debate, both the definition of reasonable regulations and the role of government to legislate food choices are at stake. In the name of public health and safety, state governments have the responsibility to shape health policies and to regulate healthy eating choices, especially since doing so offers a potentially large social benefit for a relatively small cost.

Debates surrounding the government's role in regulating food have a long history in the United States. According to Lorine Goodwin, a food historian, nineteenth-century reformers who sought to purify the food supply were called "fanatics" and "radicals" by critics who argued that consumers should be free to buy and eat what they want (77). Thanks to regulations, though, such as the 1906 federal Pure Food and Drug Act, food, beverages, and medicine are largely free from toxins. In addition, to prevent contamination and the spread of disease, meat and dairy products are now inspected by government agents to ensure that they

Use Times New Roman or another easy-to-read **font.**

Use a **1-inch margin** on all sides of the page, and **double-space** the text.

Formatting the paper: Other concerns

Group projects   If you are writing a group project, create a cover page with all members' names, the professor's name, the course, and the date, all left-aligned on separate double-spaced lines. Center the title on a new line a few spaces down. Starting on the first text page, include all members' last names and the page number, aligned top and right, on every page. If the names will not all fit on a single line, include only the page number.

Capitalization, italics, and quotation marks   In titles of works, capitalize all words except articles (*a, an, the*), prepositions (*to, from, between,* and so on), coordinating conjunctions (*and, but, or, nor, for, so, yet*), and the *to* in infinitives—unless the word is first or last in the title or subtitle. Follow these guidelines in your paper even if the title appears in all capital or all lowercase letters in the source.

Italicize the titles of books, journals, magazines, and other long works, such as websites. Use quotation marks around the titles of articles, short stories, poems, and other short works.

Long quotations   When a quotation is longer than four typed lines of prose or three lines of poetry, set it off from the text by indenting the entire quotation one-half inch from the left margin. Do not use quotation marks when a quotation has been set off from the text by indenting. See page 301 for an example.

Headings   While headings are generally not needed for brief essays, readers may find them helpful for long or complex essays. Place each heading in the same style and size. If you need subheadings (level 2, level 3), be consistent in styling them. Place headings at the left margin without any indent. Capitalize headings as you would titles.

Visuals   MLA classifies visuals as tables and illustrations (labeled "figures" and including graphs, charts, maps, photographs, and drawings). Place visuals in your essay as near as possible to the relevant text. Label and number each table ("Table 1"), and provide a clear title. Capitalize as you would the title of a work (see above). Place the table number and title on separate lines above the table, flush with the left margin.

For a table that you have borrowed or adapted, give the source below the table in a note like the following:

Source: Boris Groysberg and Michael Slind. "Leadership Is a Conversation." *Harvard Business Review*, June 2012, p. 83.

All other visuals should be labeled "Figure" (usually abbreviated "Fig."), numbered, and captioned. The label and caption should appear on the same line underneath the visual, flush left. Capitalize the caption as you would a sentence; include source information. If your caption includes full source information and you do not cite the source anywhere else in your essay, it is not necessary to include an entry in your list of works cited. Remember to refer to each visual within your text (*see table 1*; *as shown in figure 2*), indicating how the visual contributes to the point you are making. See page 360 for an example of a figure in a paper.

Preparing the list of works cited

Begin the list of works cited on a new page at the end of the paper. Center the title "Works Cited" one inch from the top of the page. Double-space throughout. See pages 364 and 365 for a sample list of works cited.

Alphabetizing the list   Alphabetize the list by the last names of the authors (or editors); if a work has no author or editor, alphabetize by the first word of the title other than *A, An,* or *The.*

Indenting   Do not indent the first line of each works cited entry, but indent any additional lines one-half inch. This technique, called a hanging indent, highlights the names of the authors, making it easy for readers to scan the alphabetized list. See the works cited list that begins on page 364.

URLs and DOIs   Do not insert line breaks, spaces, or hyphens into URLs or DOIs in works cited entries. If the entire URL moves to another line, creating a short line, you may leave it that way. See also the instruction on page 329 for treating URLs and DOIs.

51b Sample MLA research paper

Below is a research paper on the topic of the role of government in legislating food choices, written by Sophie Harba, a student in a composition class. Harba's paper is documented with in-text citations and a list of works cited in MLA style. Annotations in the margins of the paper draw your attention to Harba's use of MLA style and her effective writing.

Harba 1

Sophie Harba

Professor Baros-Moon

Engl 1101

9 November 2015

Title is centered.

What's for Dinner? Personal Choices vs. Public Health

Opening question engages readers.

Should the government enact laws to regulate healthy eating choices? Many Americans would answer an emphatic "No," arguing that what and how much we eat should be left to individual choice rather than unreasonable laws. Others might argue that it would be unreasonable for the government not to enact legislation, given the rise of chronic diseases that result from harmful diets. In this debate, both the definition of reasonable regulations and the role of government to legislate food choices are at stake. In the name of public health and safety, state governments have the responsibility to shape health policies and to regulate healthy eating choices, especially since doing so offers a potentially large social benefit for a relatively small cost.

Writer highlights the research conversation.

Thesis answers the question and presents main point.

Signal phrase names the author. Page number is in parentheses.

Debates surrounding the government's role in regulating food have a long history in the United States. According to Lorine Goodwin, a food historian, nineteenth-century reformers who sought to purify the food supply were called "fanatics" and "radicals" by critics who argued that consumers should be free to buy and eat what they want (77). Thanks to

Marginal annotations indicate MLA-style formatting and effective writing.

Harba 2

regulations, though, such as the 1906 federal Pure Food and Drug Act,
food, beverages, and medicine are largely free from toxins. In addition,
to prevent contamination and the spread of disease, meat and dairy
products are now inspected by government agents to ensure that they
meet health requirements. Such regulations can be considered reasonable
because they protect us from harm with little, if any, noticeable
consumer cost. It is not considered an unreasonable infringement on
personal choice that contaminated meat or arsenic-laced cough drops
are *un*available at our local supermarket. Rather, it is an important
government function to stop such harmful items from entering the
marketplace.

Even though our food meets current safety standards, there is a
need for further regulation. Not all food dangers, for example, arise from
obvious toxins like arsenic and *E. coli*. A diet that is low in nutritional
value and high in sugars, fats, and refined grains—grains that have
been processed to increase shelf life but that contain little fiber, iron,
and B vitamins—can be damaging over time (United States, Department
of Agriculture 36). A graph from the government's *Dietary Guidelines for
Americans, 2010* shows that Americans consume about three times more
fats and sugars and twice as many refined grains as is recommended but
only half of the recommended foods (see fig. 1).

Michael Pollan, who has written extensively about Americans'
unhealthy eating habits, notes that "[t]he Centers for Disease Control
estimates that fully three quarters of US health care spending goes to
treat chronic diseases, most of which are preventable and linked to
diet: heart disease, stroke, type 2 diabetes, and at least a third of all
cancers." In fact, the amount of money the United States spends to treat
chronic illnesses is increasing so rapidly that the Centers for Disease
Control has labeled chronic disease "the public health challenge of

---

Harba provides historical background and introduces a key term, *reasonable*.

Harba establishes common ground with the reader.

Transition helps readers move from one paragraph to the next.

No page number is available for this web source.

Harba 3

Harba uses
a graph to
illustrate
Americans'
poor nutritional
choices.

How Do Typical American Diets Compare to Recommended Intake Levels or Limits?

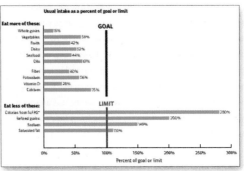

Visual includes
a caption with a
figure number
and source
information.
A full entry
for this source
appears in the
works cited list.

Fig. 1. United States, Department of Agriculture, fig. 5-1.

Harba
emphasizes the
urgency of her
argument.

the 21st century" (United States, Department of Health 1). In fighting
this epidemic, the primary challenge is not the need to find a cure; the
challenge is to prevent chronic diseases from striking in the first place.

Harba treats
both sides fairly.

Legislation, however, is not a popular solution when it comes to
most Americans and the food they eat. According to a nationwide poll,
seventy-five percent of Americans are opposed to laws that restrict or
put limitations on access to unhealthy foods (Neergaard and Agiesta).
When New York mayor Michael Bloomberg proposed a regulation in 2012
banning the sale of soft drinks in servings greater than twelve ounces in
restaurants and movie theaters, he was ridiculed as "Nanny Bloomberg."

No page
number is
provided for
a one-page
source.

In California in 2011, legislators failed to pass a law that would impose
a penny-per-ounce tax on soda, which would have funded obesity
prevention programs. And in Mississippi, legislators passed "a ban on
bans—a law that forbids . . . local restrictions on food or drink" (Conly).

Why is the public largely resistant to laws that would limit
unhealthy choices or penalize those choices with so-called fat taxes?
Many consumers and civil rights advocates find such laws to be an
unreasonable restriction on individual freedom of choice. As health
policy experts Mello and others point out, opposition to food and
beverage regulation is similar to the opposition to early tobacco
legislation: the public views the issue as one of personal responsibility
rather than one requiring government intervention (2602). In other
words, if a person eats unhealthy food and becomes ill as a result,
that is his or her choice. But those who favor legislation claim that
freedom of choice is a myth because of the strong influence of food and
beverage industry marketing on consumers' dietary habits. According
to one nonprofit health advocacy group, food and beverage companies
spend roughly two billion dollars per year marketing directly to children.
As a result, kids see nearly four thousand ads per year encouraging
them to eat unhealthy food and drinks ("Facts"). As was the case with
antismoking laws passed in recent decades, taxes and legal restrictions
on junk food sales could help to counter the strong marketing messages
that promote unhealthy products.

The United States has a history of state and local public health
laws that have successfully promoted a particular behavior by punishing
an undesirable behavior. The decline in tobacco use as a result of
antismoking taxes and laws is perhaps the most obvious example.
Another example is legislation requiring the use of seat belts, which
have significantly reduced fatalities in car crashes. One government
agency reports that seat belt use saved an average of more than
fourteen thousand lives per year in the United States between 2000 and
2010 (United States, Department of Transportation 231). Perhaps seat
belt laws have public support because the cost of wearing a seat belt
is small, especially when compared with the benefit of saving fourteen
thousand lives per year.

Harba
anticipates
objections
to her idea.
She counters
opposing views
and supports
her argument.

Shortened title
provided in
parentheses for
a source with no
named author.

Analogy
extends
Harba's
argument.

Government
or organization
author's name
is shortened in
parentheses.

Harba introduces a quotation with a signal phrase and shows readers why she chose to use the source.

Laws designed to prevent chronic disease by promoting healthier food and beverage consumption also have potentially enormous benefits. To give just one example, Marion Nestle, New York University professor of nutrition and public health, notes that "a 1% reduction in intake of saturated fat across the population would prevent more than 30,000 cases of coronary heart disease annually and save more than a billion dollars in health care costs" (7). Few would argue that saving lives and dollars is not an enormous benefit. But three-quarters of Americans say they would object to the costs needed to achieve this benefit—the regulations needed to reduce saturated fat intake.

Harba acknowledges critics and counter-arguments.

Why do so many Americans believe there is a degree of personal choice lost when regulations such as taxes, bans, or portion limits on unhealthy foods are proposed? Some critics of anti-junk-food laws believe that even if state and local laws were successful in curbing chronic diseases, they would still be unacceptable. Bioethicist David Resnik emphasizes that such policies, despite their potential to make our society healthier, "open the door to excessive government control over food, which could restrict dietary choices, interfere with cultural, ethnic, and religious traditions, and exacerbate socioeconomic inequalities" (31). Resnik acknowledges that his argument relies on "slippery slope" thinking, but he insists that "social and political pressures" regarding food regulation make his concerns valid (31). Yet the social and political pressures that Resnik cites are really just the desire to improve public health, and limiting access to unhealthy, artificial ingredients seems a small price to pay. As legal scholars L. O. Gostin and K. G. Gostin

Including the source's credentials makes Harba more credible.

explain, "[I]nterventions that do not pose a truly significant burden on individual liberty" are justified if they "go a long way towards safeguarding the health and well-being of the populace" (214).

To improve public health, advocates such as Bowdoin College philosophy professor Sarah Conly contend that it is the government's duty

Harba 6

to prevent people from making harmful choices whenever feasible and
whenever public benefits outweigh the costs. In response to critics who
claim that laws aimed at stopping us from eating whatever we want
are an assault on our freedom of choice, Conly offers a persuasive
counterargument:

> [L]aws aren't designed for each one of us individually. Some of us
> can drive safely at 90 miles per hour, but we're bound by the same
> laws as the people who can't, because individual speeding laws aren't
> practical. Giving up a little liberty is something we agree to when we
> agree to live in a democratic society that is governed by laws.

As Conly suggests, it's important to move from either/or thinking
(either we have complete freedom of choice *or* we have government
regulations and lose any freedom) to seeing health as a matter of public
good, not individual liberty. Proposals such as Mayor Bloomberg's that
seek to limit portions of unhealthy beverages aren't about giving up
liberty; they are about asking individuals to choose substantial public
health benefits at a very small cost.

Despite arguments in favor of regulating unhealthy food as a
means to improve public health, public opposition has stood in the
way of legislation. Americans freely eat as much unhealthy food as they
want, and manufacturers and sellers of these foods have nearly unlimited
freedom to promote such products and drive increased consumption,
without any requirements to warn the public of potential hazards. Yet
mounting scientific evidence points to unhealthy food as a significant
contributing factor to chronic disease, which is straining our health care
system, decreasing Americans' quality of life, and leading to unnecessary
premature deaths. Americans must consider whether to allow the costly
trend of rising chronic disease to continue in the name of personal
choice or whether to support the regulatory changes and public health
policies that will reverse that trend.

Signal phrase names the author.

Long quotation is set off from the text. Quotation marks are omitted.

Quotation is followed by comments that connect the source to Harba's argument.

Conclusion sums up Harba's argument and provides closure.

Harba 7

Works Cited

Conly, Sarah. "Three Cheers for the Nanny State." *The New York Times*, 25
Mar. 2013, p. A23.

"The Facts on Junk Food Marketing and Kids." *Prevention Institute*, www
.preventioninstitute.org/focus-areas/were-not-buying-it-get
-involved/were-not-buying-it-the-facts-on-junk-food-marketing
-and-kids. Accessed 16 Oct. 2015.

Goodwin, Lorine Swainston. *The Pure Food, Drink, and Drug Crusaders,
1879–1914*. McFarland, 2006.

Gostin, L. O., and K. G. Gostin. "A Broader Liberty: J. S. Mill, Paternal-
ism, and the Public's Health." *Public Health*, vol. 123, no. 3, Mar.
2009, pp. 214–21, https://doi.org/10.1016/j.puhe.2008.12.024.

Mello, Michelle M., et al. "Obesity—the New Frontier of Public
Health Law." *The New England Journal of Medicine*, vol. 354,
no. 24, 15 June 2006, pp. 2601–10, https://doi.org/10.1056
/NEJMhpr060227.

Neergaard, Lauran, and Jennifer Agiesta. "Obesity's a Crisis but We Want
Our Junk Food, Poll Shows." *The Huffington Post*, 4 Jan. 2013,
www.huffingtonpost.com/2013/01/04/obesity-junk-food
-government-intervention-poll_n_2410376.html.

Nestle, Marion. *Food Politics: How the Food Industry Influences Nutrition
and Health*. U of California P, 2013.

Pollan, Michael. "The Food Movement, Rising." *The New York Review of
Books*, 10 June 2010, www.nybooks.com/articles/2010/06/10
/food-movement-rising.

Resnik, David. "Trans Fat Bans and Human Freedom." *The American
Journal of Bioethics*, vol. 10, no. 3, Mar. 2010, pp. 27–32.

Works cited list
begins on a new
page. Heading
is centered.

Access date
used for an
undated online
source.

List is
alphabetized
by authors' last
names (or by
title if no author).

First line of
each entry is at
the left margin;
extra lines are
indented ½".

Double-
spacing is used
throughout.

Harba 8

United States, Department of Agriculture and Department of Health and
Human Services. *Dietary Guidelines for Americans, 2010.* 2010,
health.gov/dietaryguidelines/dga2010/dietaryguidelines2010.pdf.

---, Department of Health and Human Services, Centers for Disease
Control and Prevention. National Center for Chronic Disease
Prevention and Health Promotion. *The Power of Prevention.* 2009,
www.cdc.gov/chronicdisease/pdf/2009-Power-of-Prevention.pdf.

---, Department of Transportation, National Highway Traffic Safety
Administration. *Traffic Safety Facts 2010: A Compilation of Motor
Vehicle Crash Data from the Fatality Analysis Reporting System
and the General Estimates System.* 2010, www.nrd.nhtsa.dot.gov
/Pubs/811659.pdf.

Author names
are standardized
for multiple
government
sources.

52 Documenting sources in APA style

In most social science classes, you will be asked to use the APA system for documenting sources, which is set forth in the *Publication Manual of the American Psychological Association*, 7th ed. (APA, 2020).

APA recommends in-text citations that refer readers to a list of references. An in-text citation gives the author of the source (often in a signal phrase), the year of publication, and often a page number in parentheses. At the end of the paper, a list of references provides publication information for each cited source; the list is alphabetized by authors' last names (or by titles for works with no authors). The direct link between the in-text citation and the entry in the reference list is highlighted in the following example.

IN-TEXT CITATION

Bell (2010) reported that students engaged in this kind of learning performed better on both project-based assessments and standardized tests (pp. 39–40).

ENTRY IN THE LIST OF REFERENCES

Bell, S. (2010). Project-based learning for the 21st century: Skills for the future. *The Clearing House, 83*(2), 39–43.

For a reference list that includes this entry, see 53b.

52a APA in-text citations

APA's in-text citations provide the author's last name and the year of publication, usually before the cited material, and a page number in parentheses directly after the cited material. In the models in this section, certain elements of the citation are underlined.

NOTE: APA style requires the use of the past tense or the present perfect tense in signal phrases introducing cited material: Smith (2021) reported; Smith (2021) has argued.

List of APA in-text citation models

List of APA reference list models

List of **APA reference list** models (*cont.*)

1. Basic format for a quotation Ordinarily, introduce the quotation with a signal phrase that includes the author's last name followed by the year of publication in parentheses. Put the page number (preceded by "p.," or "pp." for more than one page) in parentheses after the quotation. For sources from the web without page numbers, see item 3 in this section.

Çubukçu (2012) argued that for a student-centered approach to work, students must maintain "ownership for their goals and activities" (p. 64).

If the author is not named in the signal phrase, place the author's name, the year, and the page number in parentheses after the quotation: (Çubukçu, 2012, p. 64). (See items 6 and 14 for citing sources that lack authors.)

NOTE: Do not include a month in an in-text citation, even if the entry in the reference list includes the month.

2. Basic format for a summary or a paraphrase As for a quotation (see item 1), include the author's last name and the year either in a signal phrase introducing the material or in parentheses following it. A page number or other locator is not required for a summary or a paraphrase, but include one if it would help readers find the information or if your instructor requires it.

Watson (2008) offered a case study of the Cincinnati Public Schools Virtual High School, in which students were able to engage in highly individualized instruction according to their own needs, strengths, and learning styles, using 10 teachers as support (p. 7).

The Cincinnati Public Schools Virtual High School brought students together to engage in highly individualized instruction according to their own needs, strengths, and learning styles, using 10 teachers as support (Watson, 2008, p. 7).

3. Quotation from a source without page numbers If your source does not include page numbers, include another locator — information from the source such as a section heading, paragraph number, figure or table number, slide number, or time stamp — to help readers find the cited passage. See the examples on the next page.

3. Quotation from a source without page numbers (*cont.*)

Lopez (2020) has noted that ". . ." (Symptoms section).

Myers (2019) extolled the benefits of humility (para. 5).

Brezinski and Zhang (2017) traced the increase . . . (Figure 3).

The American Immigration Council has recommended that ". . ." (Slide 5).

In a recent TED Talk, Gould (2019) argued that ". . ." (13:27).

If you shorten a long heading, place it in quotation marks: ("How to Apply" section).

4. Work with two authors   Name both authors in the signal phrase or in parentheses each time you cite the work. In the signal phrase, use "and" between the authors' names; in the parentheses, use "&."

According to Donitsa-Schmidt and Zuzovsky (2014), "demographic growth in the school population" can lead to teacher shortages (p. 426).

In the United States, most public school systems are struggling with teacher shortages, which are projected to worsen as the number of applicants to education schools decreases (Donitsa-Schmidt & Zuzovsky, 2014, p. 420).

5. Work with three or more authors   Use the first author's name followed by "et al." (Latin for "and others") in either a signal phrase or a parenthetical citation.

In 2013, Harper et al. studied teachers' perceptions of project-based learning (PBL) before and after participating in a PBL pilot program.

Researchers studied teachers' perceptions of project-based learning (PBL) before and after participating in a PBL pilot program (Harper et al., 2013).

6. Work with an unknown or anonymous author   If the author is unknown, include the work's title (shortened if more than a few words) in the in-text citation.

Collaboration increases significantly among students who own or have regular access to a laptop ("Tech Seeds," 2015).

All titles in in-text citations are set in title case: Capitalize the first and last words of a title and subtitle, all significant words, and any words of four letters or more. For books and most stand-alone works (except websites), italicize the title; for most articles and other parts of larger works, set the title in quotation marks.

Only in rare cases in which "Anonymous" is specified as the author, use the word "Anonymous" in the author position: (Anonymous, 2021). (Also use the word "Anonymous" at the start of the reference list entry.)

NOTE: Titles are treated differently in reference list entries. See 52b.

7. Organization as author   If the author is an organization or a government agency, name the <u>organization</u> in the signal phrase or in parentheses the first time you cite the source.

> According to the <u>International Society for Technology in Education</u> (2016), "Student-centered learning moves students from passive receivers of information to active participants in their own discovery process" (What Is It? section).

For an organization with a long name, you may abbreviate the name of the organization in citations after the first.

FIRST CITATION	(Texas Higher Education Coordinating Board [THECB], 2019)
LATER CITATIONS	(THECB, 2019)

For a work by a government agency or large organization with multiple, nested departments, list the most specific agency or department as the author, as in the reference list (see item 33 in 52b).

8. Authors with the same last name   To avoid confusion, use <u>first initials</u> with the last names in your in-text citations. If authors share the same initials, spell out each author's first name.

> Research by <u>E.</u> Smith (2019) revealed that . . .

> One 2018 study contradicted . . . (<u>R.</u> Smith, p. 234).

9. Two or more works by the same author in the same year In your reference list, you will use <u>lowercase letters</u> ("a," "b," and so on) with the year to order the entries (see item 8 in 52b). Use those same letters with the year in the in-text citations.

> Research by Durgin (2013<u>b</u>) has yielded new findings about the role of smartphones in the classroom.

10. Two or more works in the same parentheses Put the works in the same order that they appear in the reference list, separated by semicolons: (Nazer, 2015; Serrao et al., 2014).

11. Multiple citations to the same work in one paragraph If you give the <u>author's name</u> in the text of your paper (not in parentheses) and you mention that source again in the text of the same paragraph, give only the author's name, not the <u>date</u>, in the later citation. If any subsequent reference in the same paragraph is in parentheses, include both the author and the date in the parentheses.

> Bell (<u>2010</u>) has argued that the chief benefit of student-centered learning is that it can connect students with "real-world tasks," thus making learning more engaging as well as more comprehensive (p. 42). For example, <u>Bell</u> observed a group of middle-school students who wanted to build a social justice monument for their school. Students engaged in this kind of learning performed better on both project-based assessments and standardized tests (<u>Bell, 2010</u>).

12. Part of a source (section, figure) To cite a specific part of a source, such as a section of a web page or a figure or table, identify the <u>element</u> in parentheses. Don't abbreviate terms such as "Figure," "Chapter," or "Section"; "page" is abbreviated "p." (or "pp." for more than one page). Cite the source as a whole in your reference list.

> The data support the finding that peer relationships are difficult to replicate in a completely online environment (Hanniman, 2010, <u>Figure 8-3</u>).

13. Indirect source (source quoted in another source) When a published source is quoted in a source written by someone else, cite the original source first; include "<u>as cited in</u>" before the author and date of the source you read. In the following example, Chow is the author of the source in the reference list; that source contains a quotation by Brailsford.

> Brailsford (1990) commended the writer and educator's "sure understanding of the thoughts of young people" (as cited in Chow, 2019, para. 9).

14. Web source Cite sources from the web as you would cite any other source, giving the author and the year when that information is available.

> Atkinson (2011) found that children who spent at least four hours a day engaged in online activities in an academic environment were less likely to want to play video games or watch TV after school.

Usually a page number is not available; occasionally a web source will lack an author or a date (see items 14a–14c).

a. No page numbers When quoting a web source that lacks stable numbered pages, include a paragraph number or a section heading, or both, to help readers locate the passage being cited.

Some sources have numbered paragraphs; if a source lacks both numbered paragraphs and headings, count the paragraphs manually. When quoting an audio or video source, use a time stamp to indicate the start of the quotation.

> Crush and Jayasingh (2015) pointed out that several other school districts in low-income areas had "jump-started their distance learning initiatives with available grant funds" (Funding Change section, para. 6).

If a heading in a source is long, you may use a shortened version of the heading in quotation marks: (Gregor, 2017, "What Happens When" section).

b. Unknown author If no author is named in the source, mention the title of the source in a signal phrase or give the first word or two of the title in parentheses (see also item 6). (If an organization serves as the author, see item 7.)

> A student's IEP may, in fact, recommend the use of mobile technology ("Considerations," 2012).

c. Unknown date When the source does not give a date, use the abbreviation "n.d." (for "no date").

> Administrators believe 1-to-1 programs boost learner engagement (Magnus, n.d.).

15. An entire website   If you mention an entire website from which you did not pull specific information, give the URL in the text of your paper but do not include it in the reference list.

> The Berkeley Center for Teaching and Learning website (https://teaching.berkeley
> .edu/) shares ideas for using mobile technology in the classroom.

16. Personal communication   Interviews that you conduct, memos, letters, email messages, and similar communications that would be difficult for your readers to retrieve should be cited in the text only, not in the reference list. (Use the first initial with the last name either in your text sentence or in parentheses.)

> One of Yim's colleagues, who has studied the effect of social media on children's
> academic progress, has contended that the benefits of this technology for
> children under 12 years old are few (F. Johnson, personal communication,
> October 20, 2021).

17. Course materials   Cite lecture notes from your instructor or your own class notes as personal communication (see item 16). If your instructor's material contains publication information, cite as you would the appropriate source. See also item 56 in 52b.

18. Work available in multiple versions   If you consulted a reprinted, republished, or translated work, include both the date of original publication and the date of the version you used, and separate the dates with a slash: (Padura, 2009/2014).

19. Sacred or classical text   Identify the text (specifying the version or edition you used), the publication date(s), and the relevant part (book, chapter, verse).

> Peace activists have long cited the biblical prophet's vision of a world without
> war: "And they shall beat their swords into plowshares, and their spears into pruning
> hooks; nation shall not lift up sword against nation, neither shall they learn
> war any more" (*Holy Bible Revised Standard Edition*, 1952/2004, Isaiah 2:4).

52b APA list of references

▸ List of APA reference list models, 367
▸ General guidelines for the reference list, 375

As you gather sources for an assignment, you will likely find them in print, on the web, and in other places. The information you will need for the reference list at the end of your paper will differ slightly for some sources, but the main principles apply to all sources: You should identify an author, a creator, or a producer whenever possible, give a title, and provide the date on which the source was produced. In most cases, you will provide page numbers or other locator or retrieval information.

Section 52b provides specific requirements for and examples of many of the sources you are likely to encounter. When you cite sources, your goals are to show that the sources you've used are reliable and relevant to your work, to provide your readers with enough information so that they can find your sources easily, and to provide that information in a consistent way according to APA conventions.

In the list of references, include only sources that you quote, summarize, or paraphrase in your paper.

General guidelines for the reference list

In APA style, the alphabetical list of works cited, which appears at the end of the paper, is titled "References." In general, an APA-style reference consists of four parts:

- the **author's** (or authors') name(s).
- the **date** of publication.
- the **title** of the work.
- the **source** of the work (the retrieval information).

Insert a period following each of these four parts.

Authors

- The author is the person or people most responsible for the work. For a book or article, for example, the author is the person or people who wrote it; for a movie, the person most responsible is the director; for a government report, the author might be the specific agency that produced the work.

GENERAL GUIDELINES FOR THE REFERENCE LIST (*cont.*)

- Alphabetize entries in the list of references by authors' last names; if a work has no author, alphabetize it by its title.
- For all authors' names, put the last name first, followed by a comma; use initials for the first and middle names.
- With two or more authors, separate the names with commas. Include names for up to twenty authors, with an ampersand (&) before the last author's name. For twenty-one or more authors, list the first nineteen authors, an ellipsis, and the last author.
- If the author is a company or an organization, give the name in typical order.

Dates

- Put the date of publication immediately after the first element of the citation. Enclose the date in parentheses, followed by a period (outside the parentheses).
- Use the date as given in the publication. Generally, give the year for books and journals (2021); the year and month for monthly magazines (2021, April); and the year, month, and day for weekly magazines and for newspapers (2021, April 9). Use the season when a publication gives the season. For web sources, use the date of posting or update, if it is available. Use "(n.d.)" if no date is given.

Titles

- Italicize the titles and subtitles of books, journals, and other stand-alone works. If a book title contains another book title or an article title, do not italicize the internal title and do not put quotation marks around it.
- Use no italics or quotation marks for the titles of articles. If an article title contains another article title or a term usually placed in quotation marks, use quotation marks around the internal title or term. If it contains a title or term usually italicized, place the title or term in italics.
- For books and articles, capitalize only the first word of the title and subtitle and all proper nouns.
- For the titles of journals, magazines, and newspapers, capitalize all words of four letters or more (and all nouns, pronouns, verbs, adjectives, and adverbs of any length).

GENERAL GUIDELINES FOR THE REFERENCE LIST (*cont.*)

Source information

- When a source lists other key contributors such as editors or translators, provide their names in typical order and their roles in parentheses: (B. Yu, Trans.).

- For multimedia sources or sources where the format may be unclear, include the source type in brackets: [Podcast episode]; [Advertisement].

- In publishers' names, omit business designations such as "Inc." or "Ltd." Otherwise, write the publisher's name exactly how it appears in the source.

- For online sources, list the name of the website in the publisher position: Twitter; YouTube; U.S. Census Bureau.

- If the publisher is the same as the author, do not repeat the name in the publisher position.

- Provide locations only for works associated with a single location (such as a conference presentation).

- Include the volume and issue numbers for any journals, magazines, or other periodicals that have them. Italicize the volume number and put the issue number, not italicized, in parentheses: *26*(2).

- When an article appears on consecutive pages, provide the range of pages: 87–96. When an article does not appear on consecutive pages, give all page numbers: A1, A17.

- Use "p." and "pp." only before page numbers for selections in edited books. Do not use "p." and "pp." with magazines, journals, and newspapers.

URLs, DOIs, and other retrieval information

- For articles and books from the web, use the DOI (digital object identifier) if the source has one. If a source does not have a DOI, give the URL.

- If a URL or DOI is long and complicated and your readers are not likely to be able to use it to access the source, you may use a permalink (if the website provides one) or create one using a shortening service such as shortdoi. org or bitly.com.

- Do not include a period after URLs or DOIs.

- Use a retrieval date for a web source only if the content is likely to change (such as content on a website's home page or in a social media profile).

General guidelines for listing authors

The formatting of authors' names in items 1–11 applies to all sources in print and on the web—books, articles, websites, and so on. For more models of specific source types, see items 12–59.

1. Single author

Yanagihara, H. (2015). *A little life.* Doubleday.

2. Two to twenty authors   List up to twenty authors by last names followed by initials. Use an ampersand (&) before the name of the last author. (See items 4 and 5 in 52a for citing works with multiple authors in the text of your paper.)

Kim, E. H., Hollon, S. D., & Olatunji, B. O. (2016). Clinical errors in cognitive-behavior therapy. *Psychotherapy, 53*(3), 325–330. https://doi.org/10.1037/pst0000074

3. Twenty-one or more authors   List the first nineteen authors, followed by an ellipsis (. . .) and the last author's name.

Sharon, G., Cruz, N. J., Kang, D.-W., Gandal, M. J., Wang, B., Kim, Y.-M., Zink, E. M., Casey, C. P., Taylor, B. C., Lane, C. J., Bramer, L. M., Isern, N. G., Hoyt, D. W., Noecker, C., Sweredoski, M. J., Moradian, A., Borenstein, E., Jansson, J. K., Knight, R., . . . Mazmanian, S. K. (2019). Human gut microbiota from autism spectrum disorder promote behavioral symptoms in mice. *Cell, 177*(6), 1600–1618. https://doi.org/10.1016/j.cell.2019.05.004

4. Organization as author

American Psychiatric Association. (2013). *Diagnostic and statistical manual of mental disorders* (5th ed.).

5. Unknown author   Begin the entry with the work's title. Alphabetize by the first word in the title (not including the articles "The," "A," or "An").

Pushed out. (2019, August 24). *The Economist, 432*(9157), 19–20.

6. Author using a screen name, pen name, or stage name Use the author's real name, if known, and give the screen name or pen name in brackets exactly as it appears in the source. If only the screen name is known, begin with that name and do not use brackets. (See also items 58 and 59 on citing screen names in social media.)

dr.zachary.smith. (2019, October 3). What problem are they trying to solve? [Comment on the article "Georgia is purging voter rolls again"]. *Slate.* https://fyre.it/sjSPFyza.4

If the author uses just a single name ("Prince," "Sophocles") or a two-part name in which the two parts are essential ("Cardi B"), give the name with no abbreviations or alterations.

7. Two or more works by the same author Use the author's name for all entries. List the entries by year, the earliest first.

Abdurraqib, H. (2017). *They can't kill us until they kill us.* Two Dollar Radio.

Abdurraqib, H. (2021). *A little devil in America: Notes in praise of Black performance.* Random House.

8. Two or more works by the same author in the same year List the works by date. In the parentheses, add "a," "b," and so on after the year. (Use these same letters when giving the year in the in-text citations.) If the works have identical dates, list the works alphabetically by title. (See also item 9 in 52a.)

Conover, E. (2019a, June 8). Gold's origins tied to collapsars. *Science News, 195*(10), 10. https://bit.ly/31JTgKD

Conover, E. (2019b, June 22). Space flames may hold secrets to soot-free fire. *Science News, 195*(11), 5. https://bit.ly/2p0Xj89

9. Editor Begin with the name(s) of the editor(s); place the abbreviation "Ed." (or "Eds." for more than one editor) in parentheses following the name(s).

Yeh, K.-H. (Ed.). (2019). *Asian indigenous psychologies in the global context.* Palgrave Macmillan.

10. Author and editor Begin with the author. After the title, place the name(s) of the editor(s) and the abbreviation "Ed." (or "Eds.") in parentheses.

Sontag, S. (2018). *Debriefing: Collected stories* (B. Taylor, Ed.). Picador.

11. Translator Begin with the author. After the title, in parentheses place the name of the translator (in normal order) and the abbreviation "Trans." (for "Translator"). Add the original date of publication at the end of the entry.

Calasso, R. (2019). *The unnamable present* (R. Dixon, Trans.). Farrar, Straus and Giroux. (Original work published 2017)

Articles and other short works

▸ Citation at a glance: Online article in a journal or magazine, 382
▸ Citation at a glance: Article from a database, 383

12. Article in a journal After the author's name, provide the title of the article first, followed by the title of the publication and other publication information. Include the volume and issue numbers and the article's page range. If an article from the web has no DOI, include the URL for the article. If an article from a database has no DOI, do not include a URL.

a. Print

Ganegoda, D. B., & Bordia, P. (2019). I can be happy for you, but not all the time: A contingency model of envy and positive empathy in the workplace. *Journal of Applied Psychology, 104*(6), 776–795.

b. Web

Bruns, A. (2019). The third shift: Multiple job holding and the incarceration of women's partners. *Social Science Research, 80*(1), 202–215. https://doi.org/dfgj

Vicary, A. M., & Larsen, A. (2018). Potential factors influencing attitudes toward veterans who commit crimes: An experimental investigation of PTSD in the legal system. *Current Research in Social Psychology, 26*(2). https://www.uiowa.edu/crisp/sites/uiowa.edu.crisp/files/crisp_vol_26_2.pdf

c. Database

Maftsir, S. (2019). Emotional change: Romantic love and the university in postcolonial Egypt. *Journal of Social History, 52*(3), 831–859. https://doi.org/10.1093/jsh/shx155

13. Article in a magazine Include the full publication date of the magazine, plus the volume and issue numbers and page range if available. If an article from the web has no DOI, use the URL for the article. If an article from a database has no DOI, do not include a URL.

a. Print

Andersen, R. (2019, April). The intention machine: A new generation of brain-machine interface can deduce what a person wants. *Scientific American, 320*(4), 24–31.

b. Web

Srinivasan, D. (2019, June 4). How digital advertising markets really work. *The American Prospect.* https://prospect.org/article/how-digital-advertising-markets-really-work

c. Database

Greengard, S. (2019, August). The algorithm that changed quantum machine learning. *Communications of the ACM, 62*(8), 15–17. https://doi.org/10.1145/3339458

14. Article in a newspaper Include the full publication date and the page and section, if available.

Finucane, M. (2019, September 25). Americans still eating too many low-quality carbs. *The Boston Globe*, B2.

Daly, J. (2019, August 2). Duquesne's med school plan part of national trend to train more doctors. *Pittsburgh Post-Gazette.* http://bit.ly/2CbUZOX

Citation at a glance

Online article in a journal or magazine `APA`

To cite an online article in a journal or magazine in APA style, include the following elements:

1. Author(s)
2. Year of publication for journal; complete date for magazine
3. Title and subtitle of article
4. Name of journal or magazine
5. Volume and issue numbers
6. DOI (digital object identifier), if article has one; otherwise, URL for article

ONLINE ARTICLE

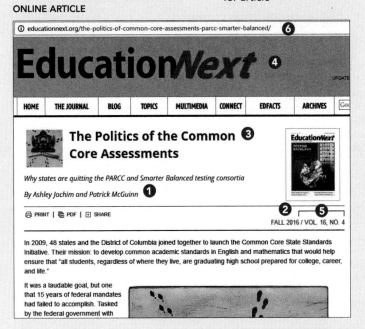

REFERENCE LIST ENTRY FOR AN ONLINE ARTICLE IN A JOURNAL OR MAGAZINE

Jochim, A., & McGuinn, P. (2016, Fall). The politics of the Common Core assessments. *Education Next, 16*(4). https://www.educationnext.org/the-politics-of-common-core-assessments-parcc-smarter-balanced/

For more on citing online articles in APA style, see items 12–14.

Citation at a glance
Article from a database APA

To cite an article from a database in APA style, include the following elements:

1 Author(s)
2 Year of publication for journal; complete date for magazine or newspaper
3 Title and subtitle of article
4 Name of periodical
5 Volume and issue numbers
6 Page number(s)
7 DOI (digital object identifier)

DATABASE RECORD

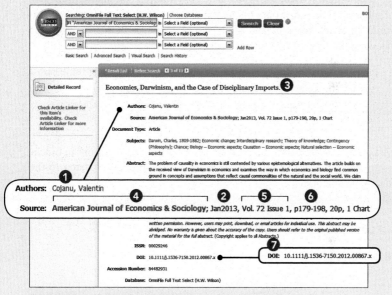

REFERENCE LIST ENTRY FOR AN ARTICLE FROM A DATABASE

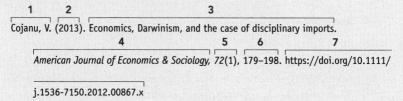

For more on citing articles from a database in APA style, see items 12–13.

15. Comment on an online article   Include the first twenty words of the comment, followed by the title of the source article in brackets.

lollyl2. (2019, September 25). My husband works in IT in a major city down South. He
is a permanent employee now, but for years [Comment on the article "The Google
workers who voted to unionize in Pittsburgh are part of tech's huge contractor
workforce"]. *Slate.* https://fyre.it/0RT8HmeL

16. Supplemental material   If an article on the web contains supplemental material that is not part of the main article, cite the material as you would an article and add the label "Supplemental material" in brackets following the title.

Blasi, D. E., Moran, S., Moisik, S. R., Widmer, P., Dediu, D., & Bickel, B. (2019). Human
sound systems are shaped by post-Neolithic changes in bite configuration
[Supplemental material]. *Science, 363*(6432). https://doi.org/10.1126/science.
aav3218

17. Letter to the editor   Insert the words "Letter to the editor" in brackets after the title of the letter. If the letter has no title, use "[Letter to the editor]" as the title.

Doran, K. (2019, October 11). When the homeless look like grandma or grandpa
[Letter to the editor]. *The New York Times.* https://nyti.ms/33foDOK

18. Editorial or other unsigned article

Gavin Newsom wants to stop rent gouging. Will lawmakers finally stand up for tenants?
[Editorial]. (2019, September 4). *Los Angeles Times.* https://lat.ms/2lBlRm1

19. Newsletter article   Cite as you would an article in a magazine, giving whatever retrieval information is available. If it is not clear that you are citing a newsletter, you may include the label "[Newsletter]" following the title.

Bond, G. (2018, Fall). Celebrities as epidemiologists. *American College of Epidemiology
Online Member Newsletter.* https://www.acepidemiology.org/assets/
ACE_Newsletter_Fall_2018%20FINAL.pdf

20. Review (book, film, performance, etc.) In brackets, give the type of work reviewed, the title, and the director for a film or the author for a book. If the review has no author or title, use the description in brackets as the title.

Douthat, R. (2019, October 14). A hustle gone wrong [Review of the film *Hustlers*, by L. Scafaria, Dir.]. *National Review, 71*(18), 47.

Hall, W. (2019). [Review of the book *How to change your mind: The new science of psychedelics,* by M. Pollan]. *Addiction, 114*(10), 1892–1893. https://doi.org/10.1111/add.14702

21. Published interview

Remnick, D. (2019, July 1). Robert Caro reflects on Robert Moses, L.B.J., and his own career in nonfiction. *The New Yorker.* https://bit.ly/2Lukm3X

22. Article in a reference work (encyclopedia, dictionary, wiki) When referencing an online, undated reference work entry, include the retrieval date. When referencing a work with archived versions, like *Wikipedia*, use the date and URL of the archived version you read.

Brue, A. W., & Wilmshurst, L. (2018). Adaptive behavior assessments. In B. B. Frey (Ed.), *The SAGE encyclopedia of educational research, measurement, and evaluation* (pp. 40–44). SAGE Publications. https://doi.org/10.4135/9781506326139.n21

Merriam-Webster. (n.d.). Adscititious. In *Merriam-Webster.com dictionary*. Retrieved September 5, 2021, from https://www.merriam-webster.com/dictionary/adscititious

Behaviorism. (2019, October 11). In *Wikipedia*. https://en.wikipedia.org/w/index.php?title=Behaviorism&oldid=915544724

23. Paper or poster presented at a conference or meeting (unpublished)

Wood, M. (2019, January 3–6). *The effects of an adult development course on students' perceptions of aging* [Poster session]. Forty-First Annual National Institute on the Teaching of Psychology, St. Pete Beach, FL, United States. https://nitop.org/resources/Documents/2019%20Poster%20Session%20II.pdf

Books and other long works

▸ Citation at a glance: Book, **387**

24. Basic format for a book

a. Print

Treuer, D. (2019). *The heartbeat of Wounded Knee: Native America from 1890 to the present.* Riverhead Books.

b. E-book Include the DOI or, if a DOI is not available, the URL for the page from which you downloaded the book.

Perlroth, N. (2021). *This is how they tell me the world ends: The cyberweapons arms race.* Bloomsbury. www.amazon.com/dp/B0877D6H28/

c. Web (or online library) Give the URL for the page where you accessed the book.

Obama, M. (2018). *Becoming.* Crown. https://books.google.com/books?id= YbtNDwAAQBAJ

d. Audiobook Include the narrator, the label "Audiobook," and the URL for the page where you accessed the audiobook.

Zuckerman, G. (2021). *A shot to save the world: The inside story of the life-or-death race for a COVID-19 vaccine* (J. Armstrong, Narr.) [Audiobook]. Penguin Audio. https://www.audible.com/pd/A-Shot-to-Save-the-World-Audiobook/0593585070

e. Database If the book has a DOI, include it. If not, do not list a URL or database name.

Kilby, P. (2019). *The green revolution: Narratives of politics, technology and gender.* Routledge. http://doi.org/dfgt

Citation at a glance

Book APA

To cite a print book in APA style, include the following elements:

1 Author(s)
2 Year of publication

3 Title and subtitle
4 Publisher

TITLE PAGE

CITY

A GUIDEBOOK FOR THE URBAN AGE

❶ P. D. SMITH

FROM COPYRIGHT PAGE

First published in Great Britain and the USA in 2012

Bloomsbury Publishing Plc, 50 Bedford Square, London WC1B 3DP
Bloomsbury USA, 175 Fifth Avenue, New York, NY 10010

❷

Copyright © 2012 by P. D. Smith

BLOOMSBURY
LONDON · BERLIN · NEW YORK · SYDNEY

❹ BLOOMSBURY
LONDON · BERLIN · NEW YORK · SYDNEY

REFERENCE LIST ENTRY FOR A PRINT BOOK

1   2   3   4

Smith, P. D. (2012). *City: A guidebook for the urban age*. Bloomsbury.

For more on citing books in APA style, see items 24–30.

25. Edition other than the first   Include the edition number (abbreviated) in parentheses after the title.

Dessler, A. E., & Parson, E. A. (2019). *The science and politics of global climate change: A guide to the debate* (3rd ed.). Cambridge University Press.

26. Selection in an anthology or a collection   An anthology is a collection of works on a common theme, often with different authors for the selections and usually with an editor for the entire volume.

a. Entire anthology

Lindert, J., & Marsoobian, A. T. (Eds.). (2018). *Multidisciplinary perspectives on genocide and memory.* Springer.

b. Selection in an anthology

Pettigrew, D. (2018). The suppression of cultural memory and identity in Bosnia and Herzegovina. In J. Lindert & A. T. Marsoobian (Eds.), *Multidisciplinary perspectives on genocide and memory* (pp. 187–198). Springer.

27. Multivolume work   If you have used only one volume of a multivolume work, indicate the volume number after the title of the complete work; if the volume has its own title, add that title after the volume number.

a. All volumes

Zeigler-Hill, V., & Shackelford, T. K. (Eds.). (2018). *The SAGE handbook of personality and individual differences* (Vols. I–III). SAGE Publications.

b. One volume, with title

Zeigler-Hill, V., & Shackelford, T. K. (Eds.). (2018). *The SAGE handbook of personality and individual differences: Vol. II. Origins of personality and individual differences.* SAGE Publications.

28. Dictionary or other reference work

Leong, F. T. L. (Ed.). (2008). *Encyclopedia of counseling* (Vols. 1–4). SAGE Publications.

29. Republished book

Fremlin, C. (2017). *The hours before dawn.* Dover Publications. *(Original work published 1958)*

30. Book in a language other than English Place the English translation, not italicized, in brackets.

Carminati, G. G., & Méndez, A. (2012). *Étapes de vie, étapes de soins* [Stages of life, stages of care]. Médecine & Hygiène.

31. Dissertation If you accessed the dissertation from a specialty database, indicate it at the end of the citation.

Bacaksizlar, N. G. (2019). *Understanding social movements through simulations of anger contagion in social media* [Doctoral dissertation, University of North Carolina at Charlotte]. ProQuest Dissertations & Theses.

32. Conference proceedings

Srujan Raju, K., Govardhan, A., Padmaja Rani, B., Sridevi, R., & Ramakrishna Murty, M. (Eds.). (2018). *Proceedings of the third international conference on computational intelligence and informatics.* Springer.

33. Government document If no author is listed, begin with the department that produced the document. Any broader organization listed can be included as the publisher of the document, as in the first example below. If a specific report number is provided, include it after the title.

National Park Service. (2019, April 11). *Travel where women made history: Ordinary and extraordinary places of American women.* U.S. Department of the Interior. https://www.nps.gov/subjects/travelwomenshistory/index.htm

33. Government document (*cont.*)

Berchick, E. R., Barnett, J. C., & Upton, R. D. (2019, September 10). *Health insurance coverage in the United States: 2018* (Report No. P60-267). U.S. Census Bureau. https://www.census.gov/library/publications/2019/demo/p60-267.html

34. Report from a private organization

Ford Foundation International Fellowships Program. (2019). *Leveraging higher education to promote social justice: Evidence from the IFP alumni tracking study.* https://p.widencdn.net/kei61u/IFP-Alumni-Tracking-Study-Report-5

35. Legal source   The title of a court case is italicized in an in-text citation, but it is not italicized in the reference list.

Sweatt v. Painter, 339 U.S. 629 (1950). http://www.law.cornell.edu/supct/html/historics/USSC_CR_0339_0629_ZS.html

36. Sacred or classical text   Cite a sacred or classical text as a book, using the title, year, and editor/translator (if any) of the version you are using. If an original date is known, include it at the end of the citation. If the year is approximate, include "ca." (for "circa"); use "B.C.E." for ancient texts.

The Holy Bible 1611 edition: King James version. (2006). Hendrickson Publishers. (Original work published 1611)

Homer. (2018). *The odyssey* (E. Wilson, Trans.). W. W. Norton & Company. (Original work published ca. 725–675 B.C.E.)

Websites and parts of websites

▶ Citation at a glance: Page from a website, 392

37. Entire website   If you retrieved specific information from the home page of a website, include the website name, retrieval date, and URL in your reference list entry. If you only mention the website in the body of your paper, do not include it in your reference list. See items 14 and 15 in 52a for advice about how to cite web sources in the text of your paper.

38. Page from a website Use one of the models below only when your source doesn't fit into any other category. These models are for content found on an interior page of a website and not published elsewhere. The website name follows the page title unless the author and website name are the same.

National Institute of Mental Health. (2016, March). *Seasonal affective disorder*. National Institutes of Health. https://www.nimh.nih.gov/health/topics/ seasonal-affective-disorder/index.shtml

BBC News. (2019, October 31). *California fires: Goats help save Ronald Reagan Presidential Library*. https://www.bbc.com/news/world-us-canada-50248549

39. Document on a website Most documents published on websites fall into other categories, such as an article, a government document, or a report from a private organization (items 12–14, 33, and 34).

Tahseen, M., Ahmed, S., & Ahmed, S. (2018). *Bullying of Muslim youth: A review of research and recommendations*. The Family and Youth Institute. http://www.thefyi. org/wp-content/uploads/2018/10/FYI-Bullying-Report.pdf

40. Blog post Cite a blog post as you would an article in a periodical. Treat a comment on a blog post as you would a comment on an online article (see item 15).

Fister, B. (2019, February 14). Information literacy's third wave. *Library Babel Fish*. https://www.insidehighered.com/blogs/library-babel-fish/information-literacy% E2%80%99s-third-wave

Audio, visual, and multimedia sources

41. Podcast series or episode

Joffe-Walt, C. (Host). (2020). *Nice white parents* [Audio podcast]. The New York Times. https://open.spotify.com/show/7oBSLCZFCgpdCaBjIG8mLV

Longoria, J. (Host & Producer). (2019, April 19). Americanish [Audio podcast episode]. In J. Abumrad & R. Krulwich (Hosts), *Radiolab*. WNYC Studios. https://www. wnycstudios.org/podcasts/radiolab/articles/americanish

Citation at a glance

Page from a website APA

To cite a page from a website in APA style, include the following elements:

1 Author(s)

2 Date of publication or most recent update ("n.d." if there is no date)

3 Title of web page

4 Name of website (if not the same as author)

5 URL of web page

PAGE FROM A WEBSITE

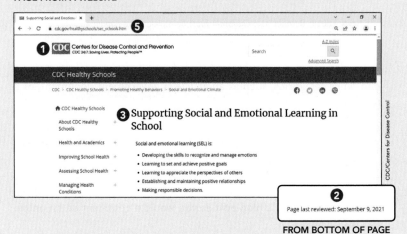

FROM BOTTOM OF PAGE

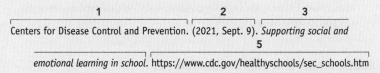

REFERENCE LIST ENTRY FOR A PAGE FROM A WEBSITE

        1   2   3

Centers for Disease Control and Prevention. (2021, Sept. 9). *Supporting social and*

                            5

emotional learning in school. https://www.cdc.gov/healthyschools/sec_schools.htm

For more on citing documents from websites in APA style, see items 37–39.

42. Video or audio on the web (YouTube, TED Talk)

The New York Times. (2018, January 9). *Taking a knee and taking down a monument* [Video]. YouTube. https://www.youtube.com/watch?v=qY34DQCdUvQ

Wray, B. (2019, May). *How climate change affects your mental health* [Video]. TED Conferences. https://www.ted.com/talks/britt_wray_how_climate_change_ affects_your_mental_health

43. Transcript of an audio or video file

Gopnik, A. (2019, July 10). *A separate kind of intelligence* [Video transcript]. Edge. https://www.edge.org/conversation/alison_gopnik-a-separate-kind-of-intelligence

44. Film   If the film is a special version, such as an extended cut, include that information in brackets after the title.

Peele, J. (Director). (2017). *Get out* [Film]. Universal Pictures.

Hitchcock, A. (Director). (1959). *The essentials collection: North by northwest* [Film; special ed. on DVD]. Metro-Goldwyn-Mayer; Universal Pictures Home Entertainment.

45. TV or radio series or episode

Burns, K., Duncan, D., & Dunfey, J. (Producers). (2019). *Country music* [TV series]. Florentine Films; WETA-TV; PBS.

Guy, S. (Writer), Lenis, C. (Writer), & Williams, R. R. (Director). (2021, May 26). The rice kingdom (Season 1, Episode 2) [TV series episode]. In Das, S., Jagger, K., Martz, G., Piligian, C., Toback, F., & Williams, R. R. (Executive Producers), *High on the hog: How African American cuisine transformed America*. Netflix Studios.

46. Music recording

Nielsen, C. (2014). *Carl Nielsen: Symphonies 1 & 4* [Album recorded by New York Philharmonic Orchestra]. Dacapo Records. (Original work published 1892–1916)

Carlile, B. (2018). The mother [Song]. On *By the way, I forgive you*. Low Country Sound; Elektra.

47. Lecture, speech, address, or recorded interview Cite the speaker or interviewee as the author.

Warren, E. (2019, September 16). *Senator Elizabeth Warren speech in Washington Square Park* [Speech video recording]. C-SPAN. https://www.c-span.org/video/?4643141/senator-elizabeth-warren-campaigns-york-city

48. Data set or graphic representation of data (chart, table)

Reid, L. (2019). *Smarter homes: Experiences of living in low carbon homes 2013–2018* [Data set]. UK Data Service. https://doi.org/10.5255/UKDA-SN-853485

Pew Research Center. (2018, November 15). *U.S. public is closely divided about overall health risk from food additives* [Chart]. https://www.pewresearch.org/science/2018/11/19/public-perspectives-on-food-risks/

49. Mobile app Begin with the developer of the app, if known.

Google. (2019). *Google Earth* (Version 9.3.3) [Mobile app]. App Store. https://apps.apple.com/us/app/google-earth/id293622097

50. Video game

ConcernedApe. (2016). *Stardew Valley* [Video game]. Chucklefish.

51. Map

Desjardins, J. (2017, November 17). *Walmart nation: Mapping the largest employers in the U.S.* [Map]. Visual Capitalist. https://www.visualcapitalist.com/walmart-nation-mapping-largest-employers-u-s/

52. Advertisement

America's Biopharmaceutical Companies [Advertisement]. (2018, September). *The Atlantic, 322*(2), 2.

Centers for Disease Control and Prevention. (n.d.). *A tip from a former smoker: Beatrice* [Advertisement]. U.S. Department of Health and Human Services. https://www.cdc.gov/tobacco/campaign/tips/resources/ads/pdf-print-ads/beatrices-tip-print-ad-7x10.pdf

53. **Work of art or photograph** When citing a physical piece of art such as a painting or sculpture, include the location of the piece. If you viewed the piece online or in a book, also include the website and URL or publication information for the source.

O'Keeffe, G. (1931). *Cow's skull: Red, white, and blue* [Painting]. Metropolitan Museum of Art, New York, NY, United States. https://www.metmuseum.org/art/collection/search/488694

Browne, M. (1963). *The burning monk* [Photograph]. Time. http://100photos.time.com/photos/malcolm-browne-burning-monk

54. **Brochure or fact sheet**

National Council of State Boards of Nursing. (2018). *A nurse manager's guide to substance use disorder in nursing* [Brochure].

World Health Organization. (2019, July 15). *Immunization coverage* [Fact sheet]. https://www.who.int/news-room/fact-sheets/detail/immunization-coverage

55. **Press release**

New York University. (2019, September 5). *NYU Oral Cancer Center awarded $2.5 million NIH grant to study cancer pain* [Press release]. https://www.nyu.edu/about/news-publications/news/2019/september/nyu-oral-cancer-center-awarded--2-5-million-nih-grant-to-study-c.html

56. **Lecture notes or other course materials** Cite posted materials as you would a document on a website (see item 39). Cite material from your instructor that is not available to others as personal communication in the text of your paper (see item 16 in 52a).

Chatterjee, S., Constenla, D., Kinghorn, A., & Mayora, C. (2018). *Teaching vaccine economics everywhere: Costing in vaccine planning and programming* [Lecture notes and slides]. Department of Population, Family, and Reproductive Health, Johns Hopkins University. http://ocw.jhsph.edu/index.cfm/go/viewCourse/course/TeachVaccEconCosting/coursePage/lectureNotes/

Personal communication and social media

57. Email and other messages   Email and text messages, letters, and other personal communication are not included in the list of references. See item 16 in 52a for citing these sources in the text of your paper.

58. Social media post (Twitter, Instagram)   If the writer's real name and screen name are given, put the real name first, followed by the screen name in brackets. If only the screen name is known, begin with the screen name without brackets. For the title, include up to the first twenty words (including hashtags or emojis) of the title, caption, or post. After the title, list any attachments (such as a photo or link) and the type of post in separate brackets. List the website or app in the publisher position. Include the URL for the post. Cite posts that are not accessible to all readers as personal communication in the text of your paper.

National Science Foundation [@NSF]. (2019, October 13). *Understanding how forest structure drives carbon sequestration is important for ecologists, climate modelers and forest managers, who are working on* [Thumbnail with link attached] [Tweet]. Twitter. https://twitter.com/NSF/status/1183388649263652864

Smithsonian [@smithsonian]. (2019, October 7). *You're looking at a ureilite meteorite under a microscope. When illuminated with polarized light, they appear in dazzling colors, influenced* [Photograph]. Instagram. https://www.instagram.com/p/B3VI27yHLQG/

59. Social media profile or highlight   Because profiles are designed to change over time, include the date you viewed the page.

National Science Foundation [@NSF]. (n.d.). *Tweets* [Twitter profile]. Twitter. Retrieved August 15, 2022, from https://twitter.com/NSF

Smithsonian [@smithsonian]. (n.d.). *#Apollo50* [Highlight]. Instagram. Retrieved January 5, 2021, from https://www.instagram.com/stories/highlights/17902787752343364/

53 APA format; sample research paper

The guidelines in this section are consistent with advice given in the *Publication Manual of the American Psychological Association*, 7th ed. (APA, 2020), and with typical requirements for undergraduate papers. For a sample APA paper, see 53b.

53a APA format

The guidelines in this section describe APA's recommendations for formatting the text of a paper written for an undergraduate college course and for preparing the reference list.

Formatting the paper

Font If your instructor does not require a specific font, use one that is standard and easy to read (such as 12-point Times New Roman).

Title page Put the page number 1 at the right margin one-half inch from the top of the page. A few lines down the page, center the full title of your paper in bold. After a blank line, include your name, and then add the following assignment details on separate lines: the department and the school, the course code and name, your instructor's name, and the due date. See page 402 for a sample title page.

Page numbers and running head Starting with the title page, number all pages in the upper-right corner one-half inch from the top of the page. Professional (submitted for publication) papers also require a running head, a shortened version of the paper's title (no more than 50 characters) on every page. If your assignment requires one, type the running head in the upper-left corner in all capital letters. See page 414 for an example of a running head.

Margins, line spacing, and paragraph indents   Use margins of one inch on all sides of the page. Left-align the text. Double-space all text throughout the paper. Indent the first line of each paragraph one-half inch.

Capitalization, italics, and quotation marks   In headings and in titles of works that appear in the text of the paper, capitalize all words of four letters or more (and all nouns, pronouns, verbs, adjectives, and adverbs of any length). Capitalize the first word following a colon in a title or a heading, and capitalize the first word following a colon in the body of your paper if the word begins a complete sentence.

In the body of your paper, italicize the titles of books, journals, magazines, and other long works, including websites. Use quotation marks around the titles of articles, short stories, and other short works named in the body of your paper.

NOTE: APA has different requirements for titles in the reference list. See page 400.

Long quotations   When a quotation is forty or more words, indent it one-half inch from the left margin. Double-space the quotation. Do not use quotation marks around it. (See p. 407 for an example. See also 49b for more information about integrating long quotations.)

Footnotes   Insert footnotes using the footnote function in your word processing program. The callout number in the text should immediately follow a word or any mark of punctuation except a dash. The text of the footnote should be single-spaced.

Abstract   If your assignment requires an abstract—a 150-to-250-word summary paragraph—include it on a new page after the title page. Center the word "Abstract" (in bold) one inch from the top of the page. Double-space the abstract and do not indent the first or subsequent lines. For an example, see page 414.

Headings   Although headings are not always necessary, their use is encouraged in the social sciences. For most undergraduate papers, one level of heading is usually sufficient. (See the paper in 53b.)

First-level headings are centered and boldface. In research papers and laboratory reports, the major headings are "Method," "Results," and "Discussion." In other types of papers, the major headings should be informative and concise, conveying the structure of the paper. In all headings, capitalize the first and last words and all words of four or more letters (and nouns, pronouns, verbs, adjectives, and adverbs of any length).

First-Level Heading Centered

Second-Level Heading Aligned Left

Third-Level Heading Aligned Left

Visuals APA classifies visuals as tables and figures (figures include graphs, charts, drawings, and photographs). Place each visual immediately after the paragraph in which it is called out, or place it on the following page if it does not fit on the same page as the callout.

Number each table or figure (Table 1, Table 2; Figure 1, Figure 2) and provide a clear title. The label and title should appear on separate lines above the visual, flush left and double-spaced. Type the number in bold font; italicize the title.

Table 2

Effect of Nifedipine (Procardia) on Blood Pressure in Women

If you have used data from an outside source or have taken or adapted the visual from a source, give the source information in a note below the table. Begin with the word "Note," italicized and followed by a period. Notes can also include additional information or context for the visual. For an example of a visual with a note, see page 405.

Preparing the list of references

Begin your list of references on a new page at the end of the paper. Center the title "References" in bold one inch from the top of the page. Double-space throughout. For a sample reference list, see page 412.

Indenting entries Type the first line of each entry at the left margin and indent any additional lines one-half inch.

Alphabetizing the list Alphabetize the reference list by the last names of the authors (or editors) or by the first word of an organization name (if the author is an organization). When a work has no author or editor, alphabetize by the first word of the title other than "A," "An," or "The."

If your list includes two or more works by the same author, arrange those entries by year, the earliest first. If your list includes two or more works by the same author in the same year, arrange those works alphabetically by title. Add the letters "a," "b," and so on within the parentheses after the year. For journal articles, use only the year and the letter: (2012a). For articles in magazines and newspapers, use the full date and the letter in the reference list: (2012a, July 7); use only the year and the letter in the in-text citation.

Authors' names Invert all authors' names and use initials instead of first names. Separate the names with commas. For two to twenty authors, use an ampersand (&) before the last author's name. For twenty-one or more authors, give the first nineteen authors, followed by an ellipsis and the last author (see item 3 in 52b).

Titles of books and articles In the reference list, italicize the titles and subtitles of books. Do not italicize or use quotation marks around the titles of articles and other stand-alone works. For both books and articles, capitalize only the first word of the title and subtitle (and all proper nouns). Capitalize names of journals, magazines, and newspapers as you would capitalize them normally (see 39c).

Abbreviations for page numbers Abbreviations for "page" and "pages" ("p." and "pp.") are used before page numbers of selections in anthologies and other edited books (see item 26 in 52b). Do not use "p." or "pp." before page numbers of articles in journals and magazines (see items 12 and 13 in 52b).

Breaking a URL or DOI   Do not insert any line breaks into a URL or
DOI (digital object identifier). Any line breaks that your word processor
makes automatically are acceptable. Do not add a period at the end of a
URL or DOI.

53b Sample APA research paper

On the following pages is a research paper on the use of educational
technology in the shift to student-centered learning, written by April Bo
Wang, a student in an education class. Wang's assignment was to write
a literature review paper documented with APA-style citations and references. Following Wang's paper is a sample abstract and running head,
used for professional papers. (If you are not sure what your assignment
requires, check with your instructor.)

1

All pages are numbered, starting with the title page.

Technology and the Shift From Teacher-Delivered to Student-Centered Learning: A Review of the Literature

Paper title is boldface, followed by one blank (double-spaced) line. Writer's name, department and school, course, instructor, and date follow on separate double-spaced lines.

April Bo Wang

Department of Education, Glen County Community College

EDU 107: Education, Technology, and Media

Dr. Julien Gomez

October 29, 2017

Marginal annotations indicate APA-style formatting and effective writing.

2

Technology and the Shift From Teacher-Delivered to
Student-Centered Learning: A Review of the Literature

In the United States, most public school systems are struggling with teacher shortages, which are projected to worsen as the number of applicants to education schools decreases (Donitsa-Schmidt & Zuzovsky, 2014, p. 420). Citing federal data, *The New York Times* reported a 30% drop in "people entering teacher preparation programs" between 2010 and 2014 (Rich, 2015, para. 10). Especially in science and math fields, the teacher shortage is projected to escalate in the next 10 years (Hutchison, 2012). In recent decades, instructors and administrators have viewed the practice of student-centered learning as one promising solution. Unlike traditional teacher-delivered (also called "transmissive") instruction, student-centered learning allows students to help direct their own education by setting their own goals and selecting appropriate resources for achieving those goals. Though student-centered learning might once have been viewed as an experimental solution in understaffed schools, it is gaining credibility as an effective pedagogical practice. What is also gaining momentum is the idea that technology might play a significant role in fostering student-centered learning. This literature review will examine three key questions:

1. In what ways is student-centered learning effective?
2. Can educational technology help students drive their own learning?
3. How can public schools effectively combine teacher talent and educational technology?

In the face of mounting teacher shortages, public schools should embrace educational technology that promotes student-centered learning in order to help all students become engaged and successful learners.

Sources provide background information and context.

In-text citation for a quotation from a source without page numbers includes a paragraph number or another locator.

Wang sets up her organization by posing three questions.

Wang states her thesis.

In What Ways Is Student-Centered Learning Effective?

According to the International Society for Technology in Education (2016), "Student-centered learning moves students from passive receivers of information to active participants in their own discovery process. What students learn, how they learn it, and how their learning is assessed are all driven by each individual student's needs and abilities" (What Is It? section). The results of student-centered learning have been positive, not only for academic achievement but also for student self-esteem. In this model of instruction, the teacher acts as a facilitator, and the students actively participate in the process of learning and teaching. With guidance, students decide on the learning goals most pertinent to themselves, they devise a learning plan that will most likely help them achieve those goals, they direct themselves in carrying out that learning plan, and they assess how much they learned (Çubukçu, 2012, Introduction section). The major differences between student-centered learning and instructor-centered learning are summarized in Table 1.

Bell (2010) has argued that the chief benefit of student-centered learning is that it can connect students with "real-world tasks," thus making learning more engaging as well as more comprehensive (p. 42). For example, Bell observed a group of middle-school students who wanted to build a social justice monument for their school. They researched social justice issues, selected several to focus on, and then designed a three-dimensional playground to represent those issues. In doing so, they achieved learning goals in the areas of social studies, physics, and mathematics and practiced research and teamwork. Students engaged in this kind of learning performed better on both project-based assessments and standardized tests (Bell, 2010).

Wang uses a source to define the key term "student-centered learning."

Locator is included for a paraphrase to help readers find the source in a long article without page numbers.

Page number or other locator is not necessary for a paraphrase from a short article.

4

Table 1

Comparison of Two Approaches to Teaching and Learning

Teaching and learning period	Instructor-centered approach	Student-centered approach
Before class	• Instructor prepares lecture/instruction on new topic. • Students complete homework on previous topic.	• Students read and view new material, practice new concepts, and prepare questions ahead of class. • Instructor views student practice and questions, identifies learning opportunities.
During class	• Instructor delivers new material in a lecture or prepared discussion. • Students — unprepared — listen, watch, take notes, and try to follow along with the new material.	• Students lead discussions of the new material or practice applying the concepts or skills in an active environment. • Instructor answers student questions and provides immediate feedback.
After class	• Instructor grades homework and gives feedback about the previous lesson. • Students work independently to practice or apply the new concepts.	• Students apply concepts/skills to more complex tasks, some of their own choosing, individually and in groups. • Instructor posts additional resources to help students.

Note. Adapted from *The Flipped Class Demystified*, by New York University, n.d. (https://www.nyu.edu/faculty/teaching-and-learning
-resources/instructional-technology-support/instructional-design
-assessment/flipped-classes/the-flipped-class-demystified.html).

Wang creates a table to compare and contrast two key concepts for her readers.

5

In a citation
of a work with
three or more
authors, the first
author's name,
followed by
"et al.," is given
in parentheses
or in a signal
phrase.

A Stanford study came to a similar conclusion; researchers examined four schools that had moved from teacher-driven instruction to student-centered learning (Friedlaender et al., 2014). The study focused on students from a mix of racial, cultural, and socioeconomic backgrounds, with varying levels of English-language proficiency. The researchers predicted that this mix of students, representing differing levels of academic ability, would benefit from a student-centered approach. Through interviews, surveys, and classroom observations, the researchers identified key characteristics of the new student-centered learning environments at the four schools:

- teachers who prioritized building relationships with students
- support structures for teachers to improve and collaborate on instruction

Authors and
year are given
earlier in the
paragraph,
so only page
numbers are
provided at
the end of the
paraphrase.

- a shift in classroom activity from lectures and tests to projects and performance-based assessments (pp. 5–7)

After the schools designed their curriculum to be personalized to individual students rather than standardized across a diverse student body and to be inclusive of skills such as persistence as well as traditional academic skills, students outperformed peers on state tests and increased their rates of high school and college graduation (Friedlaender et al., 2014, p. 3).

Headings,
centered
and boldface,
help readers
follow the
organization.

Can Educational Technology Help Students Drive Their Own Learning?

When students engage in self-directed learning, they rely less on teachers to deliver information and require less face-to-face time with teachers. For content delivery, many school districts have begun to use educational technology resources that, in recent years, have become more available, more affordable, and easier to use. For the purposes of this paper, the term "educational technology resources" encompasses the following: distance learning, by which students learn from a remote

6

instructor online; other online education programming such as slide
shows and video or audio lectures; interactive online activities, such
as quizzing or games; and the use of computers, tablets, smartphones,
SMART Boards, or other such devices for coursework.

Much like student-centered learning, the use of educational
technology began in many places as a temporary measure to keep classes
running despite teacher shortages. A Horn and Staker study (2011)
examined the major patterns over time for students who subscribed to
distance learning, for example. A decade ago, students who enrolled
in distance learning often fell into one of the following categories:
They lived in a rural community that had no alternative for learning;
they attended a school where there were not enough qualified teachers
to teach certain subjects; or they were homeschooled or homebound.
But faced with tighter budgets, teacher shortages, increasingly diverse
student populations, and rigorous state standards, schools recognized
the need and the potential for distance learning across the board.

As the teacher shortage has intensified, educational technology
resources have become more tailored to student needs and more
affordable. Pens that convert handwritten notes to digital text and
organize them, backpacks that charge electronic devices, and apps
that create audiovisual flash cards are just a few of the more recent
innovations. Some educational technology resources entertain students
while supporting student-centered learning. Svokos (2015) described
popular educational games developed by the nonprofit organization
GlassLab and used in thousands of U.S. classrooms:

> Some of the company's games are education versions of existing
> ones—for example, its first release was SimCity EDU—while others
> are originals. Teachers get real-time updates on students' progress
> as well as suggestions on what subjects they need to spend more
> time perfecting. (5. Educational Games section)

Wang develops
her thesis.

In a signal
phrase, the
word "and"
links the names
of two authors;
the date is given
in parentheses.

Quotation of
40 or more
words is
indented
without
quotation
marks.

Section title
is used for a
quotation from
an unpaginated
source.

7

Many of the companies behind these products offer institutional discounts to schools where such devices are used widely by students and teachers.

Horn and Staker (2011) concluded that the chief benefit of technological learning was that it could adapt to the individual student in a way that whole-class delivery by a single teacher could not. Their study examined various schools where technology enabled student-centered learning. For example, Carpe Diem High School in Yuma, Arizona, hired only six certified subject teachers and then outfitted its classrooms with 280 computers connected to online learning programs. The programs included software that offered "continual feedback, assessment, and incremental victory in a way that a face-to-face teacher with a class of 30 students never could. After each win, students continue to move forward at their own pace" (p. 9). Students alternated between personalized 55-minute courses online and 55-minute courses with one of the six teachers. The academic outcomes were promising. Carpe Diem ranked first in its county for student math and reading scores. Similarly, Rocketship Education, a charter network that serves low-income, predominantly Latino students, created a digital learning lab, reducing the need to hire more teachers. Rocketship's academic scores ranked in the top 15 of all California low-income public schools.

Wang uses her own analysis to shape the conversation among her sources in this synthesis paragraph.

It is clear that educational technology will continue to play a role in student and school performance. Horn and Staker (2011) acknowledged that they focused on programs in which integration of educational technology led to improved student performance. In other schools, technological learning is simply distance learning—watching a remote teacher—and not student-centered learning that allows students to partner with teachers to develop enriching learning experiences. That said, many educators seem convinced that educational technology has the potential to help them transition from traditional teacher-driven

8

learning to student-centered learning. All four schools in the Stanford study heavily relied on technology (Friedlaender et al., 2014). And indeed, Demski (2012) argued that technology is not supplemental but instead is "central" to student-centered learning (p. 33). Rather than turning to a teacher as the source of information, students are sent to investigate solutions to problems by searching online, emailing experts, collaborating with one another in a wiki space, or completing online practice. Instead of relying on a teacher for the answer to a question, students are driven to perform—driven to use technology to find those answers themselves.

How Can Public Schools Effectively Combine Teacher Talent and Educational Technology?

Some researchers have expressed doubt that schools are ready for student-centered learning—or any type of instruction—that is driven by technology. In a recent survey conducted by the Nellie Mae Education Foundation, Moeller and Reitzes (2011) reported not only that many teachers lacked confidence in their ability to incorporate technology in the classroom but that 43% of polled high school students said that they lacked confidence in their technological proficiency going into college and careers. The study concluded that technology alone would not improve learning environments. Yet others argued that students adapt quickly to even unfamiliar technology and use it to further their own learning. For example, Mitra (2013) caught the attention of the education world with his study of how to educate students in the slums of India. He installed an Internet-accessible computer in a wall in a New Delhi urban slum and left it there with no instructions. Over a few months, many of the children had learned how to use the computer, how to access information over the Internet, how to interpret information, and how to communicate this information to one another. Mitra's experiment was "not about making learning happen. [It was] about letting it

Wang uses a source to introduce a counter-argument.

Brackets indicate Wang's change in the quoted material.

9

For a direct quotation from a video, a time stamp indicates the start of the quotation.

happen" (16:31). He concluded that in the absence of teachers, even in developing countries less inundated by technology, a tool that allowed access to an organized database of knowledge (such as a search engine) was sufficient to provide students with a rewarding learning experience.

According to the Stanford study, however, the presence of teachers is still crucial (Friedlaender et al., 2014). Their roles will simply change from distributors of knowledge to facilitators and supporters of self-directed student-centered learning. The researchers asserted that teacher education and professional development programs can no longer prepare their teachers in a single instructional mode, such as teacher-delivered learning; they must instead equip teachers with a wide repertoire of skills to support a wide variety of student learning experiences. The Stanford study argued that since teachers would be partnering with students to shape the learning experience, rather than designing and delivering a curriculum on their own, the main job of a teacher would become relationship building. The teacher would establish a relationship with each student so that the teacher could support whatever learning the student pursues.

Many schools have already effectively paired a reduced faculty with educational technology to support successful student-centered learning. For example, Watson (2008) offered a case study of the Cincinnati Public Schools Virtual High School, which brought students together in a physical school building to work with an assortment of online learning programs. Although there were only 10 certified teachers in the building, students were able to engage in highly individualized instruction according to their own needs, strengths, and learning styles, using the 10 teachers as support (p. 7). Commonwealth Connections Academy (CCA), a public school in Pennsylvania, also brings students into a physical school building to engage in digital

10

curriculum. However, rather than having students identify their own learning goals and design their own curriculum around those goals, CCA uses educational technology as an assessment tool to identify areas of student weakness. It then partners students with teachers to address those areas (pp. 8–9).

Conclusion

Public education faces the opportunity for a shift from the model of teacher-delivered instruction that has characterized American public schools since their foundation to a student-centered learning model. Not only has student-centered learning proved effective in improving student academic and developmental outcomes, but it can also synchronize with technological learning for widespread adaptability across schools. Because it relies on student direction rather than an established curriculum, student-centered learning supported by educational technology can adapt to the different needs of individual students and a variety of learning environments—urban and rural, well funded and underfunded. Similarly, when student-centered learning relies on technology rather than a corps of uniformly trained teachers, it holds promise for schools that would otherwise suffer from a lack of human or financial resources.

Tone of the conclusion is objective and presents answers to Wang's three organizational questions.

References

Bell, S. (2010). Project-based learning for the 21st century: Skills for the future. *The Clearing House, 83*(2), 39–43.

Çubukçu, Z. (2012). Teachers' evaluation of student-centered learning environments. *Education, 133*(1).

Demski, J. (2012, January). This time it's personal. *THE Journal (Technological Horizons in Education), 39*(1), 32–36.

Donitsa-Schmidt, S., & Zuzovsky, R. (2014). Teacher supply and demand: The school level perspective. *American Journal of Educational Research, 2*(6), 420–429. https://doi.org/10.12691/education-2-6-14

Friedlaender, D., Burns, D., Lewis-Charp, H., Cook-Harvey, C. M., & Darling-Hammond, L. (2014). *Student-centered schools: Closing the opportunity gap* [Research brief]. Stanford Center for Opportunity Policy in Education. https://edpolicy.stanford.edu/sites/default/files/scope-pub-student-centered-research-brief.pdf

Horn, M. B., & Staker, H. (2011). *The rise of K–12 blended learning.* Innosight Institute. http://www.christenseninstitute.org/wp-content/uploads/2013/04/The-rise-of-K-12-blended-learning.pdf

Hutchison, L. F. (2012). Addressing the STEM teacher shortage in American schools: Ways to recruit and retain effective STEM teachers. *Action in Teacher Education, 34*(5/6), 541–550. https://doi.org/10.1080/01626620.2012.729483

International Society for Technology in Education. (2016). *Student-centered learning.* http://www.iste.org/connected/standards/essential-conditions/student-centered-learning

Mitra, S. (2013, February). *Build a school in the cloud* [Video]. TED. https://www.ted.com/talks/sugata_mitra_build_a_school_in_the_cloud?language=en

Annotations (margin notes): List of references begins on a new page. Heading is centered and boldface. List is alphabetized by authors' last names. All authors' names are inverted. First line of an entry is at the left margin; subsequent lines indent 1/2". Double-spacing is used throughout.

12

Moeller, B., & Reitzes, T. (2011, July). *Integrating technology with student-centered learning*. Nellie Mae Education Foundation. http://www.nmefoundation.org/research/personalization/ integrating-technology-with-student-centered-learn

Rich, M. (2015, August 9). Teacher shortages spur a nationwide hiring scramble (credentials optional). *The New York Times*. https://nyti.ms/1WaaV7a

Svokos, A. (2015, May 7). 5 innovations from the past decade that aim to change the American classroom. *Huffpost*. https://www. huffpost.com/entry/technology-changes-classrooms_n_7190910

Watson, J. (2008, January). *Blended learning: The convergence of online and face-to-face education*. North American Council for Online Learning. http://www.inacol.org/wp-content/uploads/2015/02/ NACOL_PP-BlendedLearning-lr.pdf

Additional elements: Abstract and running head

The following elements are required for professional (submitted for publication) papers.

Running head consisting of a shortened title is flush left on all pages.

Abstract appears on a new page after the title page.

Abstract is a fewer than 250-word overview of the paper.

Keywords help readers search for a paper online or in a database.

TECHNOLOGY AND STUDENT-CENTERED LEARNING   2

Abstract

In recent decades, instructors and administrators have viewed student-centered learning as a promising pedagogical practice that offers both the hope of increasing academic performance and a solution for teacher shortages. Differing from the traditional model of instruction in which a teacher delivers content from the front of a classroom, student-centered learning puts the students at the center of teaching and learning. Students set their own learning goals, select appropriate resources, and progress at their own pace. Student-centered learning has produced both positive results and increases in students' self-esteem. Given the recent proliferation of technology in classrooms, school districts are poised for success in making the shift to student-centered learning. The question for district leaders, however, is how to effectively balance existing teacher talent with educational technology.

Keywords: digital learning, student-centered learning, personalized learning, education technology, transmissive, blended

Answers to Exercises

Exercise 1–2, page 11

1. b; a is too vague
2. a; b is too broad
3. a; b is a question
4. b; a is too vague
5. b; a is a statement of fact

Exercise 2–1, page 17

Topic sentence: Quilt making has served as an important means of social, political, and artistic expression for women. *Eliminate the following sentence:* They used dyed cotton fabrics much like the fabrics quilters use today; surprisingly, quilters' basic materials haven't changed that much over the years.

Exercise 5–1, page 61

logos; ethos; pathos

Exercise 8–1, page 89

Possible revisions:

a. The Prussians defeated the Saxons in 1745.
b. Ahmed, the producer, manages the entire operation.
c. The tour guides expertly paddled the sea kayaks.
d. Correct
e. The congresswoman heard the protestors' shouts as she walked up the Capitol steps.

Exercise 9–1, page 92

Possible revisions:

a. Bluetooth technology is used with personal computers, mobile phones, and audio devices.
b. Hannah told her rock-climbing partner that she bought a new harness and that she wanted to climb Otter Cliffs.

c. It is more difficult to sustain an exercise program than to start one.
d. During basic training, I was told not only what to do but also what to think.
e. Jan wanted to drive either to wine country or to Sausalito.

Exercise 10–1, page 95

Possible revisions:

a. Oranges provide more vitamin C than any other fruit.
b. The golden eagle's wingspan is nearly as wide as the bald eagle's.
c. Looking out the family room window, Sarah saw that her favorite tree, which she had climbed as a child, was gone.
d. The graphic designers are interested in and knowledgeable about producing posters for the balloon race.
e. My town's high school is much larger than the neighboring town's high school.

Exercise 11–1, page 97

Possible revisions:

a. Using surgical gloves is a precaution now taken by dentists to prevent contact with patients' blood and saliva.
b. A career in medicine, which my brother is pursuing, requires at least ten years of challenging work.
c. The pharaohs had bad teeth because tiny particles of sand found their way into Egyptian bread.
d. Recurring bouts of flu caused the team to forfeit a record number of games.
e. This box contains the key to your future.

Exercise 12–1, page 100

Possible revisions:

a. The manager asked her employees to submit their reports on Friday if they had time.

b. Many students graduate from college with debt totaling more than fifty thousand dollars.

c. It is a myth that humans use only 10 percent of their brains.

d. When she looked in the closet, Daria found the old nightgown she used to wear to sleep.

e. Not all geese fly beyond Narragansett for the winter.

Exercise 12–2, page 101

Possible revisions:

a. To complete an online purchase with a credit card, you must enter the expiration date and the security code.

b. Though Martha was only sixteen, UCLA accepted her application.

c. As I settled in the cockpit, the pounding of the engine was muffled only slightly by my helmet.

d. After studying polymer chemistry, Letitia found computer games less complex.

e. When I was a young man, my mother enrolled me in tap dance classes.

Exercise 13–1, page 102

Possible revisions:

Version 1, first person

When online dating first became available, I thought that it would simplify romance. I believed that I could type in a list of criteria—sense of humor, college education, green eyes, good job—and a database would select the perfect mate for me. I signed up for some services and filled out my profile, confident that true love was only a few clicks away. As it turned out, however, virtual dating was no easier than traditional dating—and it has only gotten more complicated over the years. I still have to contact the people I find, exchange messages, and meet them in the real world. Although a dating app might produce a list of possibilities and screen out obviously undesirable people, it can't predict chemistry. More often than not, I find that people who seem perfect online just don't click with me in person. Dating apps and social media do help me expand my pool of potential dates, but they're no substitute for the hard work of romance.

Version 2, third person

When online dating first became available, many people thought that it would simplify romance. Hopeful singles believed that they could type in a list of criteria—sense of humor, college education, green eyes, good job—and a database would select the perfect mate. Thousands of people signed up for services and filled out their profiles, confident that true love was only a few clicks away. As it turned out, however, virtual dating was no easier than traditional dating—and it has only gotten more complicated over the years. Online daters still have to contact the people they find, exchange messages, and meet in the real world. Although a dating app might produce a list of possibilities and screen out obviously undesirable people, it can't predict chemistry. More often than not, people who seem perfect for each other online just don't click in person. Dating apps and social media do help single people expand their pool of potential dates, but they're no substitute for the hard work of romance.

Exercise 14–1, page 107

Possible revisions:

a. The X-Men comic books and Japanese woodcuts of kabuki dancers, all part of Marlena's research project on popular culture, covered the tabletop and the chairs.

b. The students organized a petition to change the school motto, which was "A man's greatest strength is his education."

c. Employees can apply for a spot in the leadership program, which teaches management and communication skills.

d. Shore houses were flooded, beaches were washed away, and Brant's Lighthouse was swallowed by the sea.

e. Laura Thackray, an engineer at Volvo Car Corporation, addressed women's safety needs by designing a pregnant crash-test dummy.

Exercise 14–2, page 108

Possible revisions:

a. These particles, known as "stealth liposomes," can hide in the body for a long time without detection.

b. Irena, a competitive gymnast majoring in biochemistry, intends to apply her athletic experience and her science degree to a career in sports medicine.

c. Because consumers and workers alike have loudly protested warehouse working conditions, some politicians have proposed stronger labor regulations for major retailers.

d. Developed in a European university, IRC (Internet relay chat) was created as a way for a group of graduate students to talk about projects from their dorm rooms.

e. The cafeteria's new menu, which has an international flavor, includes everything from pizza to pad thai.

Exercise 16–1, page 116

Possible revisions:

a. Martin Luther King Jr. set a high standard for future leaders.

b. Alice has loved cooking since she could first peek over a kitchen tabletop.

c. Bloom's race for the governorship is futile.

d. A successful graphic designer must have technical knowledge and an eye for color and balance.

e. You will set up email for all employees.

Exercise 17–1, page 121

Possible revisions:

a. Dr. Geralyn Farmer is the chief surgeon at University Hospital. Dr. Paul Green is her assistant.

b. All applicants want to know how much they will earn.

c. Elementary school teachers should understand the concept of nurturing if they intend to be effective.

d. Our company is going to hire a new I.T. employee. This employee will update the server and set up remote desktops.

e. If we do not stop polluting our environment, we will perish.

Exercise 18–1, page 124

Possible revisions:

a. John stormed into the room like a hurricane.

b. Some people insist that they'll always be available to help, even if they haven't been before.

c. The Cubs easily beat the Mets, who struggled early in the game today at Wrigley Field.

d. We worked out the problems in our relationship.

e. My mother accused me of evading her questions when in fact I was just saying the first thing that came to mind.

Exercise 20–1, page 138

Possible revisions:

a. Listening to the playlist her sister had created, Mia was overcome with a mix of emotions: happiness, homesickness, and nostalgia.

b. Cortés and his soldiers were astonished when they looked down from the mountains and saw Tenochtitlán, the magnificent capital of the Aztecs.

c. Although my spoken Spanish is not very good, I can read the language with ease.

d. There are several reasons for not eating meat. One reason is that dangerous chemicals are used throughout the various stages of meat production.

e. To learn how to sculpt beauty from everyday life is my intention in studying art and archaeology.

Exercise 21–1, page 141

Possible revisions:

a. Greta recently started working at a new company that designs and manufactures educational toys.

b. The building is being renovated, so at times we have no heat, water, or electricity.

c. I don't think I will buy the new model of smartphone. Why spend the money when my current phone works perfectly?

d. Walker's coming-of-age novel is set against a gloomy scientific backdrop; the Earth's rotation has begun to slow down.

e. City officials had good reason to fear a major earthquake: most [*or* Most] of the business district was built on landfill.

Exercise 22–1, page 148

a. One of the main reasons for elephant poaching is the profits received from selling the ivory tusks.

b. Correct

c. A number of students in the seminar were aware of the importance of joining the discussion.

d. Batik cloth from Bali, blue and white ceramics from Delft, and a bocce ball from Turin have made Angelie's room the talk of the dorm.

e. Correct

Exercise 23–1, page 152

Possible revisions:

a. Every presidential candidate must appeal to a wide variety of ethnic and social groups to win the election.

b. Either Tom Hanks or Denzel Washington will win an award for his lifetime achievement in cinema.

c. The aerobics instructor motioned for all the students to move their arms in wide, slow circles.

d. Correct

e. Applicants should be bilingual if they want to qualify for this position.

Exercise 24–1, page 154

Possible revisions:

a. Some professors say that engineering students should have hands-on experience with dismantling and reassembling machines.

b. Because she had decorated her living room with posters from chamber music festivals, her date thought that she was interested in classical music. Actually she preferred rock.

c. The high school principal congratulated the seniors who were graduating later that day.

d. Marianne told Jenny, "I am worried about my mother's illness." [*or* ". . . about your mother's illness."]

e. Though Lewis cried for several minutes after scraping his knee, eventually his crying subsided.

Exercise 25–1, page 158

a. Correct [But the writer could change the end of the sentence: . . . *than he was.*]

b. Correct [But the writer could change the end of the sentence: . . . *that she was the coach.*]

c. She appreciated his telling the truth in such a difficult situation.

d. The director has asked you and me to draft a proposal for a new recycling plan.

e. My roommate and I dreamed of renting an SUV, packing it with food, and driving two hundred miles to the shore.

Exercise 26–1, page 160

a. Correct
b. The environmental policy conference featured scholars whom I had never heard of. [or . . . scholars I had never heard of.]
c. Correct
d. Kartik always gives a holiday donation to whoever needs it.
e. The singers whom Natalia selected for the choir attended their first rehearsal last night. [or The singers Natalia selected . . .]

Exercise 27–1, page 165

a. Do you expect to perform well on the exam next week?
b. With the budget deadline approaching, our office has been handling routine correspondence more slowly than we usually do.
c. Correct
d. The customer complained that he hadn't been treated nicely by the agent on the phone.
e. Of all the smart people in my family, Uncle Roberto is the cleverest [or the most clever].

Exercise 28–1, page 171

a. The glass sculptures of the Swan Boats were prominent in the brightly lit lobby.
b. When I get the urge to exercise, I lie down until it passes.
c. Grandmother had driven our new hybrid to the sunrise church service, so we were left with the van.
d. Christos didn't know about Marlo's promotion because he never listens. He is [or He's] always talking.
e. A pile of dirty rags was lying at the bottom of the stairs.

Exercise 28–2, page 175

a. Correct
b. Discovered in 1930, Pluto is an icy dwarf planet that exists at the edge of our solar system.
c. When city planners proposed rezoning the waterfront, did they know that the mayor had promised to curb development in that neighborhood?
d. Tonight's lecture begins at 7:30. If it were earlier, I'd consider attending.
e. Correct

Exercise 29–1, page 178

a. A major league pitcher can throw a baseball more than ninety-five miles per hour.
b. The writing center tutor will help you revise your essay.
c. A reptile must adjust its body temperature to its environment.
d. Correct
e. My uncle, a cartoonist, could sketch a face in less than a minute.

Exercise 29–2, page 184

a. Freezing rain causes an icy glaze on trees.
b. I don't use the subway because I am claustrophobic.
c. Recently there have been a number of earthquakes in Turkey.
d. Whenever we eat at the café, we sit at a small table in the corner of the patio.
e. In the 1990s, entrepreneurs created new online businesses in record numbers.

Exercise 30–1, page 189

a. The cold, impersonal atmosphere of the university was unbearable.
b. An ambulance threaded its way through police cars, fire trucks, and irate citizens.
c. Correct

d. After two broken arms, three cracked ribs, and one concussion, Ken quit the varsity football team.

e. Correct

Exercise 30–2, page 196

a. Cricket, which originated in England, is also popular in Australia, South Africa, and India.

b. At the sound of the starting pistol, the horses surged forward toward the first obstacle, a sharp incline three feet high.

c. After seeing an exhibition of Western art, Gerhard Richter escaped from East Berlin and smuggled out many of his notebooks.

d. Corrie's new wet suit has an intricate blue pattern.

e. We replaced the rickety old spiral staircase with a sturdy new ladder.

Exercise 31–1, page 200

a. Correct

b. Tricia's first artwork was a bright blue clay dolphin.

c. Some modern musicians (trumpeter Jon Hassell is an example) blend several cultural traditions into a unique sound.

d. Myra liked hot, spicy foods such as chili, kung pao chicken, and buffalo wings.

e. On the display screen was a soothing pattern of light and shadow.

Exercise 32–1, page 206

a. Correct [Either *It* or *it* is correct.]

b. If we have come to fight, we are far too few; if we have come to die, we are far too many.

c. Each of the gift baskets included a greeting card, a coffee mug, and home-made cookies.

d. The news article portrays the land use proposal as reckless, although 62 percent of the town's residents support it.

e. Activist and politician Stacey Abrams tells readers of her book *Lead from the Outside* to ask themselves a powerful question: "How do I banish doubts and get out of my own way?" (xxviii).

Exercise 33–1, page 209

a. Correct

b. The innovative shoe fastener was inspired by the designer's young son.

c. Each day's menu features a different European country's dish.

d. Lottie worked overtime to increase her family's earnings.

e. Ms. Jacobs is unwilling to listen to students' complaints about computer failures.

Exercise 34–1, page 214

a. As for the advertisement "Sailors have more fun," if you consider chipping paint and swabbing decks fun, then you will have plenty of it.

b. Correct

c. After winning the lottery, Juanita said that she would give half the money to charity.

d. After the film, Vicki said, "The reviewer called this movie 'trash of the first order.' I guess you can't believe everything you read."

e. Correct

Exercise 36–1, page 219

a. A client left a [*or* their] cell phone in our conference room after the meeting.

b. The films we made of Kilauea on our research trip to Hawaii Volcanoes National Park illustrate a typical spatter cone eruption.

c. Correct

d. Of three engineering fields—chemical, mechanical, and materials—Keegan chose materials engineering for its application to toy manufacturing.

e. Correct

Exercise 38–1, page 229

a. The Williams sisters were the heroes of my entire high school tennis team.
b. The swiftly moving tugboat pulled alongside the barge and directed it away from the oil spill in the harbor.
c. We managed to get the most desirable seats in the theater.
d. As a livestock veterinarian, she cares for horses, donkeys, cows, and other large farm animals.
e. Roadblocks were set up along all the major highways leading out of the city.

Exercise 39–1, page 232

a. Assistant Dean Shirin Ahmadi recommended offering more world language courses.
b. Correct
c. Kalindi has an ambitious semester, studying differential calculus, classical Hebrew, brochure design, and Greek literature.
d. Lydia's aunt and uncle make modular houses as beautiful as modernist works of art.
e. The labs in Ohio began their research in the spring, and we expect clinical trials to start at our Cleveland lab next summer.

Exercise 40–1, page 242

a. indefinite pronoun, verb with helping verb, preposition
b. verb, adverb, noun
c. preposition, conjunction (conjunctive adverb), pronoun
d. modal verb, noun/adjective, coordinating conjunction
e. demonstrative pronoun, verb, subordinating conjunction

Exercise 41–1, page 245

a. Complete subjects: The hills and mountains, the snow atop them; simple subjects: hills, mountains, snow
b. Complete subject: points; simple subject: points
c. Complete subject: (You)
d. Complete subject: hundreds of fireflies; simple subject: hundreds
e. Complete subject: The evidence against the defendant; simple subject: evidence

Exercise 42–1, page 256

a. so that every vote would count (Adverb clause modifying *adjusted*)
b. that targets baby boomers (Adjective clause modifying *campaign*)
c. After the Tambora volcano erupted in the southern Pacific in 1815 (Adverb clause modifying *realized*); that it would contribute to the "year without a summer" in Europe and North America (Noun clause used as direct object of *realized*)
d. that at a certain point there will be no more oil to extract from the earth (Noun clause used as direct object of *implies*)
e. when you are rushing (Adverb clause modifying *are overlooked*)

Exercise 43–1, page 259

a. Complex; that are ignited in dry areas (adjective clause)
b. Compound
c. Simple
d. Complex; Before we leave for the station (adverb clause)
e. Compound-complex; when you want to leave (noun clause)

Index

A List of Charts

PART 8   Grammar Basics

PART 9   Researched Writing

MLA STYLE

APA STYLE

Editing Marks

Boldface numbers refer to sections of the handbook.

abbr	abbreviation	37a–d		⌢;	comma	30
add	add needed word	10		*no ,*	no comma	31
adj	misuse of adjective	27		;	semicolon	32a–d
adv	misuse of adverb	27		:	colon	32e–g
agr	agreement	22, 23		'	apostrophe	33
art	article (a, *an*, *the*)	29b		" "	quotation marks	34
awk	awkward			. ?	period, question mark	35a–b
cap	capital letter	39		!	exclamation point	35c
case	pronoun case	23, 24		— ( )	dash, parentheses	36a–b
cliché	cliché	18d		[ ] . . .	brackets, ellipsis	36c–d
coh	coherence	2b		/	slash	36e
coord	coordination	14		¶	new paragraph	2
cs	comma splice	21		*pass*	ineffective passive	8
dev	inadequate development	2c		*pn agr*	pronoun agreement	23
dm	dangling modifier	12d		*proof*	proofreading problem	3f
-ed	-ed ending	28d		*ref*	pronoun reference	24
effect	ineffective language	17		*run-on*	run-on sentence	21
emph	emphasis	14		*-s*	-s ending	22a, 28c
ESL	English as a second language, multilingual	29		*sexist*	sexist or noninclusive language	17e, 23a
exact	inexact language	18		*shift*	distracting shift	13
frag	sentence fragment	20		*sl*	slang	17d
fs	fused sentence	21		*sp*	misspelled word	38a
gl/us	see glossary of usage	19		*sub*	subordination	14
hyph	hyphen	38b–f		*sv agr*	subject-verb agreement	22, 28c
idiom	idioms	18c		*t*	verb tense	28f
inc	incomplete construction	10		*trans*	transition needed	2b
irreg	irregular verb	28a		*usage*	see glossary of usage	19
ital	italics	37g–h		*v*	voice	8a
jarg	jargon	17b		*var*	lack of variety in sentence structure	15
lc	lowercase	39		*vb*	verb problem	28, 29a
mix	mixed construction	11		*w*	wordy	16
mm	misplaced modifier	12a–c		//	parallelism	9
mood	mood of verb	28g		^	insert	
num	use of numbers	37e–f		#	insert space	
om	omitted word	10, 29b		◡	close up space	
p	punctuation					

A List of Grammatical Terms

Boldface numbers refer to sections of the handbook.

Detailed Menu